ASAF HANUKA

THE REALIST™

PLUG AND PLAY

Published by
ARCHAIA™

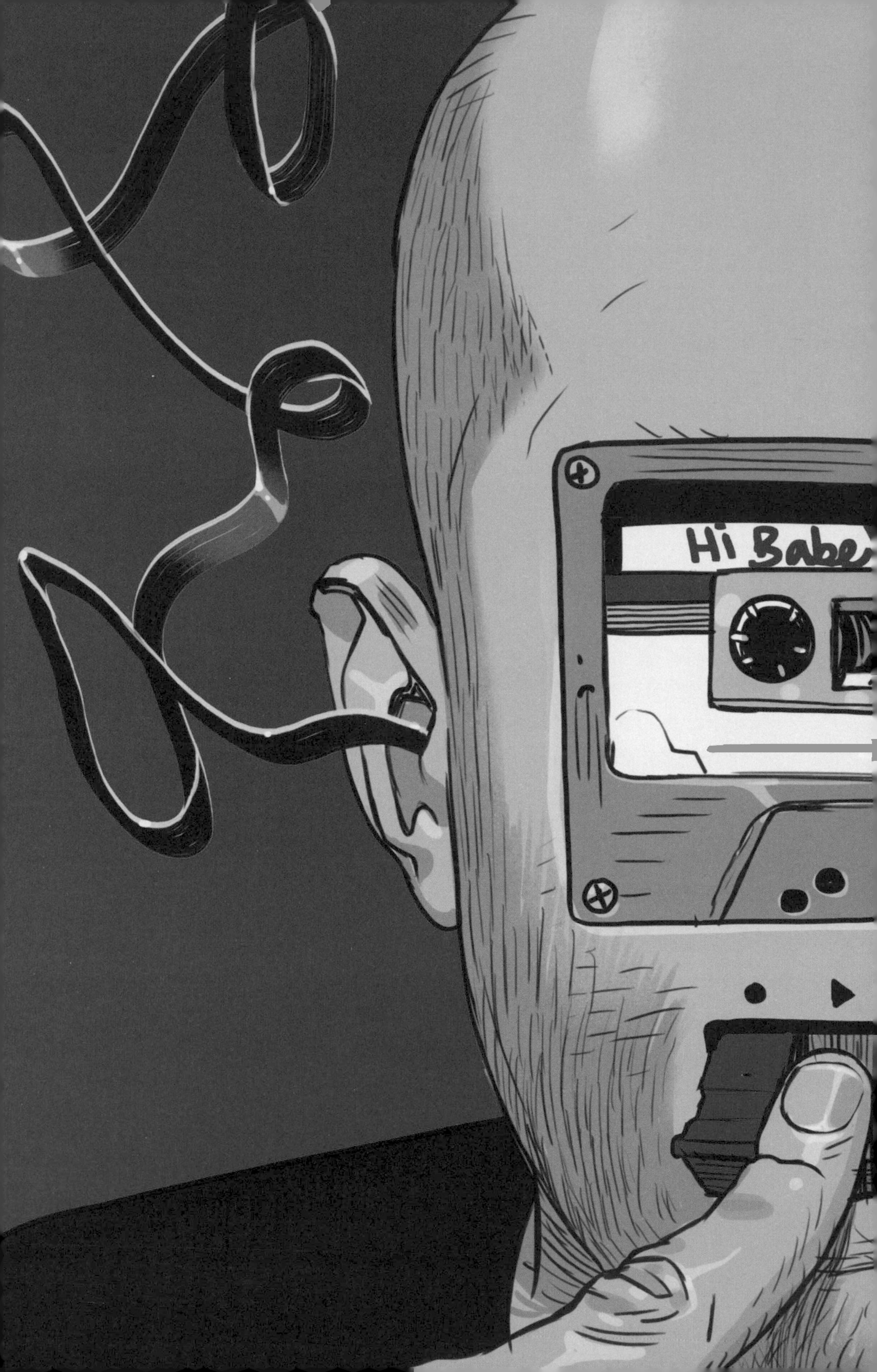
Hi Babe

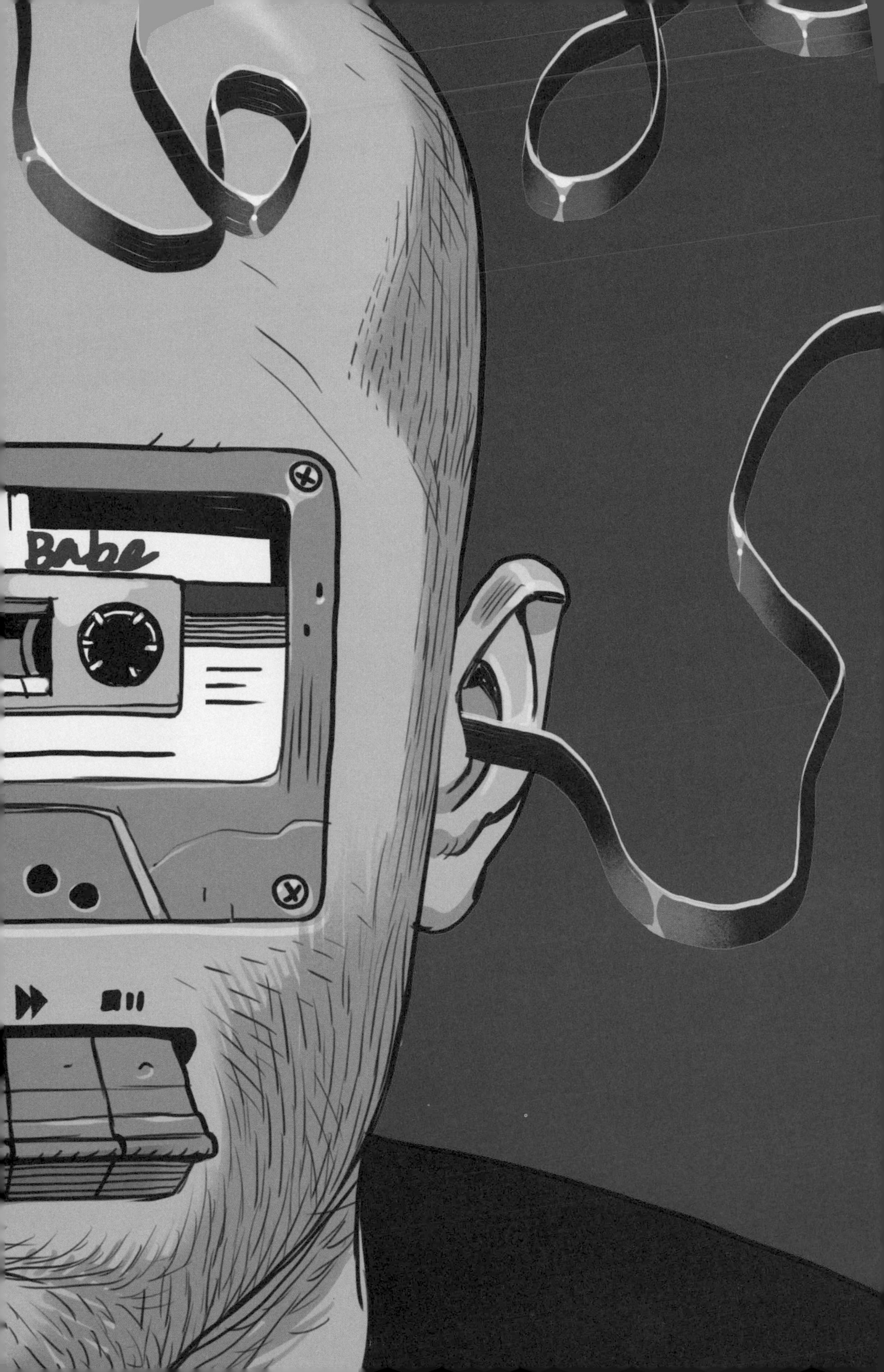
Babe

ROSS RICHIE CEO & Founder
MATT GAGNON Editor-in-Chief
FILIP SABLIK President of Publishing & Marketing
STEPHEN CHRISTY President of Development
LANCE KREITER VP of Licensing & Merchandising
PHIL BARBARO VP of Finance
BRYCE CARLSON Managing Editor
MEL CAYLO Marketing Manager
SCOTT NEWMAN Production Design Manager
KATE HENNING Operations Manager
SIERRA HAHN Senior Editor
DAFNA PLEBAN Editor, Talent Development
SHANNON WATTERS Editor
ERIC HARBURN Editor
WHITNEY LEOPARD Associate Editor
JASMINE AMIRI Associate Editor
CHRIS ROSA Associate Editor
ALEX GALER Associate Editor
CAMERON CHITTOCK Associate Editor
MATTHEW LEVINE Assistant Editor
KELSEY DIETERICH Production Designer
JILLIAN CRAB Production Designer
MICHELLE ANKLEY Production Designer
GRACE PARK Production Design Assistant
AARON FERRARA Operations Coordinator
ELIZABETH LOUGHRIDGE Accounting Coordinator
STEPHANIE HOCUTT Social Media Coordinator
JOSÉ MEZA Sales Assistant
JAMES ARRIOLA Mailroom Assistant
HOLLY AITCHISON Operations Assistant
SAM KUSEK Direct Market Representative
AMBER PARKER Administrative Assistant

ARCHAIA™

THE REALIST: PLUG AND PLAY, April 2017. Published by
Archaia, a division of Boom Entertainment, Inc. The Realist
is ™ and © 2016 Steinkis. All Rights Reserved. Archaia™ and
the Archaia logo are trademarks of Boom Entertainment, Inc.,
registered in various countries and categories. All characters,
events, and institutions depicted herein are fictional. Any
similarity between any of the names, characters, persons,
events, and/or institutions in this publication to actual names,
characters, and persons, whether living or dead, events, and/or
institutions is unintended and purely coincidental.

This edition collects material from *K.O. à Tel Aviv* Volumes
#1-3, originally published in French by Steinkis and the story
"A Complicated Question" which was originally published in
Nautilus, Winter 2015. "Obsession" was originally created for the
book "Tribute to Otomo" (2017, Kodansha.Ltd).

BOOM! Studios, 5670 Wilshire Boulevard, Suite 450, Los Angeles,
CA 90036-5679. Printed in China. First Printing.

ISBN:978-1-60886-953-4, eISBN: 978-1-61398-624-0

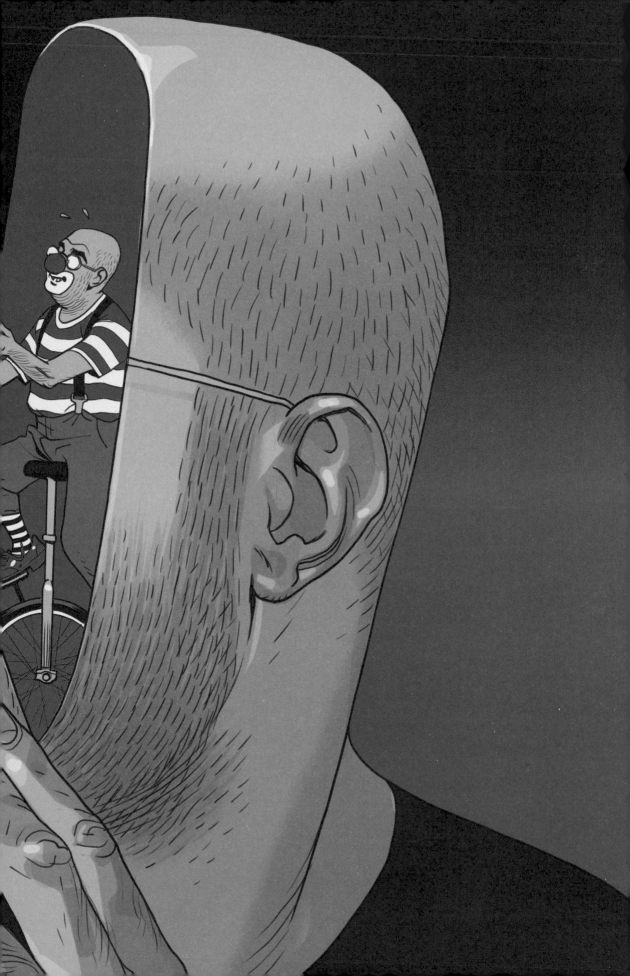

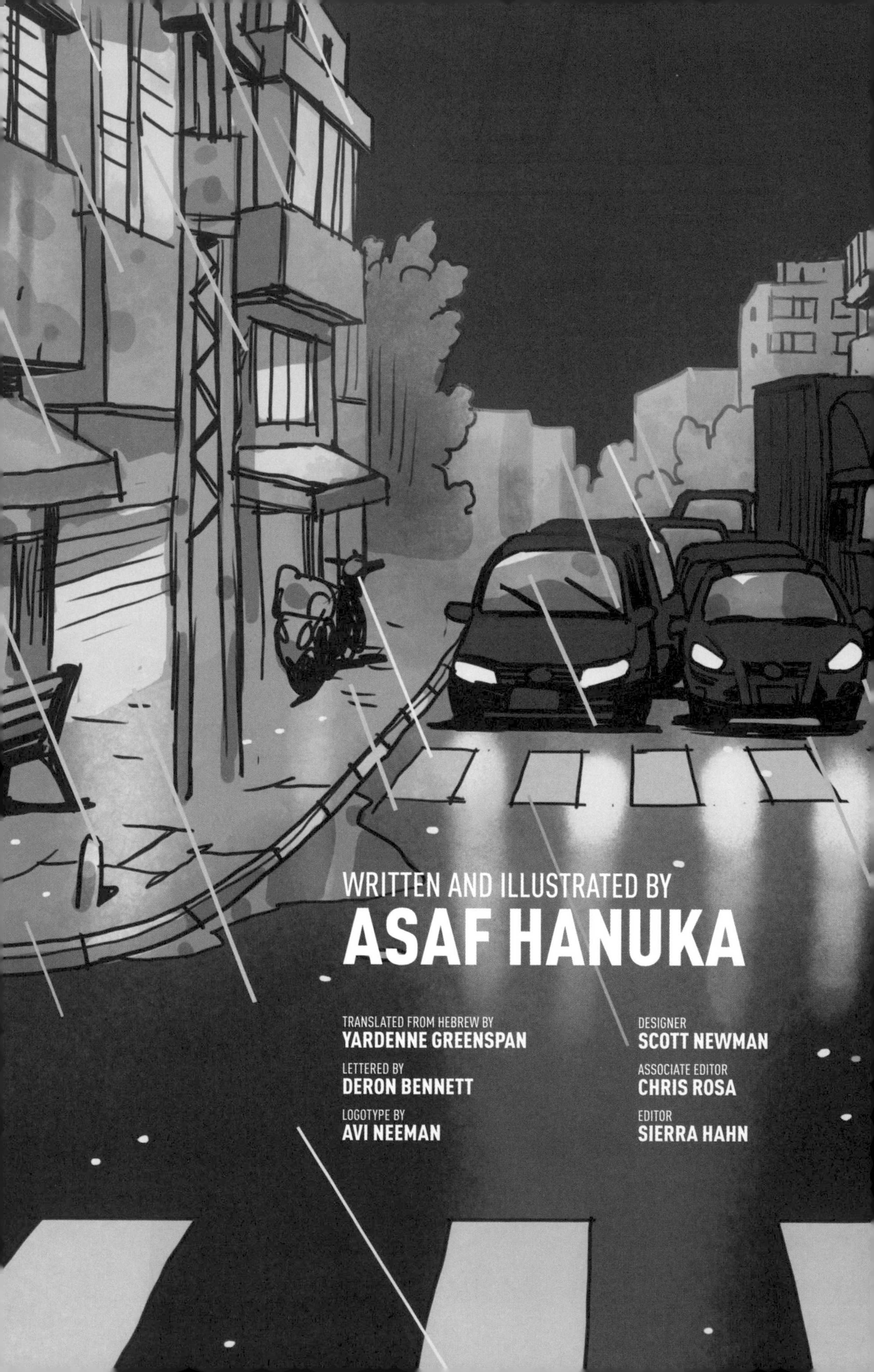

WRITTEN AND ILLUSTRATED BY

ASAF HANUKA

TRANSLATED FROM HEBREW BY
YARDENNE GREENSPAN

LETTERED BY
DERON BENNETT

LOGOTYPE BY
AVI NEEMAN

DESIGNER
SCOTT NEWMAN

ASSOCIATE EDITOR
CHRIS ROSA

EDITOR
SIERRA HAHN

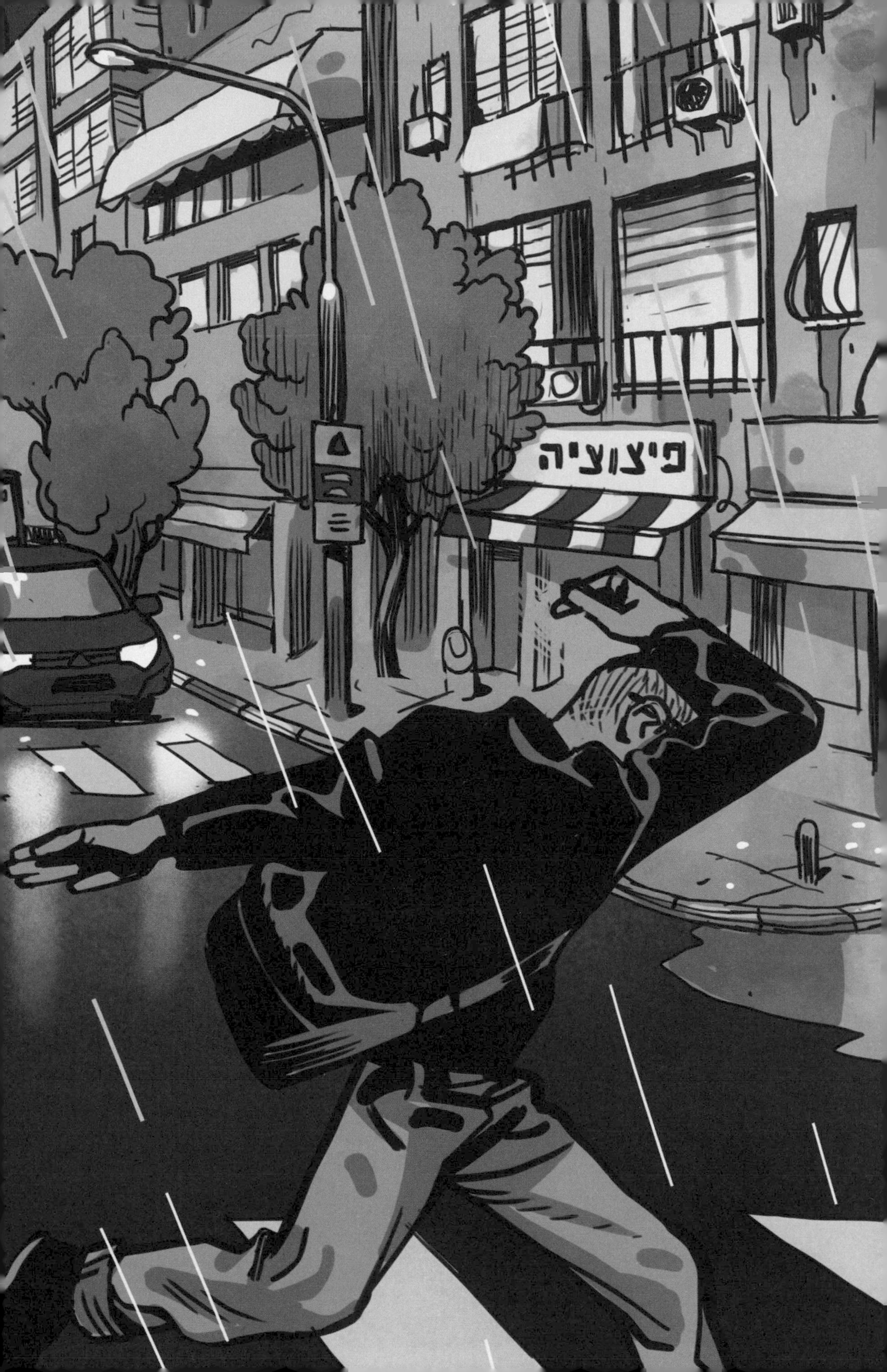
פיצוציה

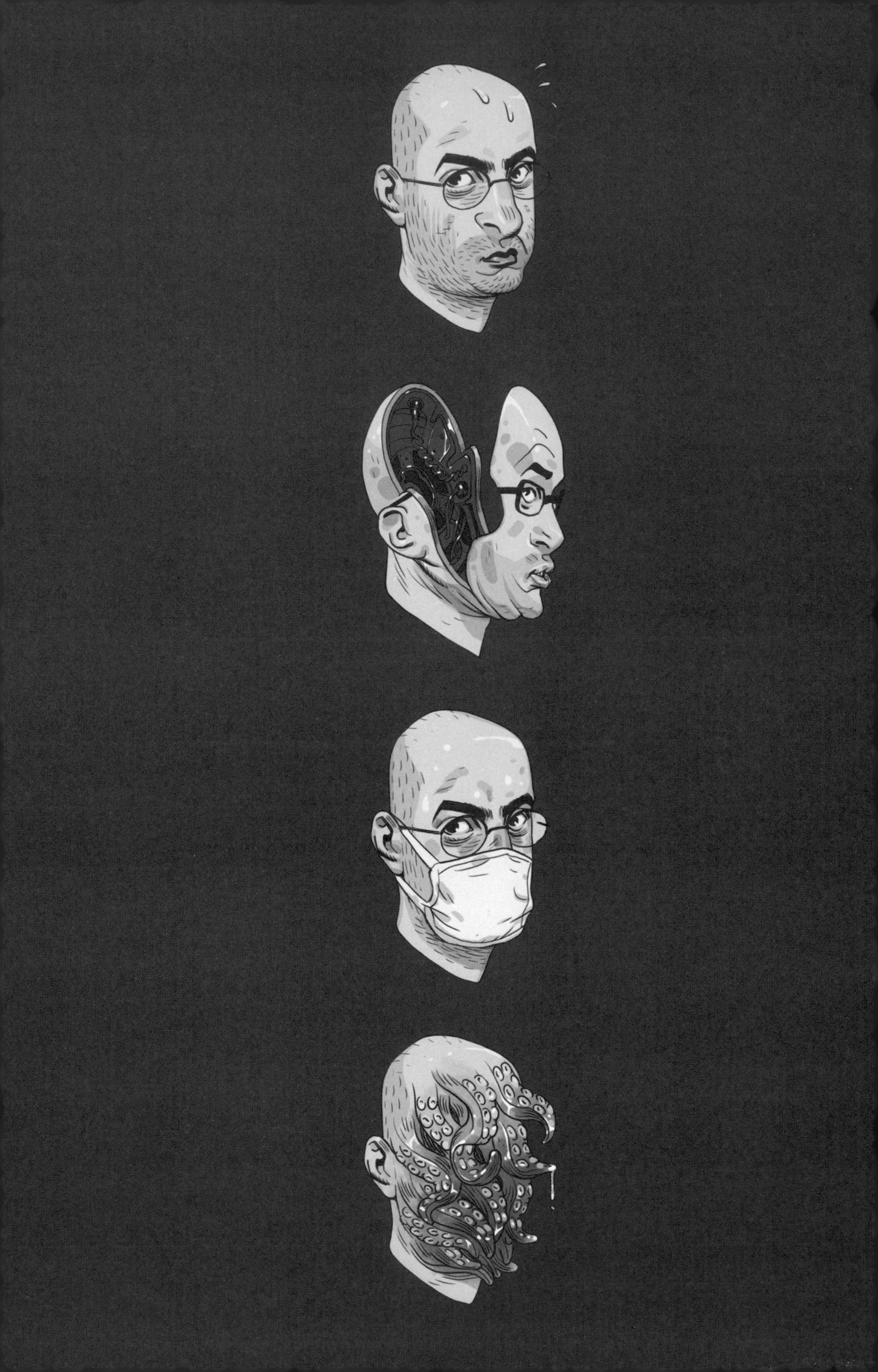

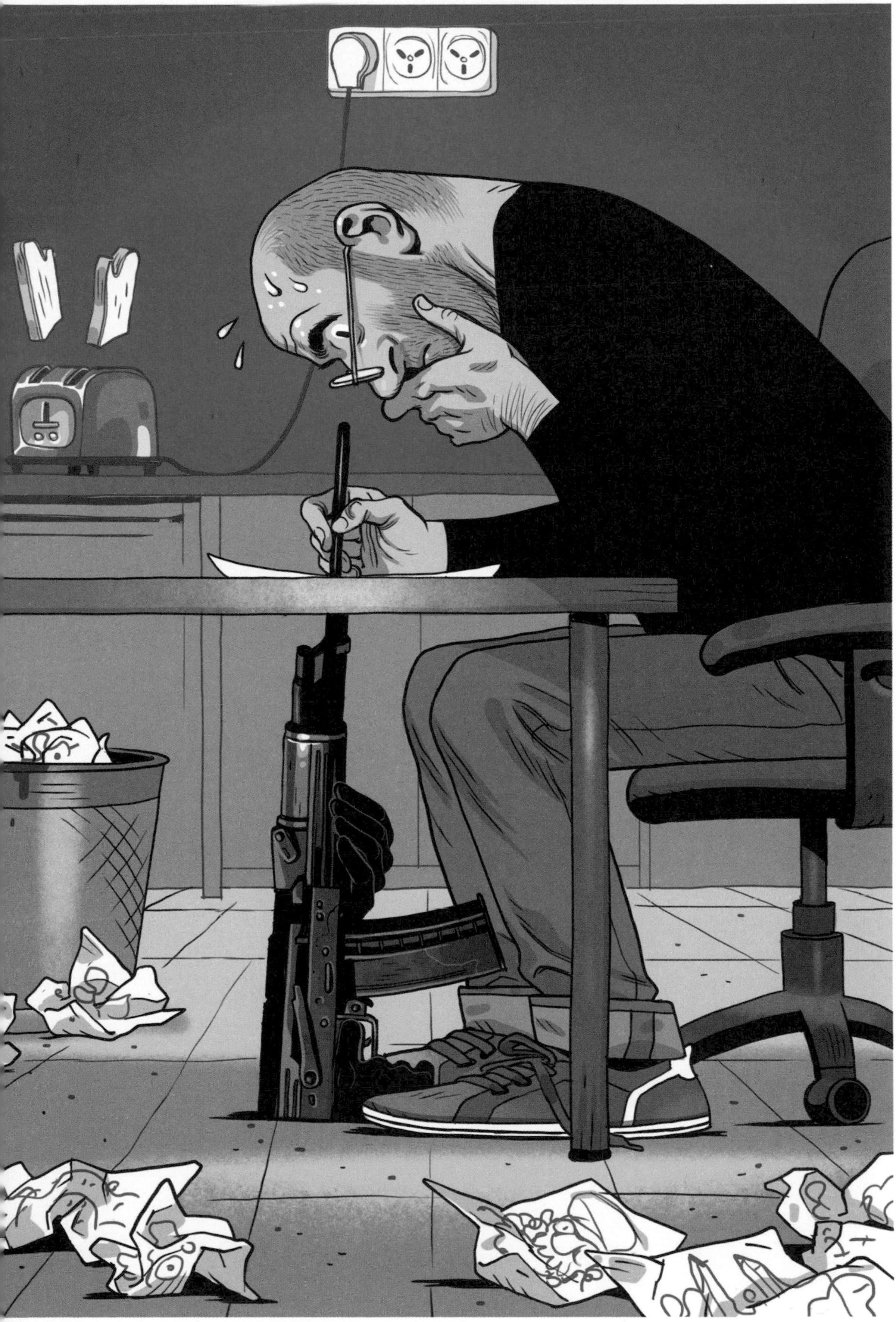

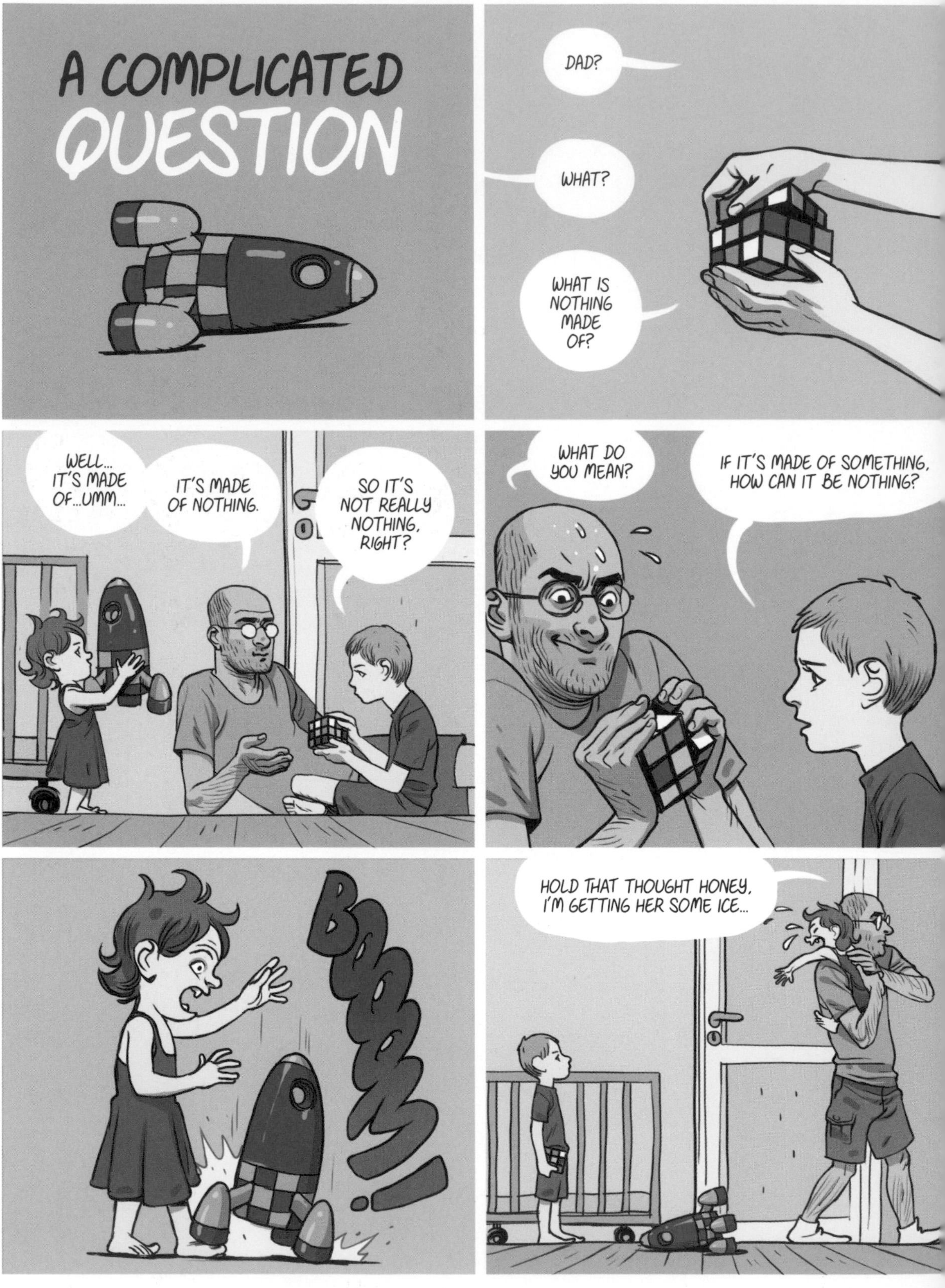
A COMPLICATED QUESTION
DAD?
WHAT?
WHAT IS NOTHING MADE OF?
WELL... IT'S MADE OF...UMM...
IT'S MADE OF NOTHING.
SO IT'S NOT REALLY NOTHING, RIGHT?
WHAT DO YOU MEAN?
IF IT'S MADE OF SOMETHING, HOW CAN IT BE NOTHING?
BOOOM!!
HOLD THAT THOUGHT HONEY, I'M GETTING HER SOME ICE...

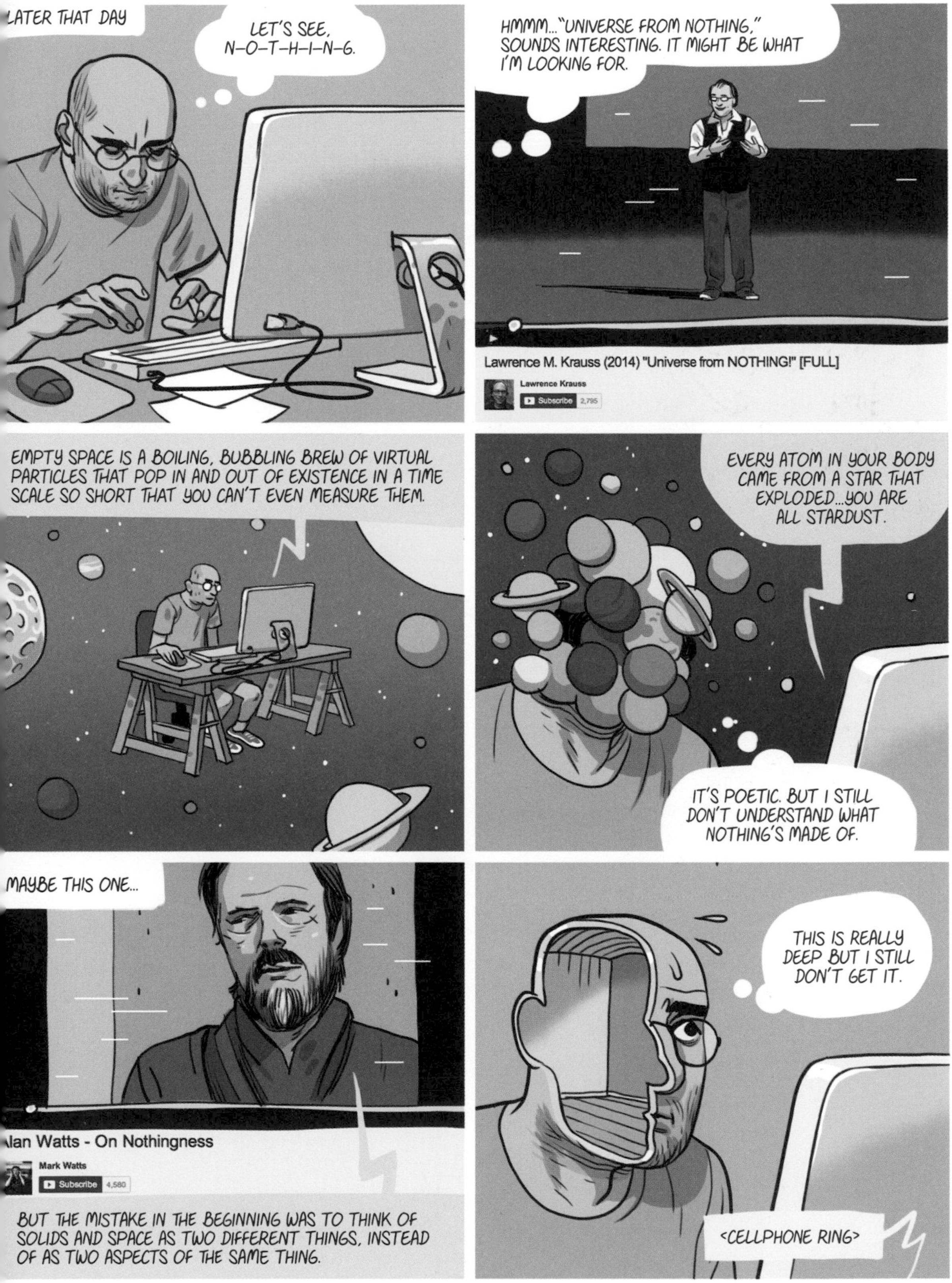
LATER THAT DAY
LET'S SEE, N-O-T-H-I-N-G.
HMMM..."UNIVERSE FROM NOTHING," SOUNDS INTERESTING. IT MIGHT BE WHAT I'M LOOKING FOR.
Lawrence M. Krauss (2014) "Universe from NOTHING!" [FULL]
Lawrence Krauss
Subscribe 2,795
EMPTY SPACE IS A BOILING, BUBBLING BREW OF VIRTUAL PARTICLES THAT POP IN AND OUT OF EXISTENCE IN A TIME SCALE SO SHORT THAT YOU CAN'T EVEN MEASURE THEM.
EVERY ATOM IN YOUR BODY CAME FROM A STAR THAT EXPLODED...YOU ARE ALL STARDUST.
IT'S POETIC. BUT I STILL DON'T UNDERSTAND WHAT NOTHING'S MADE OF.
MAYBE THIS ONE...
lan Watts - On Nothingness
Mark Watts
Subscribe 4,580
BUT THE MISTAKE IN THE BEGINNING WAS TO THINK OF SOLIDS AND SPACE AS TWO DIFFERENT THINGS, INSTEAD OF AS TWO ASPECTS OF THE SAME THING.
THIS IS REALLY DEEP BUT I STILL DON'T GET IT.
<CELLPHONE RING>

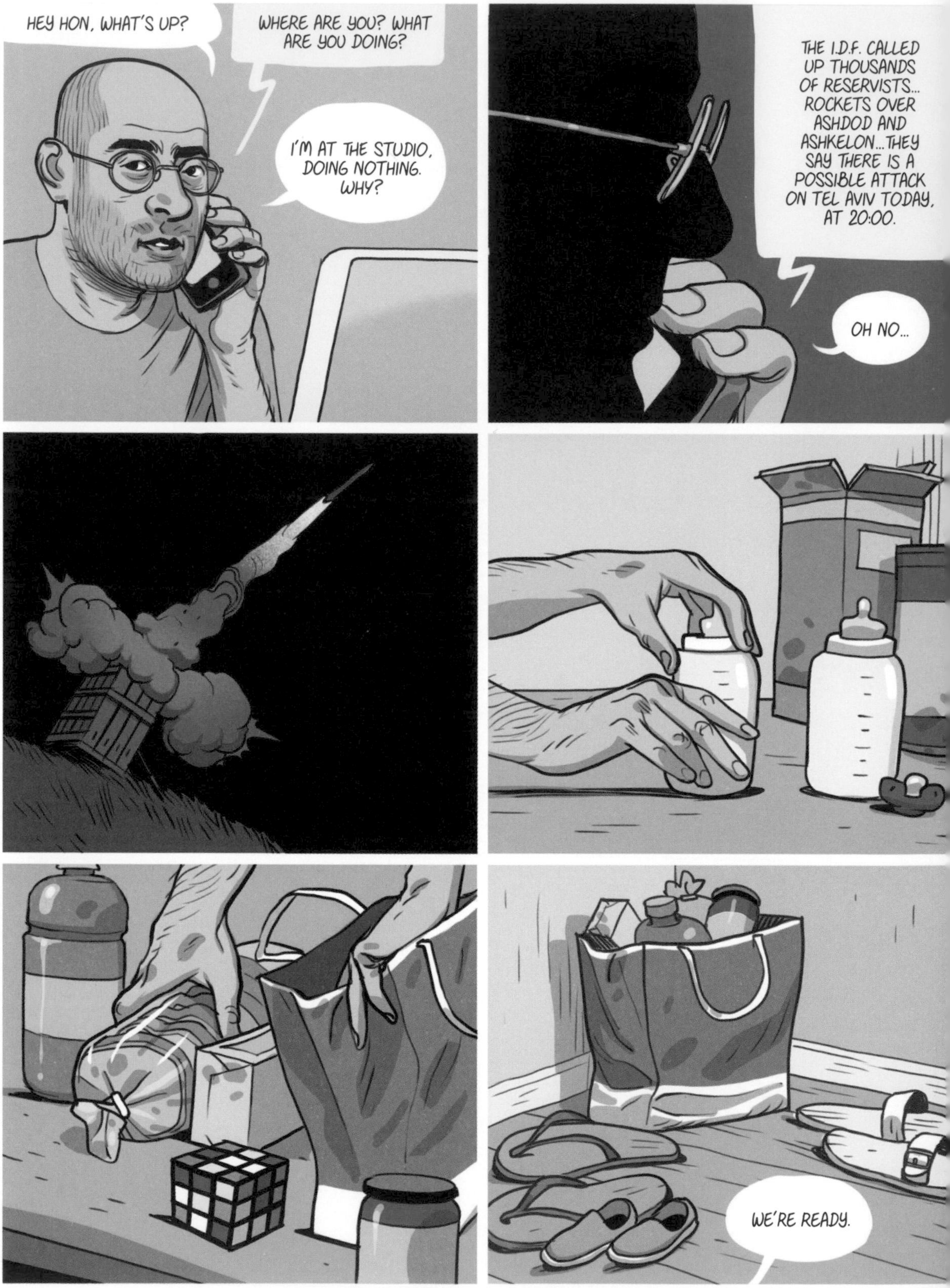
HEY HON, WHAT'S UP?
WHERE ARE YOU? WHAT ARE YOU DOING?
I'M AT THE STUDIO, DOING NOTHING. WHY?
THE I.D.F. CALLED UP THOUSANDS OF RESERVISTS... ROCKETS OVER ASHDOD AND ASHKELON...THEY SAY THERE IS A POSSIBLE ATTACK ON TEL AVIV TODAY, AT 20:00.
OH NO...
WE'RE READY.

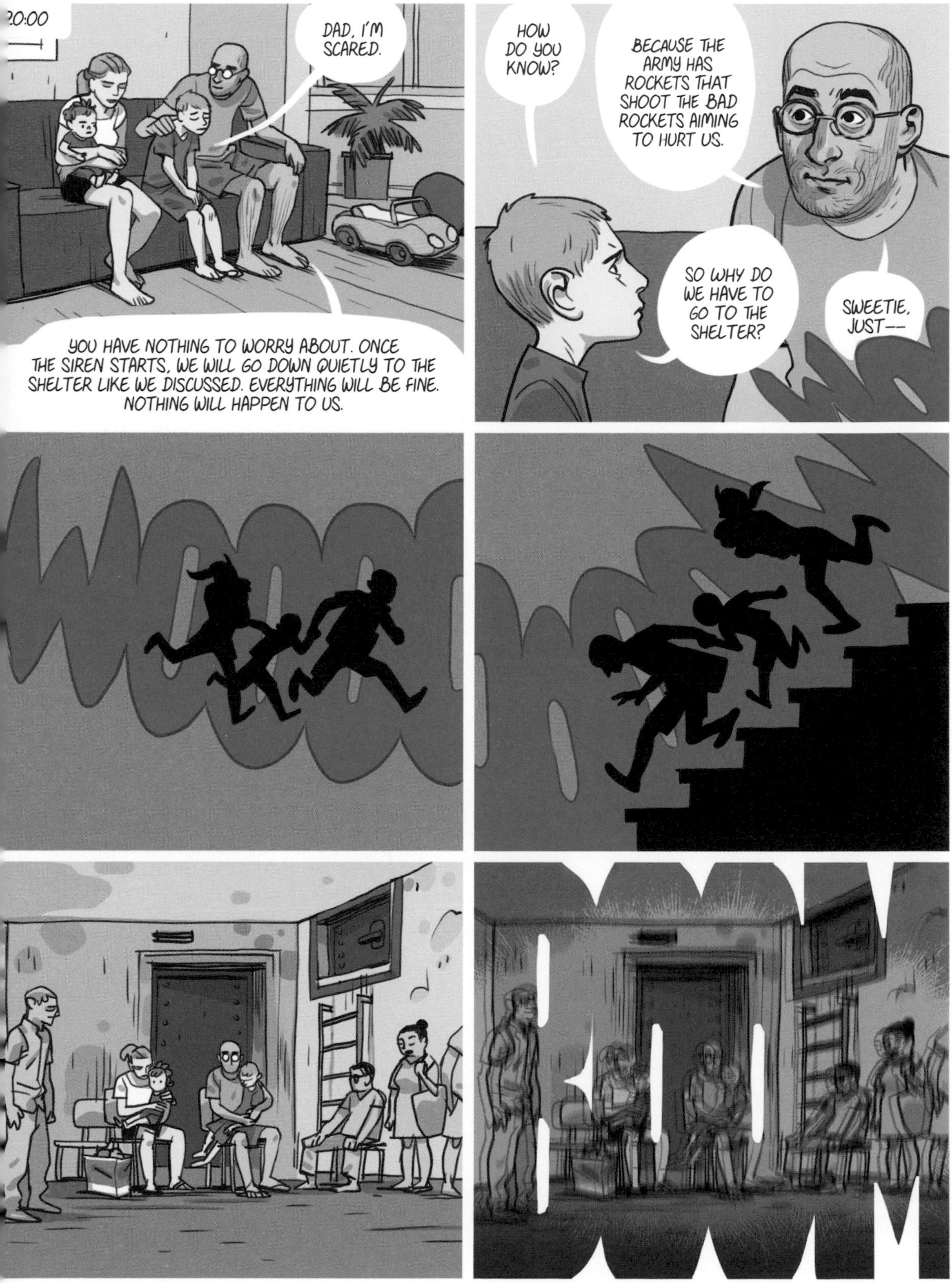
20:00
DAD, I'M SCARED.
YOU HAVE NOTHING TO WORRY ABOUT. ONCE THE SIREN STARTS, WE WILL GO DOWN QUIETLY TO THE SHELTER LIKE WE DISCUSSED. EVERYTHING WILL BE FINE. NOTHING WILL HAPPEN TO US.
HOW DO YOU KNOW?
BECAUSE THE ARMY HAS ROCKETS THAT SHOOT THE BAD ROCKETS AIMING TO HURT US.
SO WHY DO WE HAVE TO GO TO THE SHELTER?
SWEETIE, JUST--
BOOM

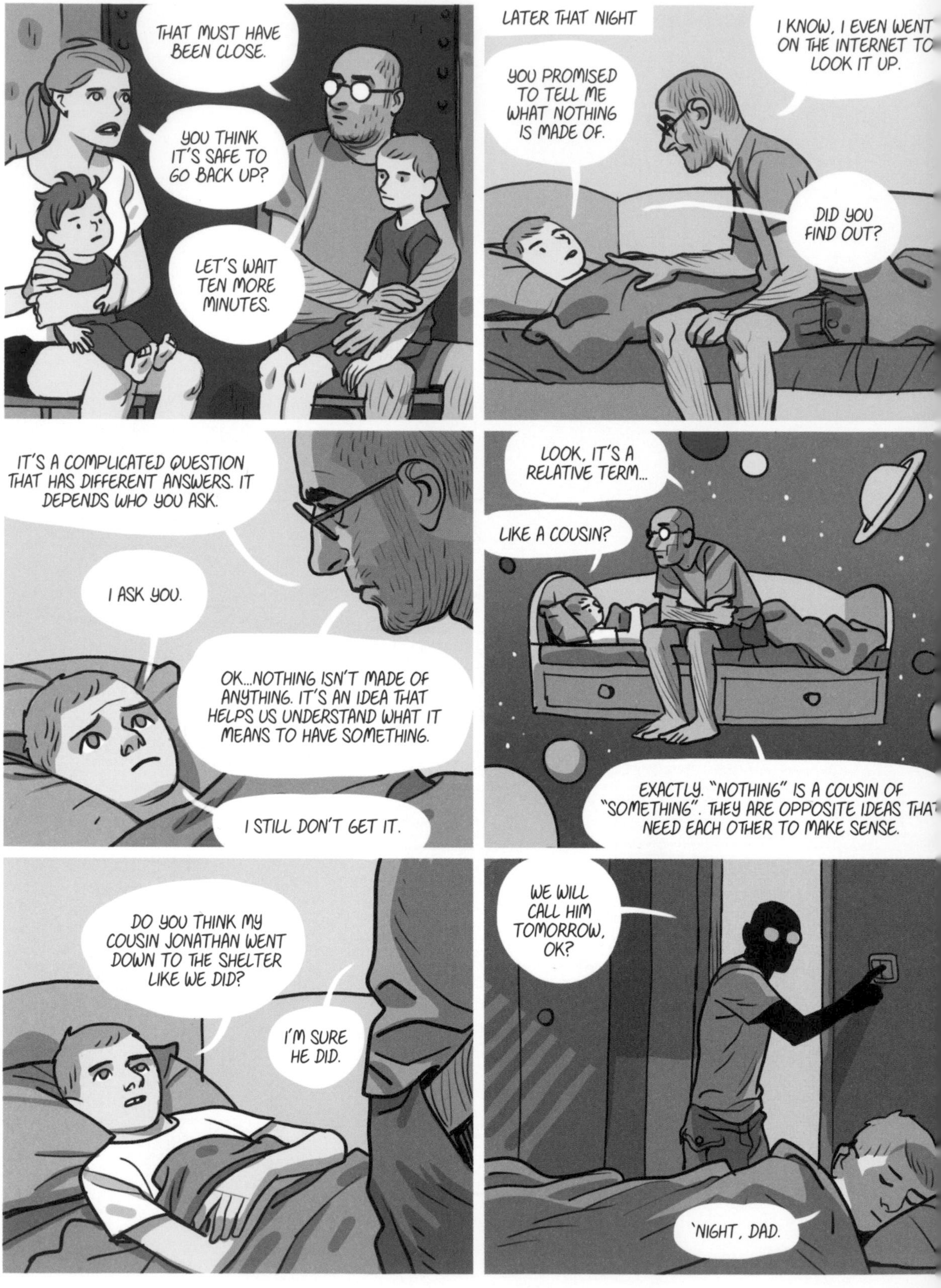
THAT MUST HAVE BEEN CLOSE.
YOU THINK IT'S SAFE TO GO BACK UP?
LET'S WAIT TEN MORE MINUTES.
LATER THAT NIGHT
YOU PROMISED TO TELL ME WHAT NOTHING IS MADE OF.
I KNOW, I EVEN WENT ON THE INTERNET TO LOOK IT UP.
DID YOU FIND OUT?
IT'S A COMPLICATED QUESTION THAT HAS DIFFERENT ANSWERS. IT DEPENDS WHO YOU ASK.
I ASK YOU.
OK...NOTHING ISN'T MADE OF ANYTHING. IT'S AN IDEA THAT HELPS US UNDERSTAND WHAT IT MEANS TO HAVE SOMETHING.
I STILL DON'T GET IT.
LOOK, IT'S A RELATIVE TERM...
LIKE A COUSIN?
EXACTLY. "NOTHING" IS A COUSIN OF "SOMETHING". THEY ARE OPPOSITE IDEAS THAT NEED EACH OTHER TO MAKE SENSE.
DO YOU THINK MY COUSIN JONATHAN WENT DOWN TO THE SHELTER LIKE WE DID?
I'M SURE HE DID.
WE WILL CALL HIM TOMORROW, OK?
'NIGHT, DAD.

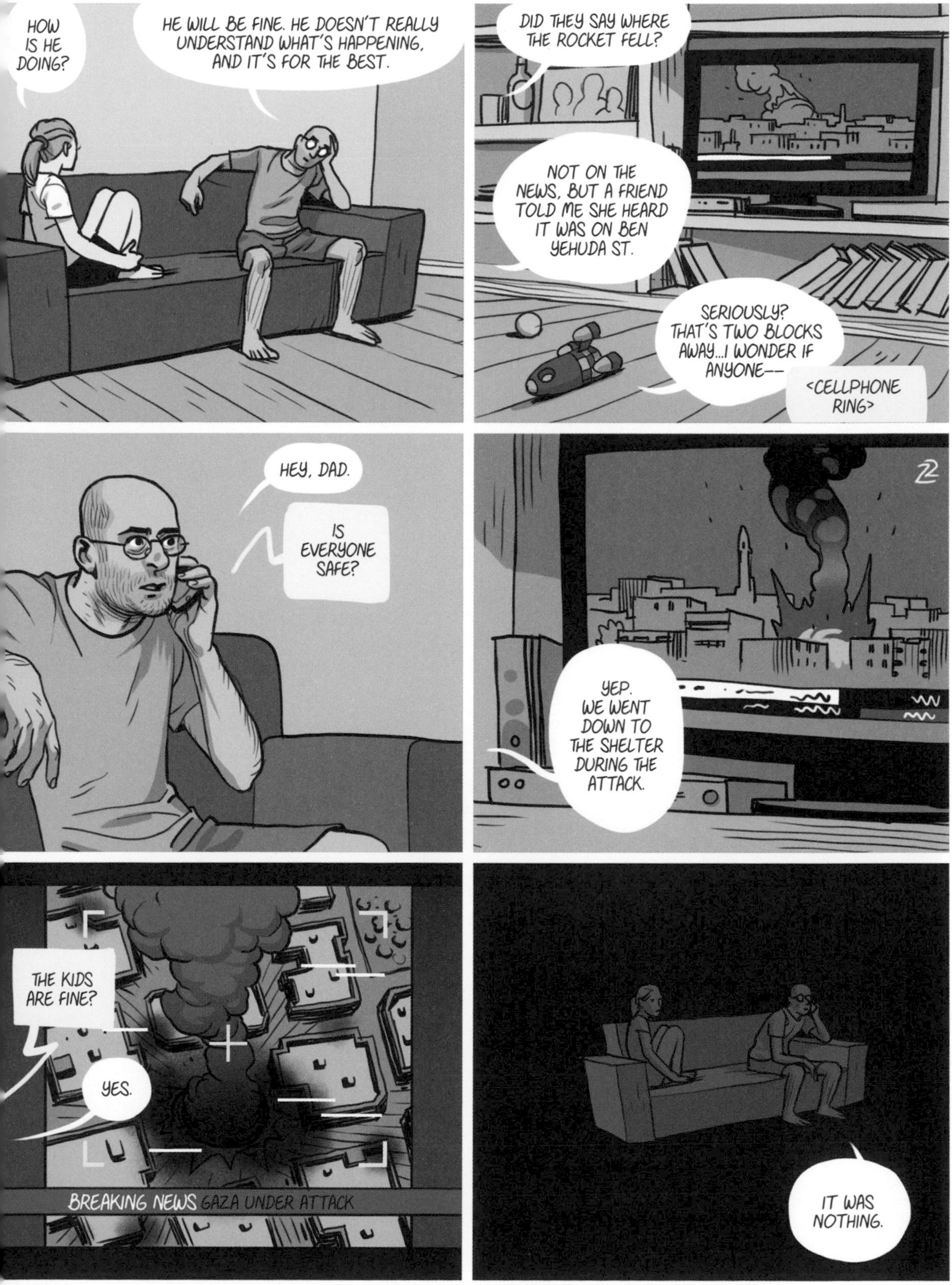
HOW IS HE DOING?
HE WILL BE FINE. HE DOESN'T REALLY UNDERSTAND WHAT'S HAPPENING, AND IT'S FOR THE BEST.
DID THEY SAY WHERE THE ROCKET FELL?
NOT ON THE NEWS, BUT A FRIEND TOLD ME SHE HEARD IT WAS ON BEN YEHUDA ST.
SERIOUSLY? THAT'S TWO BLOCKS AWAY...I WONDER IF ANYONE--
<CELLPHONE RING>
HEY, DAD.
IS EVERYONE SAFE?
YEP. WE WENT DOWN TO THE SHELTER DURING THE ATTACK.
THE KIDS ARE FINE?
YES.
BREAKING NEWS GAZA UNDER ATTACK
IT WAS NOTHING.

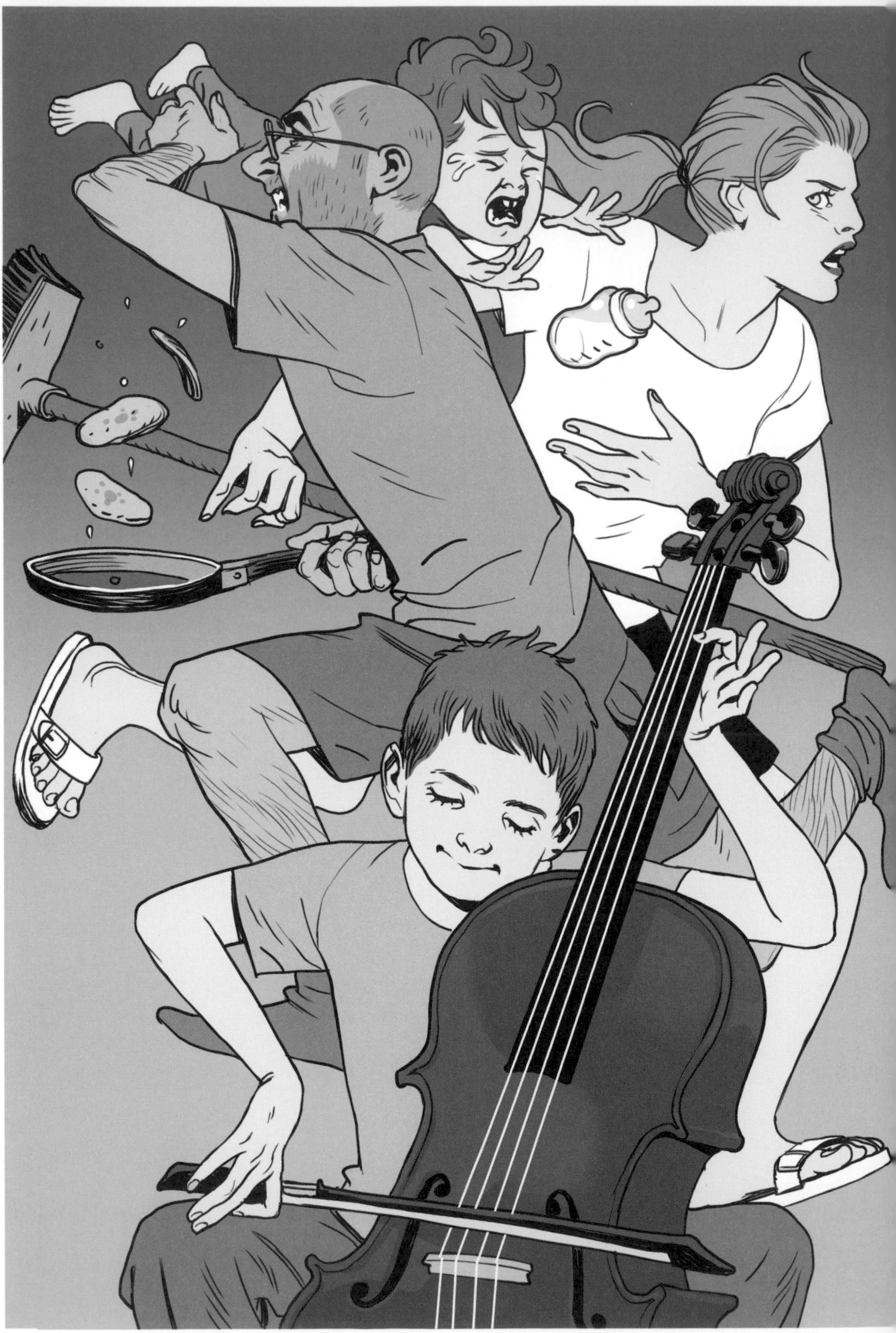

D RECEPTION

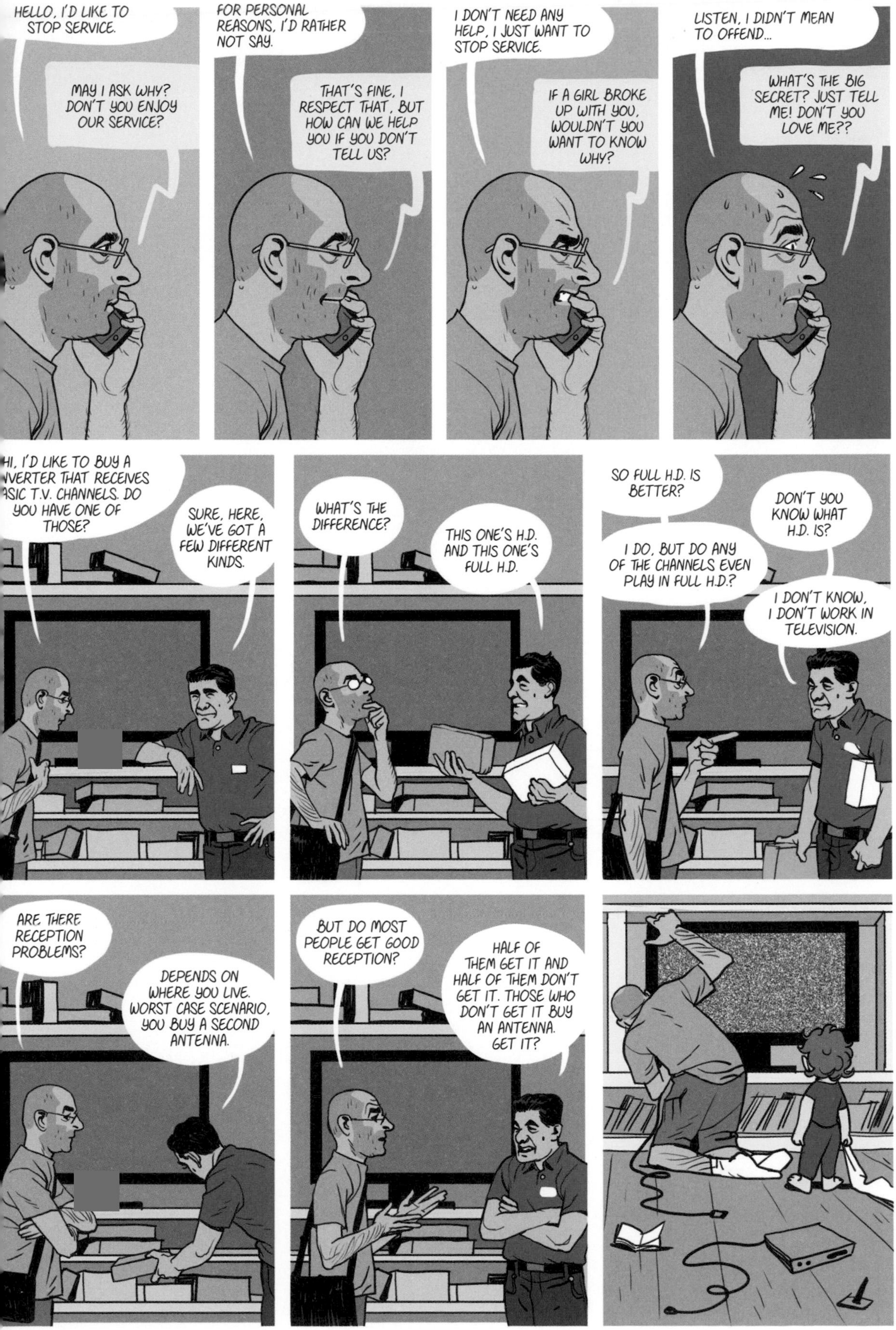
HELLO, I'D LIKE TO STOP SERVICE.
MAY I ASK WHY? DON'T YOU ENJOY OUR SERVICE?
FOR PERSONAL REASONS, I'D RATHER NOT SAY.
THAT'S FINE, I RESPECT THAT, BUT HOW CAN WE HELP YOU IF YOU DON'T TELL US?
I DON'T NEED ANY HELP, I JUST WANT TO STOP SERVICE.
IF A GIRL BROKE UP WITH YOU, WOULDN'T YOU WANT TO KNOW WHY?
LISTEN, I DIDN'T MEAN TO OFFEND...
WHAT'S THE BIG SECRET? JUST TELL ME! DON'T YOU LOVE ME??
HI, I'D LIKE TO BUY A NVERTER THAT RECEIVES ASIC T.V. CHANNELS. DO YOU HAVE ONE OF THOSE?
SURE, HERE, WE'VE GOT A FEW DIFFERENT KINDS.
WHAT'S THE DIFFERENCE?
THIS ONE'S H.D. AND THIS ONE'S FULL H.D.
SO FULL H.D. IS BETTER?
DON'T YOU KNOW WHAT H.D. IS?
I DO, BUT DO ANY OF THE CHANNELS EVEN PLAY IN FULL H.D.?
I DON'T KNOW, I DON'T WORK IN TELEVISION.
ARE THERE RECEPTION PROBLEMS?
DEPENDS ON WHERE YOU LIVE. WORST CASE SCENARIO, YOU BUY A SECOND ANTENNA.
BUT DO MOST PEOPLE GET GOOD RECEPTION?
HALF OF THEM GET IT AND HALF OF THEM DON'T GET IT. THOSE WHO DON'T GET IT BUY AN ANTENNA. GET IT?

A MILLION

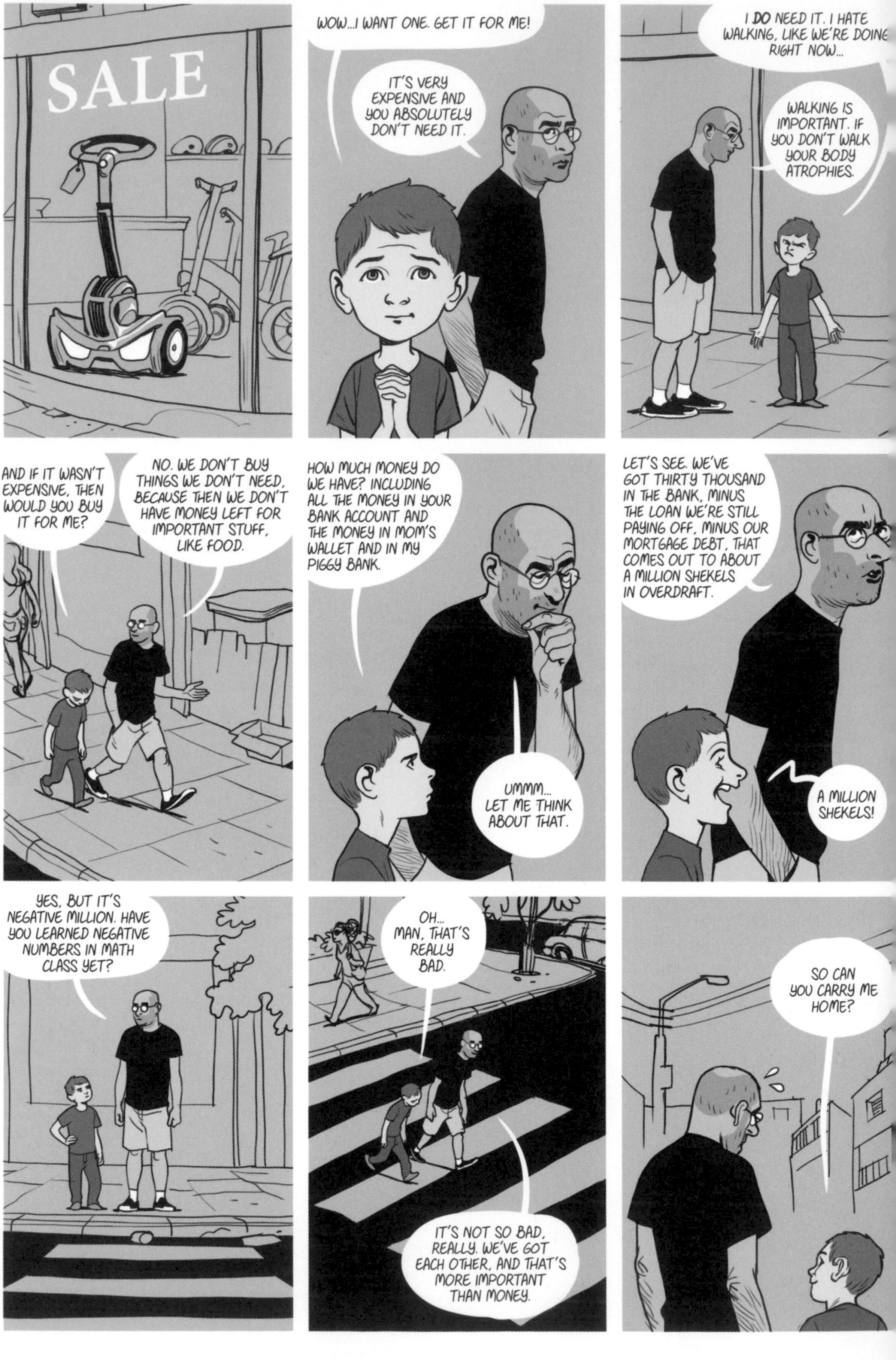
SALE
WOW...I WANT ONE. GET IT FOR ME!
IT'S VERY EXPENSIVE AND YOU ABSOLUTELY DON'T NEED IT.
I DO NEED IT. I HATE WALKING, LIKE WE'RE DOING RIGHT NOW...
WALKING IS IMPORTANT. IF YOU DON'T WALK YOUR BODY ATROPHIES.
AND IF IT WASN'T EXPENSIVE, THEN WOULD YOU BUY IT FOR ME?
NO. WE DON'T BUY THINGS WE DON'T NEED, BECAUSE THEN WE DON'T HAVE MONEY LEFT FOR IMPORTANT STUFF, LIKE FOOD.
HOW MUCH MONEY DO WE HAVE? INCLUDING ALL THE MONEY IN YOUR BANK ACCOUNT AND THE MONEY IN MOM'S WALLET AND IN MY PIGGY BANK.
UMMM... LET ME THINK ABOUT THAT.
LET'S SEE. WE'VE GOT THIRTY THOUSAND IN THE BANK, MINUS THE LOAN WE'RE STILL PAYING OFF, MINUS OUR MORTGAGE DEBT, THAT COMES OUT TO ABOUT A MILLION SHEKELS IN OVERDRAFT.
A MILLION SHEKELS!
YES, BUT IT'S NEGATIVE MILLION. HAVE YOU LEARNED NEGATIVE NUMBERS IN MATH CLASS YET?
OH... MAN, THAT'S REALLY BAD.
IT'S NOT SO BAD, REALLY. WE'VE GOT EACH OTHER, AND THAT'S MORE IMPORTANT THAN MONEY.
SO CAN YOU CARRY ME HOME?

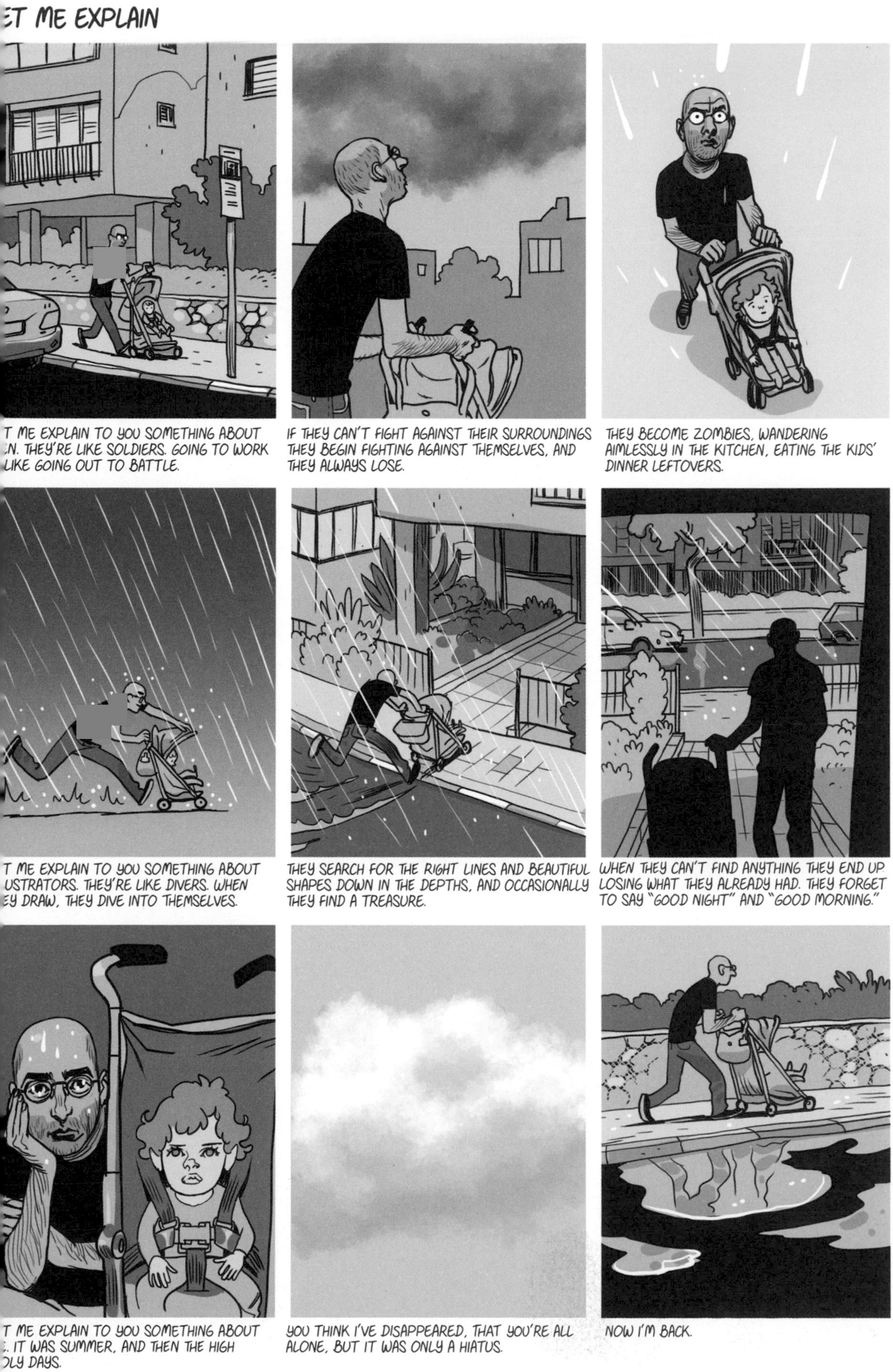

ET ME EXPLAIN
T ME EXPLAIN TO YOU SOMETHING ABOUT N. THEY'RE LIKE SOLDIERS. GOING TO WORK LIKE GOING OUT TO BATTLE.
IF THEY CAN'T FIGHT AGAINST THEIR SURROUNDINGS THEY BEGIN FIGHTING AGAINST THEMSELVES, AND THEY ALWAYS LOSE.
THEY BECOME ZOMBIES, WANDERING AIMLESSLY IN THE KITCHEN, EATING THE KIDS' DINNER LEFTOVERS.
T ME EXPLAIN TO YOU SOMETHING ABOUT USTRATORS. THEY'RE LIKE DIVERS. WHEN EY DRAW, THEY DIVE INTO THEMSELVES.
THEY SEARCH FOR THE RIGHT LINES AND BEAUTIFUL SHAPES DOWN IN THE DEPTHS, AND OCCASIONALLY THEY FIND A TREASURE.
WHEN THEY CAN'T FIND ANYTHING THEY END UP LOSING WHAT THEY ALREADY HAD. THEY FORGET TO SAY "GOOD NIGHT" AND "GOOD MORNING."
T ME EXPLAIN TO YOU SOMETHING ABOUT . IT WAS SUMMER, AND THEN THE HIGH OLY DAYS.
YOU THINK I'VE DISAPPEARED, THAT YOU'RE ALL ALONE, BUT IT WAS ONLY A HIATUS.
NOW I'M BACK.

CRASH LANDING

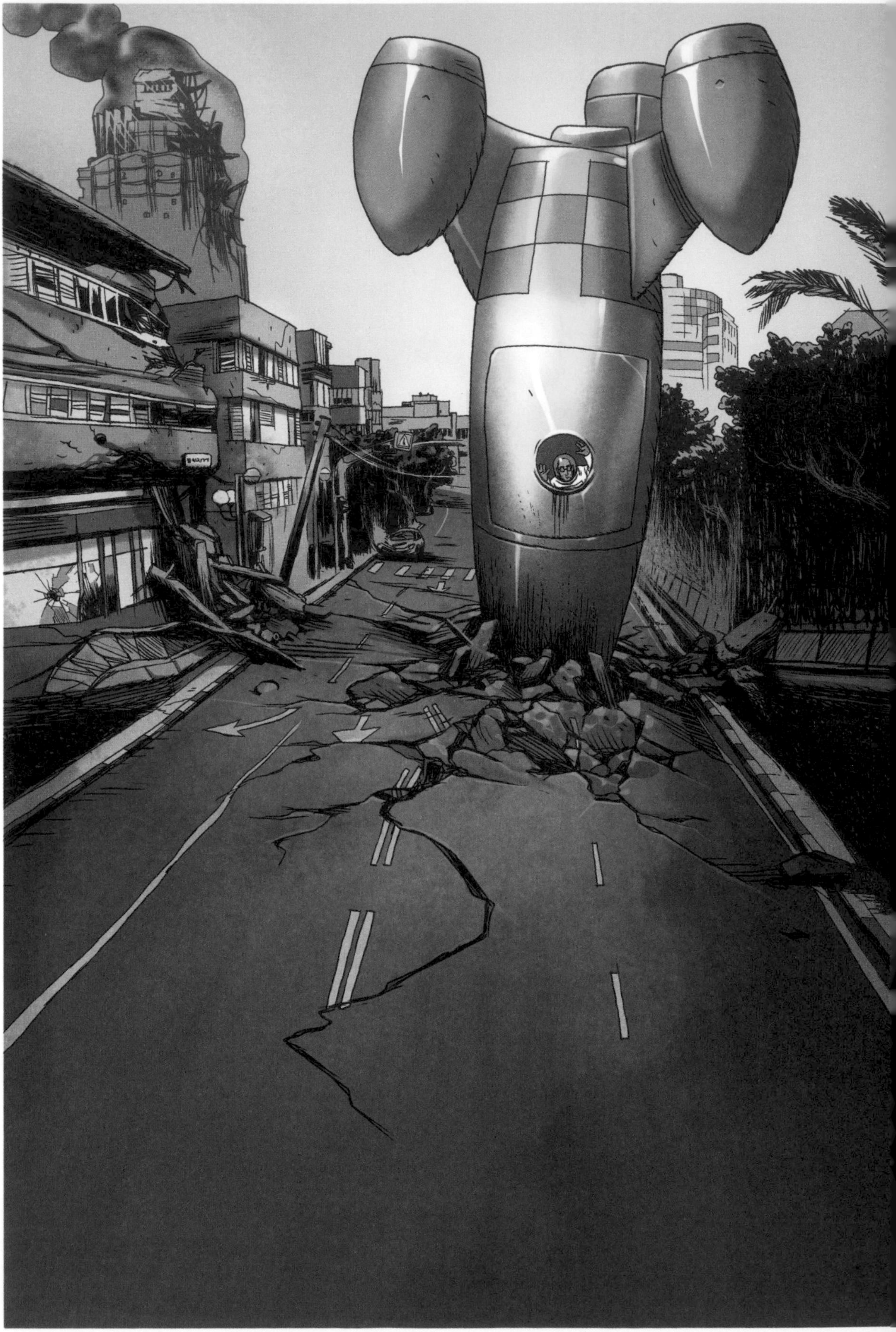

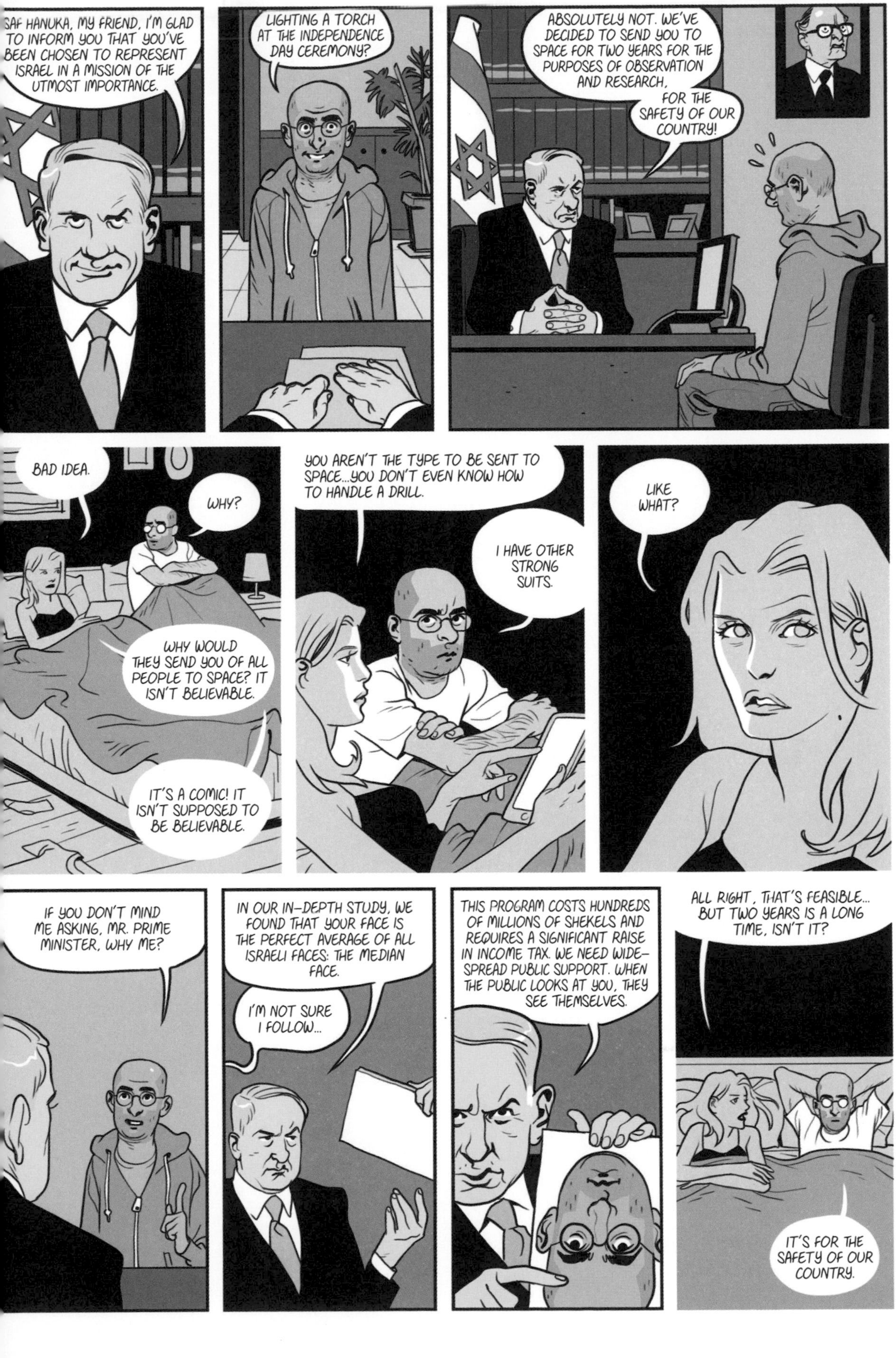
SAF HANUKA, MY FRIEND, I'M GLAD TO INFORM YOU THAT YOU'VE BEEN CHOSEN TO REPRESENT ISRAEL IN A MISSION OF THE UTMOST IMPORTANCE.
LIGHTING A TORCH AT THE INDEPENDENCE DAY CEREMONY?
ABSOLUTELY NOT. WE'VE DECIDED TO SEND YOU TO SPACE FOR TWO YEARS FOR THE PURPOSES OF OBSERVATION AND RESEARCH,
FOR THE SAFETY OF OUR COUNTRY!
BAD IDEA.
WHY?
WHY WOULD THEY SEND YOU OF ALL PEOPLE TO SPACE? IT ISN'T BELIEVABLE.
IT'S A COMIC! IT ISN'T SUPPOSED TO BE BELIEVABLE.
YOU AREN'T THE TYPE TO BE SENT TO SPACE...YOU DON'T EVEN KNOW HOW TO HANDLE A DRILL.
I HAVE OTHER STRONG SUITS.
LIKE WHAT?
IF YOU DON'T MIND ME ASKING, MR. PRIME MINISTER, WHY ME?
IN OUR IN-DEPTH STUDY, WE FOUND THAT YOUR FACE IS THE PERFECT AVERAGE OF ALL ISRAELI FACES: THE MEDIAN FACE.
I'M NOT SURE I FOLLOW...
THIS PROGRAM COSTS HUNDREDS OF MILLIONS OF SHEKELS AND REQUIRES A SIGNIFICANT RAISE IN INCOME TAX. WE NEED WIDE-SPREAD PUBLIC SUPPORT. WHEN THE PUBLIC LOOKS AT YOU, THEY SEE THEMSELVES.
ALL RIGHT, THAT'S FEASIBLE... BUT TWO YEARS IS A LONG TIME, ISN'T IT?
IT'S FOR THE SAFETY OF OUR COUNTRY.

DARK BALL

THE FIRST TEST THEY PUT ME THROUGH AT THE ISRAELI SPACE AGENCY WAS DESIGNED TO CONFIRM THAT I WASN'T CLAUSTROPHOBIC.

THEY LOCKED ME IN A DARK BALL FOR AN INDEFINITE AMOUNT OF TIME, TO TEST MY REACTION TO HERMETIC SURROUNDINGS.

TRY TO IMAGINE A CLAUSTROPHOBIC ASTRONAUT LOCKED INSIDE A SPACESHIP FOR—

Waaaaaa...

ARE YOU GOING TO PICK HER UP?

WHAT?

YOUR DAUGHTER'S CRYING...

ARE YOU EVEN HERE? I CAN'T DO EVERYTHING MYSELF!

Daddy...

IT TURNS OUT THAT LOTS OF PEOPLE HAVE MENTAL DISORDERS THAT THEY ARE NOT AWARE OF SO LONG AS THEIR DAY-TO-DAY LIFE ISN'T DISRUPTED.

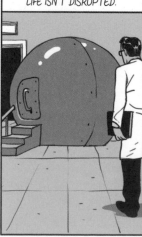

I ACTUALLY ENJOYED BEING COMPLETELY DETACHED FROM THE WORLD, AND WAS EVEN A LITTLE SORRY WHEN THEY FINALLY OPENED THE DOOR.

MY SUCCESS IN THE CLAUSTROPHOBIA TEST MADE ME THINK I MIGHT HAVE A DIFFERENT PROBLEM I'M NOT AWARE OF...

TRY TO IMAGINE A FATHER WHO, RATHER THAN PAY ATTENTION TO HIS CHILDREN, BECOMES LOCKED INSIDE—

ARE YOU PUTTING HER TO BED?

OUBLE BILL

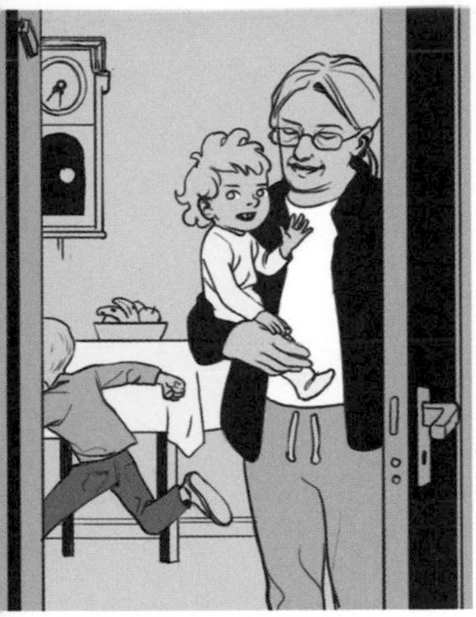

TER SEVENTEEN MONTHS, WE FELT IT OULD BE ALL RIGHT TO LEAVE THE LITTLE NE WITH HER GRANDPARENTS FOR ONE NIGHT. R ELDEST STAYED THERE TOO.

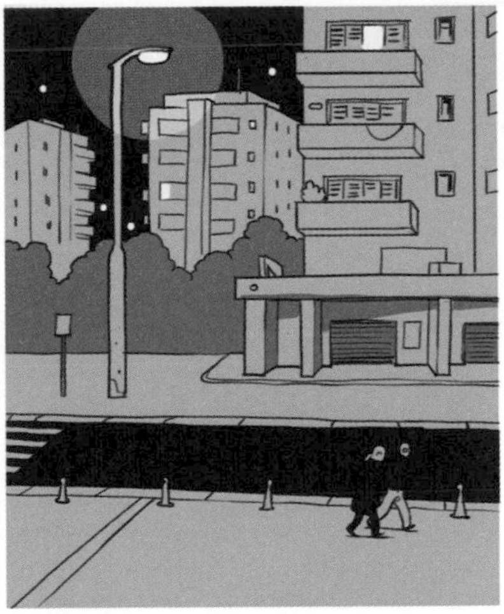

WE WANTED TO GO SEE A MOVIE, BUT IT WAS TOO LATE TO GO TO TEL AVIV, SO WE COMPROMISED FOR THE THEATER AT THE MALL IN OUR TOWN OF KIRYAT ONO.

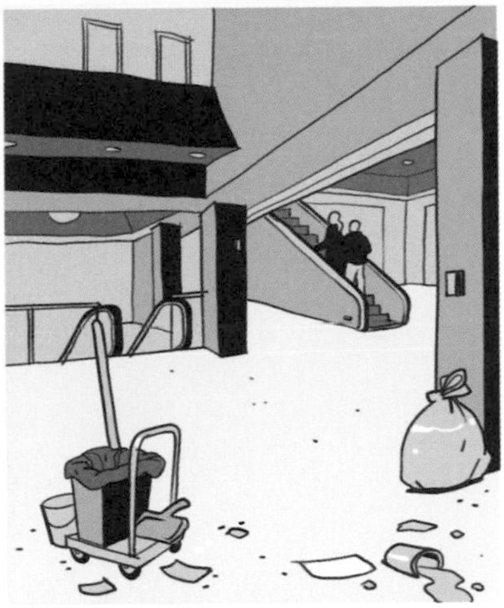

THE MOVIES LOOK THE SAME WHEREVER YOU GO ANYWAY, AND SO DO THE MALLS.

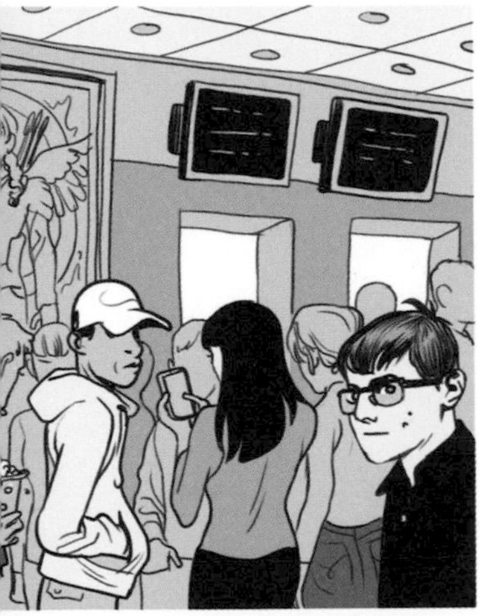

TRIED TO RECOGNIZE FAMILIAR FACES IN E TICKET LINE. WHEN I GREW UP IN KIRYAT NO, THE LAND WHERE THE MALL IS NOW WAS ST A HUGE SAND LOT.

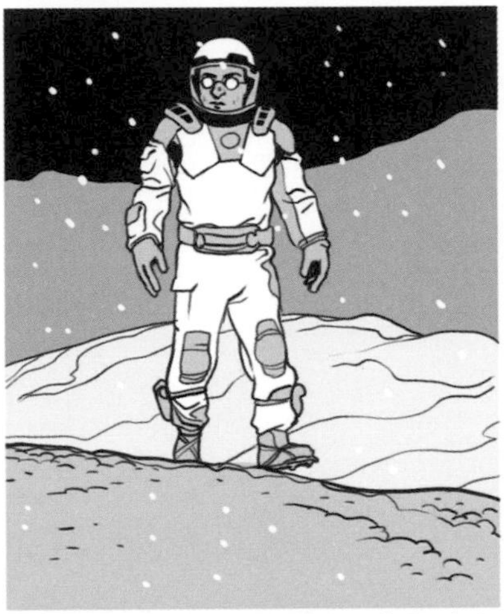

BUT THERE WERE ONLY TEENAGERS THERE, AND THEY ALL WENT TO A MOVIE ABOUT A FUTURISTIC REALITY T.V. SHOW. WE WERE GOING TO SEE A MOVIE ABOUT AN ASTRONAUT.

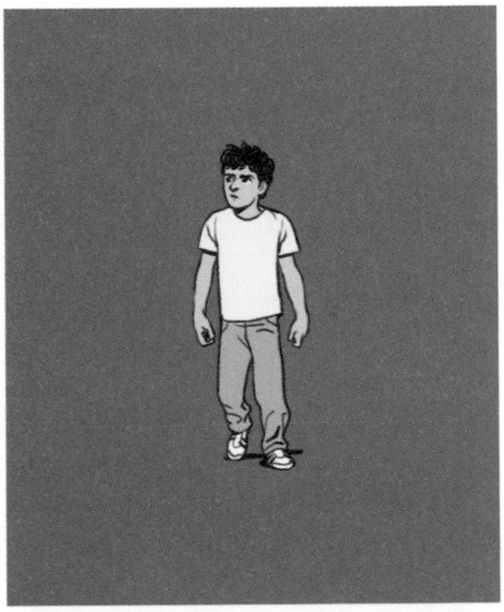

EVEN THOUGH IT'S BEEN TWENTY-FIVE YEARS SINCE I WAS THEIR AGE, I COULD RECOGNIZE ALL THEIR SOCIAL LABELS: THE "NERDS," THE "PIMPS," THE "FREAKS."

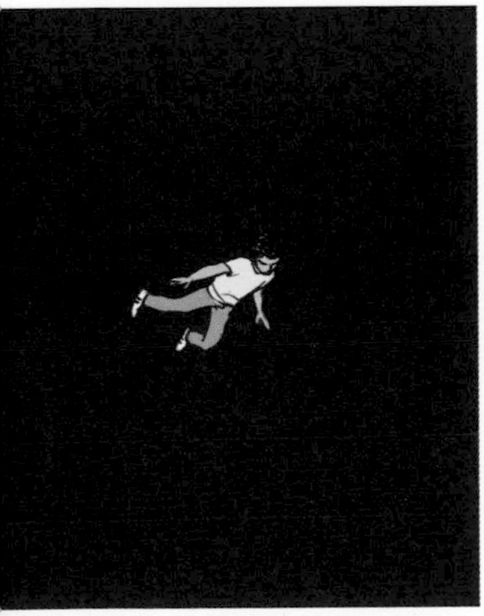

Y AGE FIFTEEN, I'D MANAGED TO TRY OUT ACH OF THESE LABELS AND GREW EQUALLY OPELESS ABOUT ALL OF THEM.

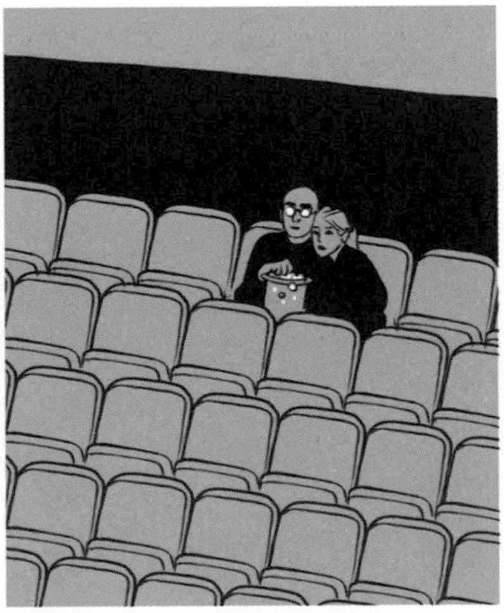

IN THE MOVIE WE WATCHED, THE ASTRONAUT HAD TO LEAVE HIS FAMILY BEHIND TO GO SAVE HUMANKIND.

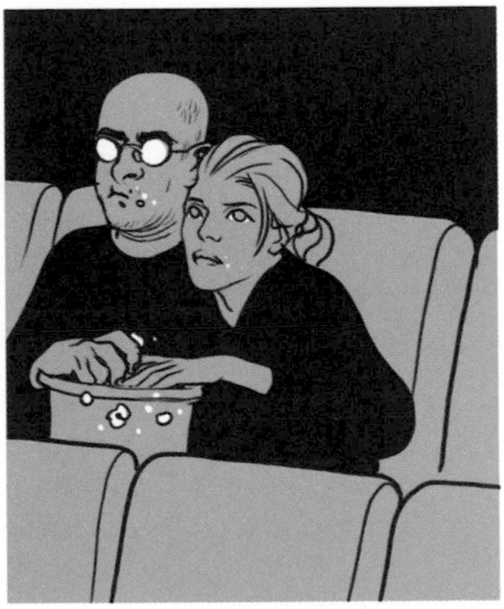

FOR ME IT WAS THE OTHER WAY AROUND. MY FAMILY SAVED ME FROM HUMANKIND.

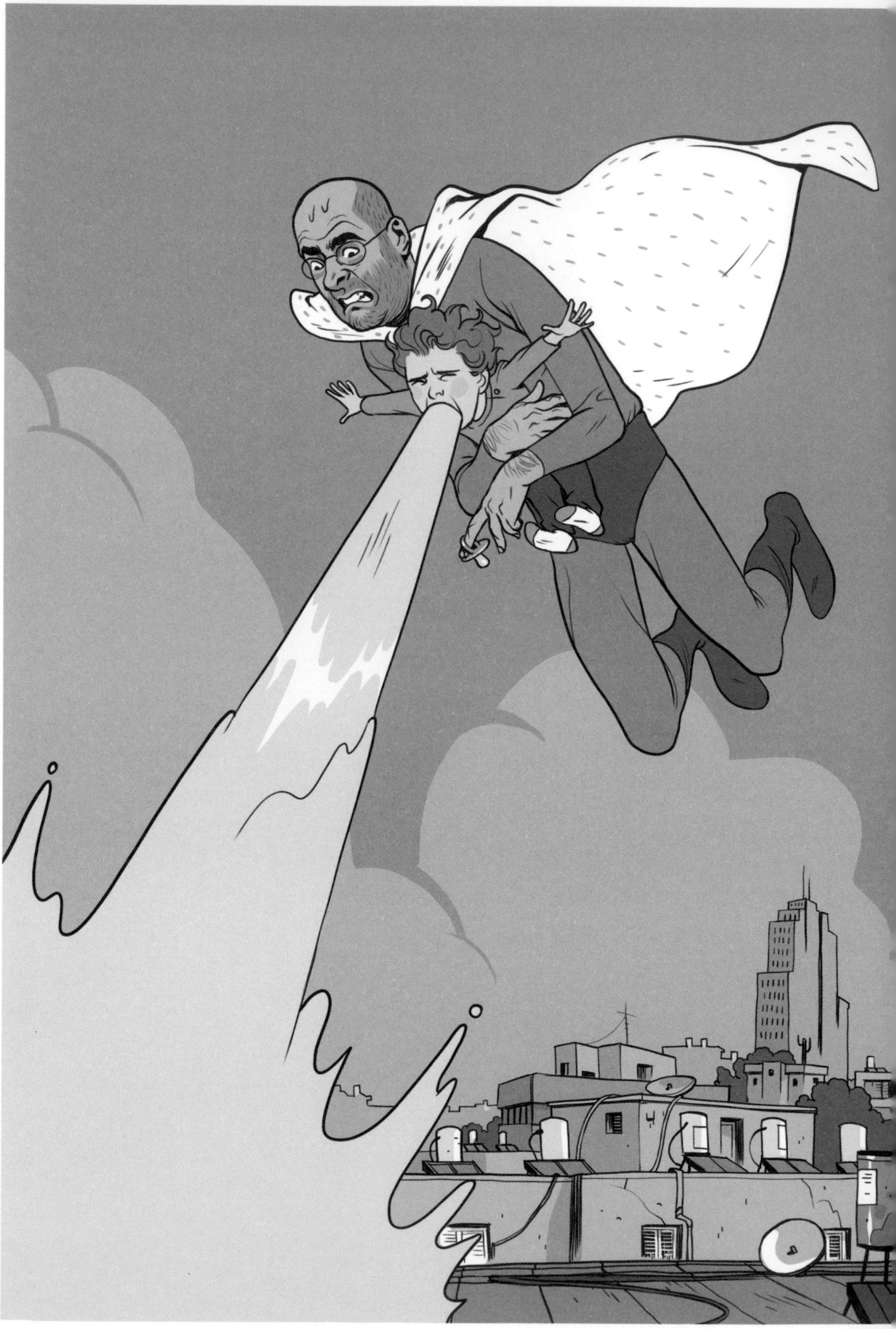

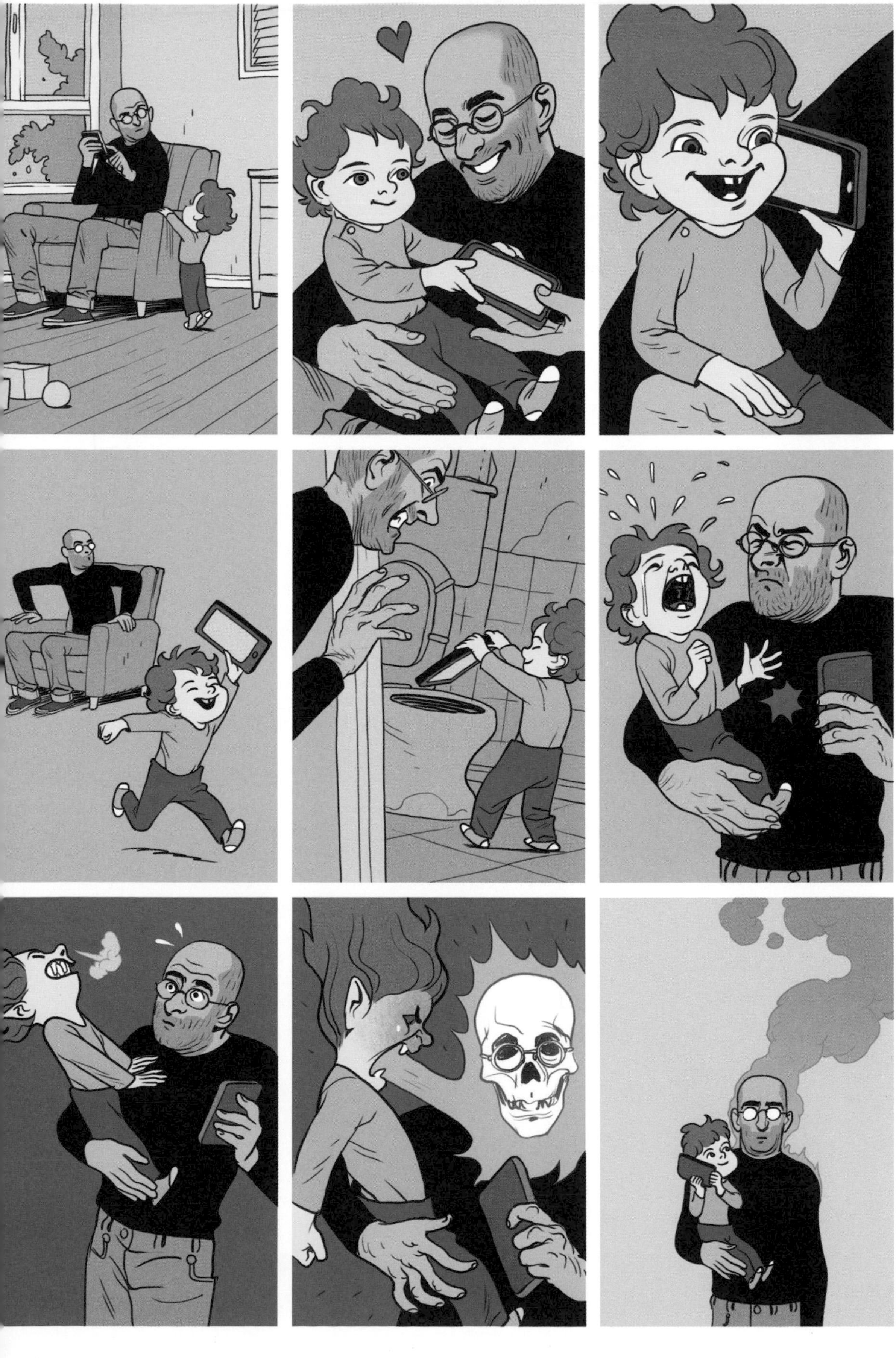

PERFECT

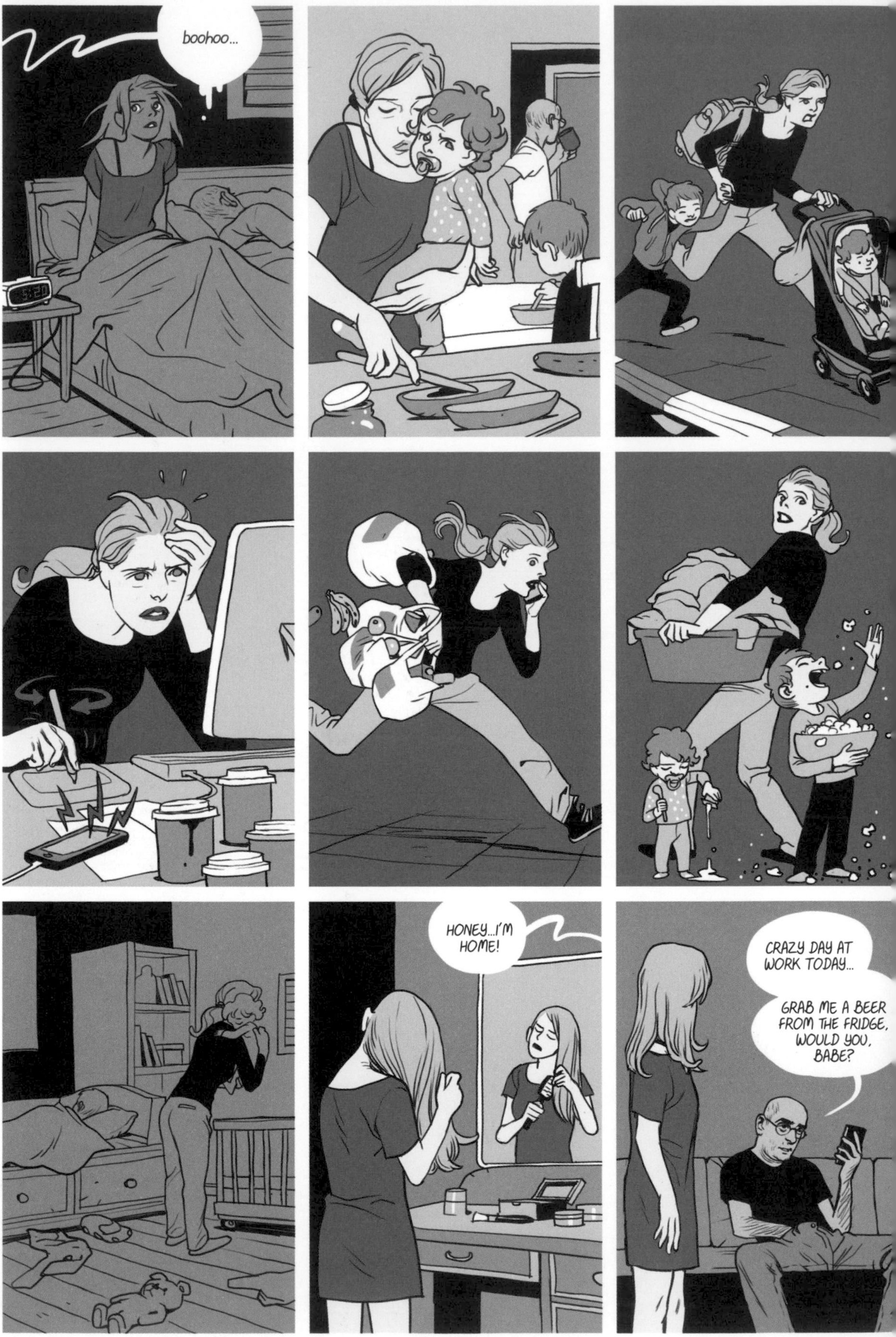
boohoo...
HONEY...I'M HOME!
CRAZY DAY AT WORK TODAY...
GRAB ME A BEER FROM THE FRIDGE, WOULD YOU, BABE?

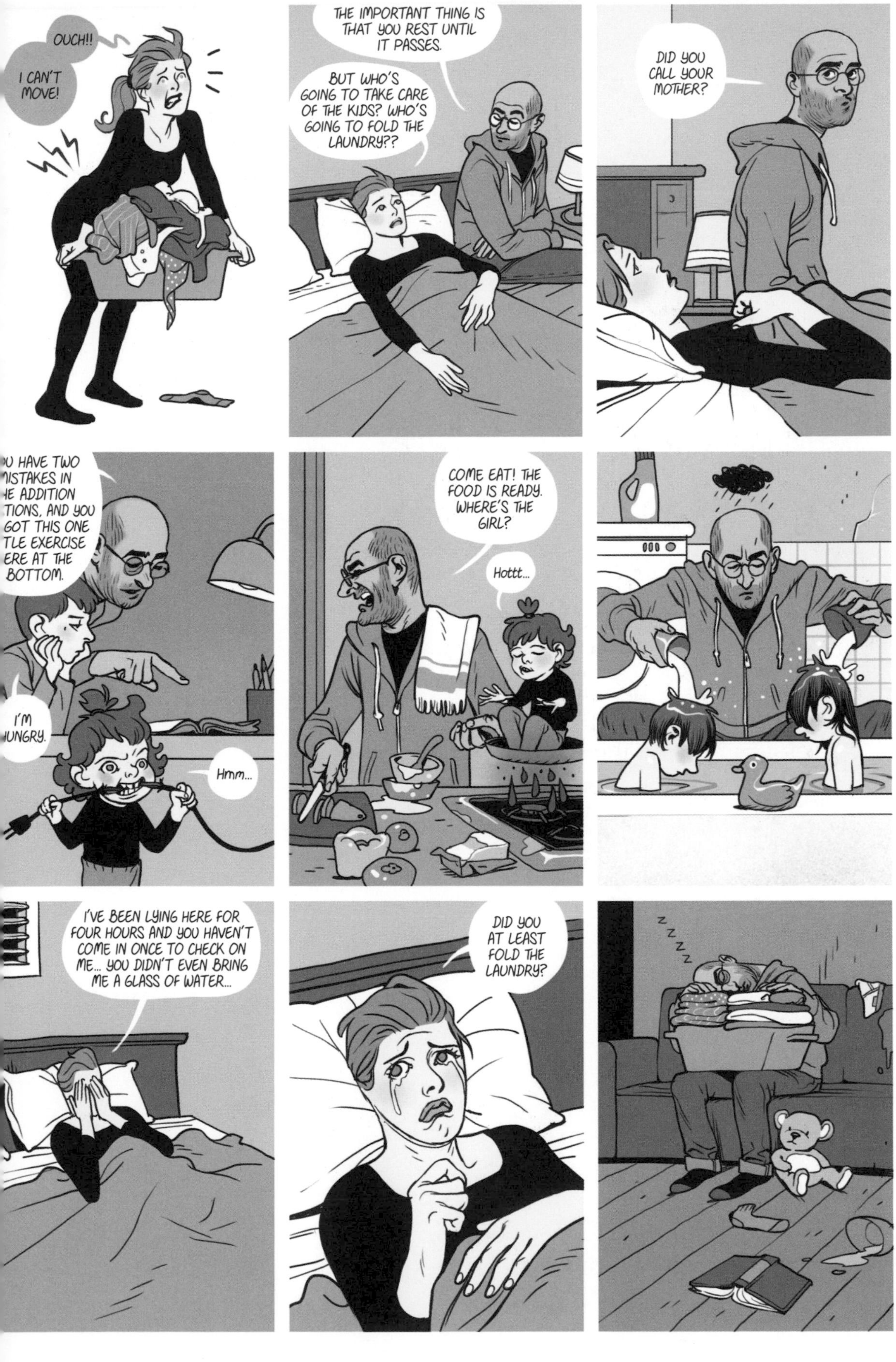
OUCH!!
I CAN'T MOVE!
THE IMPORTANT THING IS THAT YOU REST UNTIL IT PASSES.
BUT WHO'S GOING TO TAKE CARE OF THE KIDS? WHO'S GOING TO FOLD THE LAUNDRY??
DID YOU CALL YOUR MOTHER?
OU HAVE TWO MISTAKES IN HE ADDITION TIONS, AND YOU GOT THIS ONE TLE EXERCISE ERE AT THE BOTTOM.
I'M UNGRY.
Hmm...
COME EAT! THE FOOD IS READY. WHERE'S THE GIRL?
Hottt...
I'VE BEEN LYING HERE FOR FOUR HOURS AND YOU HAVEN'T COME IN ONCE TO CHECK ON ME... YOU DIDN'T EVEN BRING ME A GLASS OF WATER...
DID YOU AT LEAST FOLD THE LAUNDRY?
Z Z Z Z

TEST YOURSELF: ARE YOU A PERSON OF COLOR?

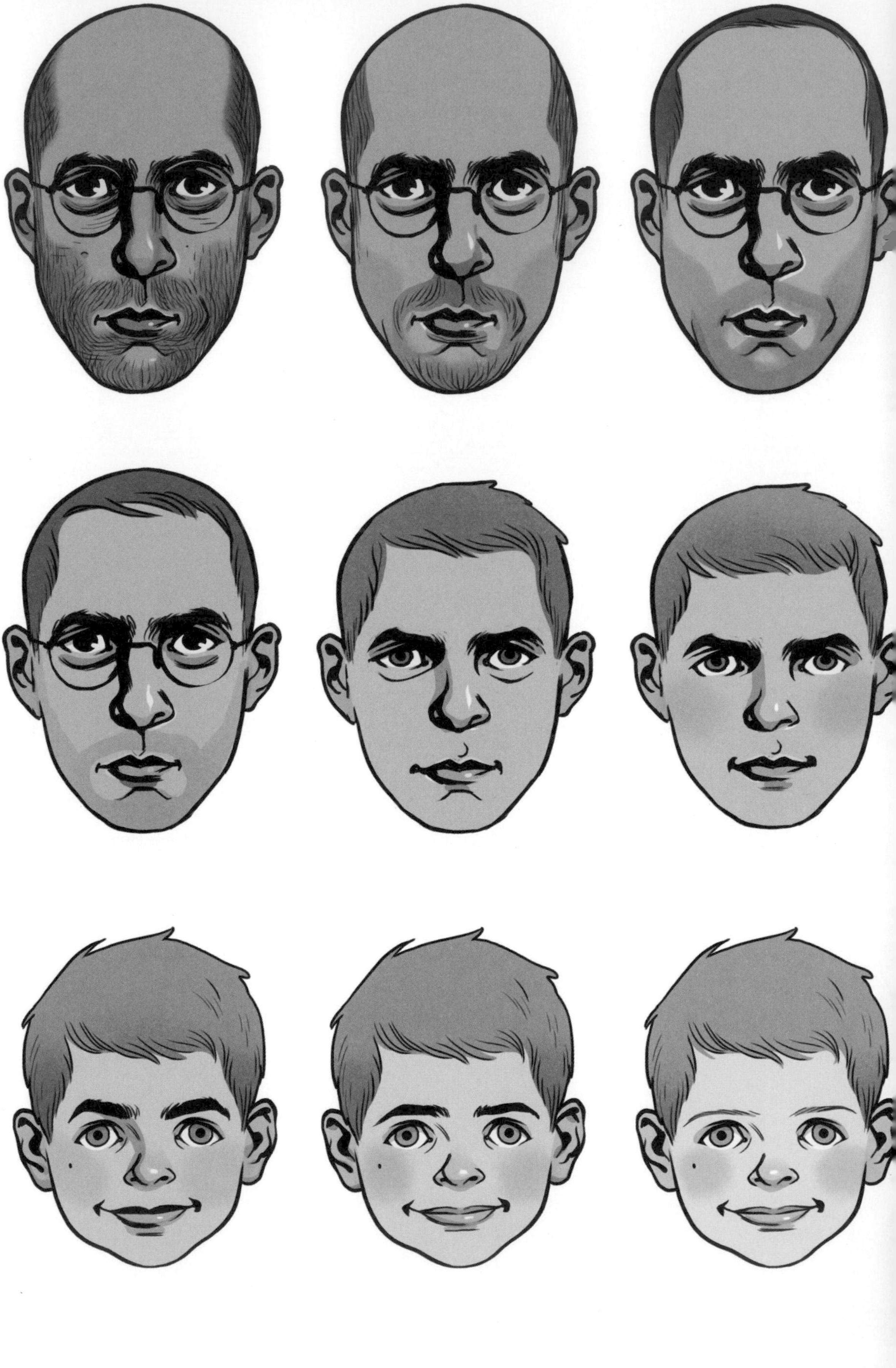

DAD...

FINISH YOUR TOAST.

WHY AREN'T YOU EVER HAPPY?

THAT'S NOT TRUE...

I'M HAPPY ALL THE TIME. YOU AND YOUR SISTER MAKE ME VERY HAPPY.

YEAH, BUT YOU NEVER LAUGH. I DON'T EVEN KNOW WHAT YOU LOOK LIKE WHEN YOU LAUGH.

HERE, I'M LAUGHING! SEE!!

ALL RIGHT, STOP IT, STOP IT! IT DOESN'T LOOK REAL.

IF YOU'RE DONE WITH YOUR TOAST GO BRUSH YOUR TEETH.

AND YOU'RE NOT EVEN TICKLISH, EITHER!

CLICK!

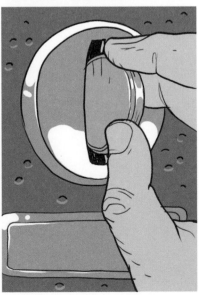

WONDER BOYZ

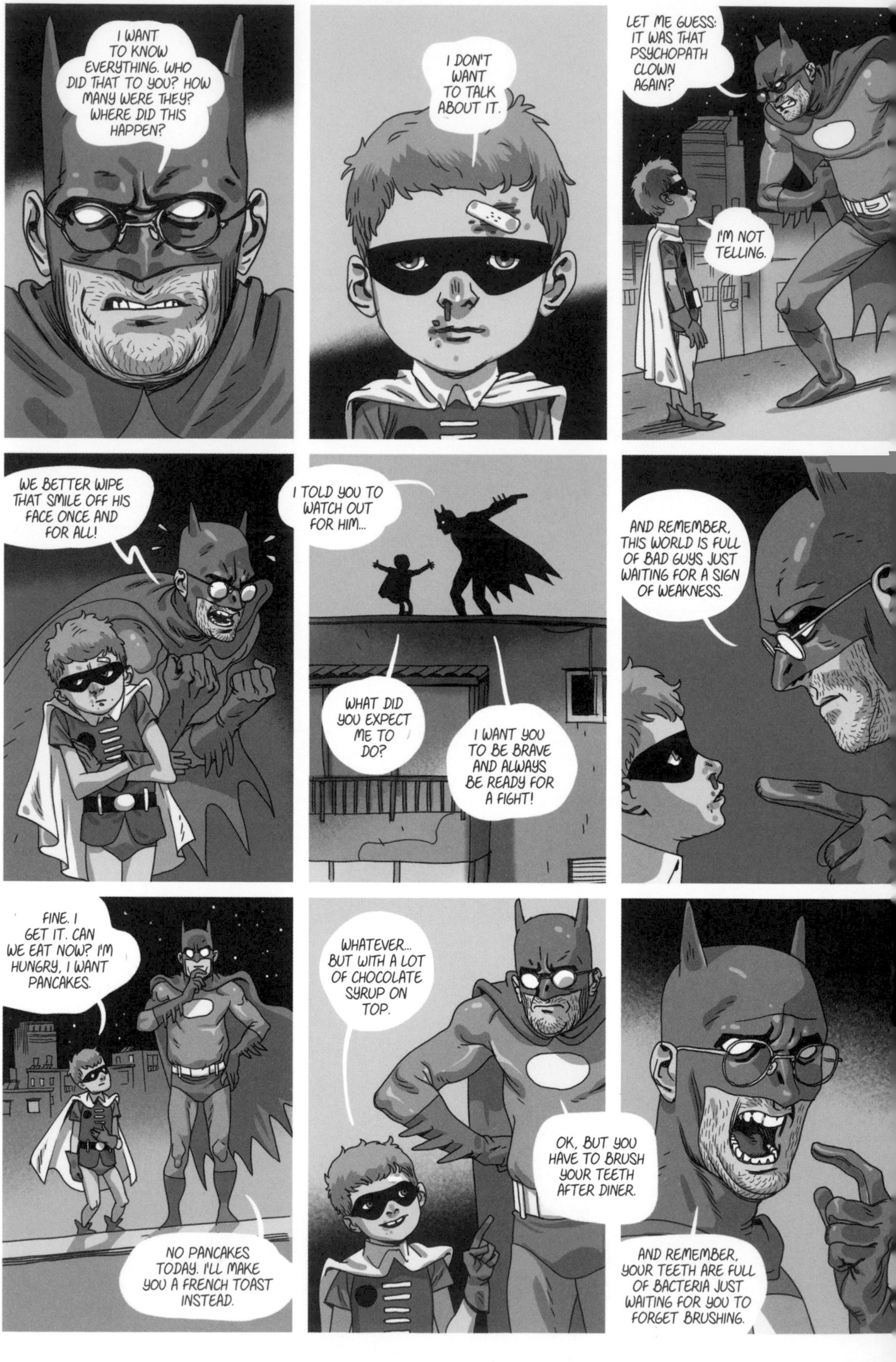

I WANT TO KNOW EVERYTHING. WHO DID THAT TO YOU? HOW MANY WERE THEY? WHERE DID THIS HAPPEN?
I DON'T WANT TO TALK ABOUT IT.
LET ME GUESS: IT WAS THAT PSYCHOPATH CLOWN AGAIN?
I'M NOT TELLING.
WE BETTER WIPE THAT SMILE OFF HIS FACE ONCE AND FOR ALL!
I TOLD YOU TO WATCH OUT FOR HIM...
WHAT DID YOU EXPECT ME TO DO?
I WANT YOU TO BE BRAVE AND ALWAYS BE READY FOR A FIGHT!
AND REMEMBER, THIS WORLD IS FULL OF BAD GUYS JUST WAITING FOR A SIGN OF WEAKNESS.
FINE. I GET IT. CAN WE EAT NOW? I'M HUNGRY, I WANT PANCAKES.
NO PANCAKES TODAY. I'LL MAKE YOU A FRENCH TOAST INSTEAD.
WHATEVER... BUT WITH A LOT OF CHOCOLATE SYRUP ON TOP.
OK, BUT YOU HAVE TO BRUSH YOUR TEETH AFTER DINER.
AND REMEMBER, YOUR TEETH ARE FULL OF BACTERIA JUST WAITING FOR YOU TO FORGET BRUSHING.

ILY ONCE A YEAR

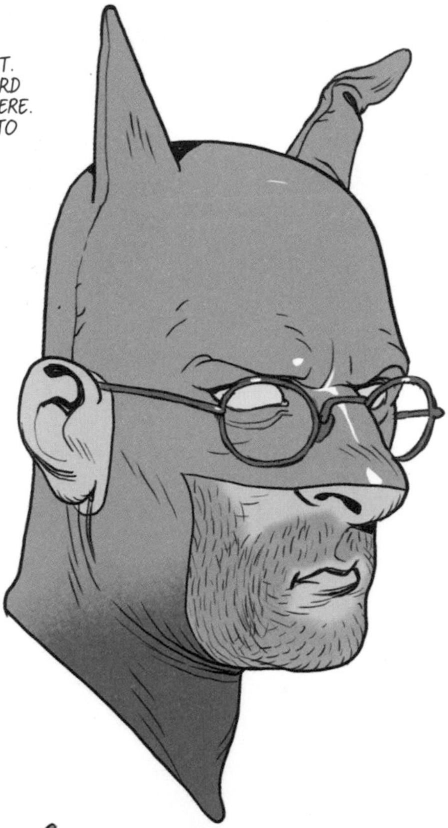

DAD: PREFERS SHADOW TO LIGHT. EVEN WHEN HE'S HOME IT'S HARD TO BE CERTAIN HE'S REALLY THERE. HE'S A SUPERHERO BUT ONLY TO THE LITTLE ONES.

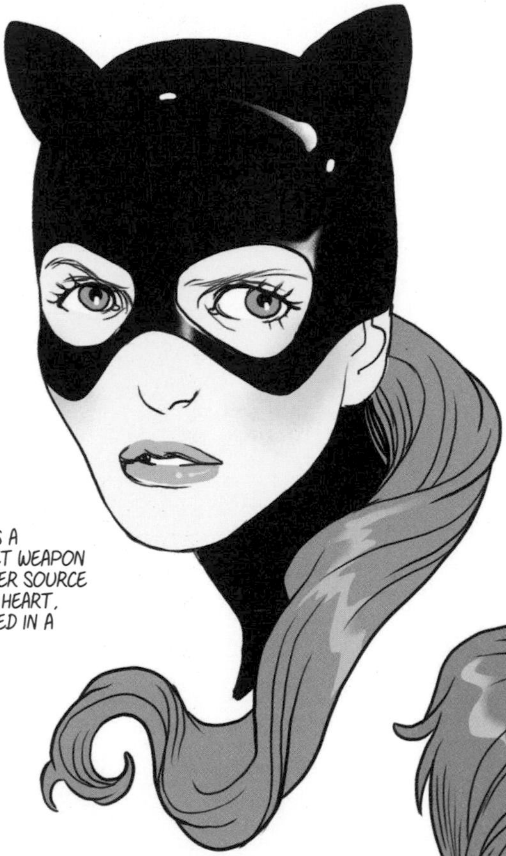

OM: HER BEAUTY IS A ISGUISE, HER SECRET WEAPON S HER BRAIN. BUT HER SOURCE F POWER IS IN HER HEART, ND IT ISN'T WRAPPED IN A OW. IT'S REAL.

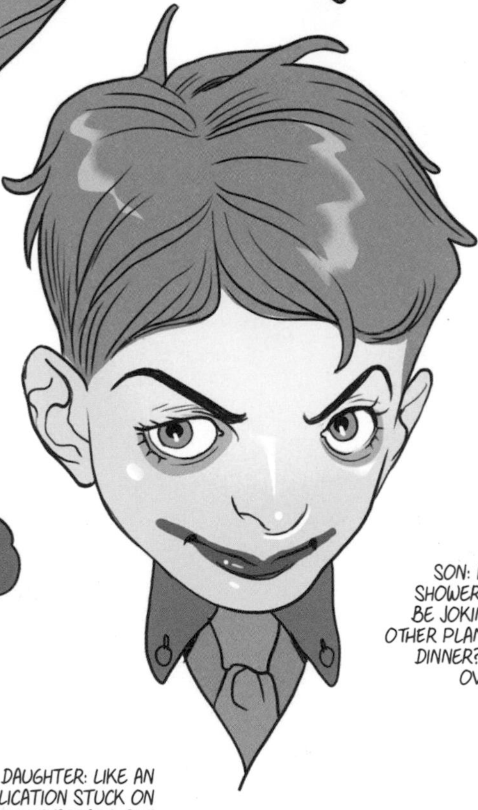

SON: HOMEWORK? SHOWER? YOU MUST BE JOKING. HE'S GOT OTHER PLANS. FINISH HIS DINNER? FIRST HAND OVER THE IPAD.

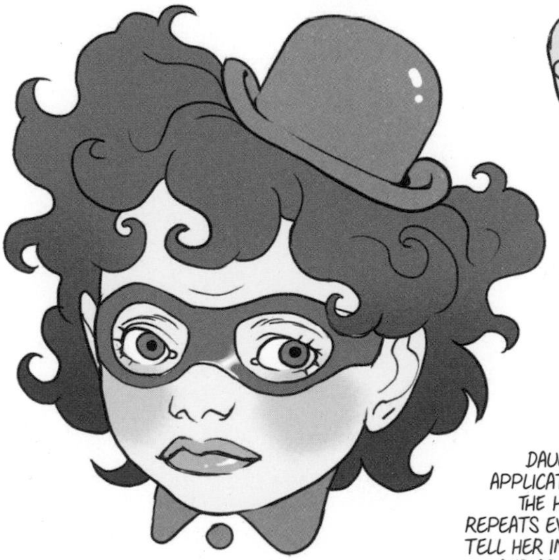

DAUGHTER: LIKE AN APPLICATION STUCK ON THE HOMEPAGE. SHE REPEATS EVERYTHING YOU TELL HER IN A CUTE VOICE AND ADDS A QUESTION MARK. QUESTION MARK?

BRILLIANT

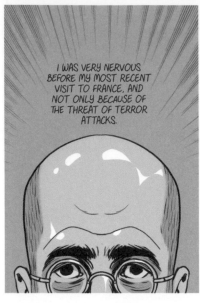

I WAS VERY NERVOUS BEFORE MY MOST RECENT VISIT TO FRANCE, AND NOT ONLY BECAUSE OF THE THREAT OF TERROR ATTACKS.

THE PURPOSE OF THE TRIP WAS TO PROMOTE A COMIC BOOK. IN FRANCE, THE CUSTOM IS TO GIVE THE BOOK TO A READER WITH A PERSONAL DEDICATION.

BUT THIS SPECIAL INTERACTION WAS OFTEN RUINED BY ONE SMALL DETAIL: A SHINY BALD HEAD. THE POOR READER, RATHER THAN ENJOY THE DEDICATION, BECOMES HYPNOTIZED BY THE SPARKLE.

I DECIDED TO GO TO WAR OVER THE HIGHEST STRATEGIC POINT IN THE BODY, AND BUY A SPECIAL PRODUCT THAT TURNS A BALD HEAD INTO A PERFECTLY MATTE SURFACE.

ANTI-SHINE

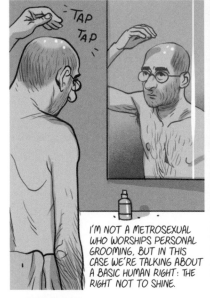

TAP TAP

I'M NOT A METROSEXUAL WHO WORSHIPS PERSONAL GROOMING, BUT IN THIS CASE WE'RE TALKING ABOUT A BASIC HUMAN RIGHT: THE RIGHT NOT TO SHINE.

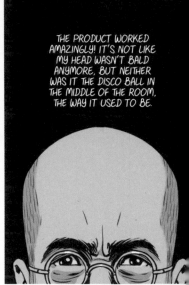

THE PRODUCT WORKED AMAZINGLY! IT'S NOT LIKE MY HEAD WASN'T BALD ANYMORE, BUT NEITHER WAS IT THE DISCO BALL IN THE MIDDLE OF THE ROOM, THE WAY IT USED TO BE.

THE SUCCESS CONTINUED AT A FANCY DINNER THROWN FOR ME BY MY PUBLISHER. I STUTTERED IN FRENCH AS USUAL, BUT THIS TIME WITHOUT A DROP OF SWEAT.

UNFORTUNATELY, THE SPELL WAS BROKEN DURING AN INTERVIEW FOR LOCAL PRESS THAT TURNED TO THE TOPIC OF ISRAELI POLITICS...

WHAT'S YOUR STANCE REGARDING THE OCCUPATION?

SIGH

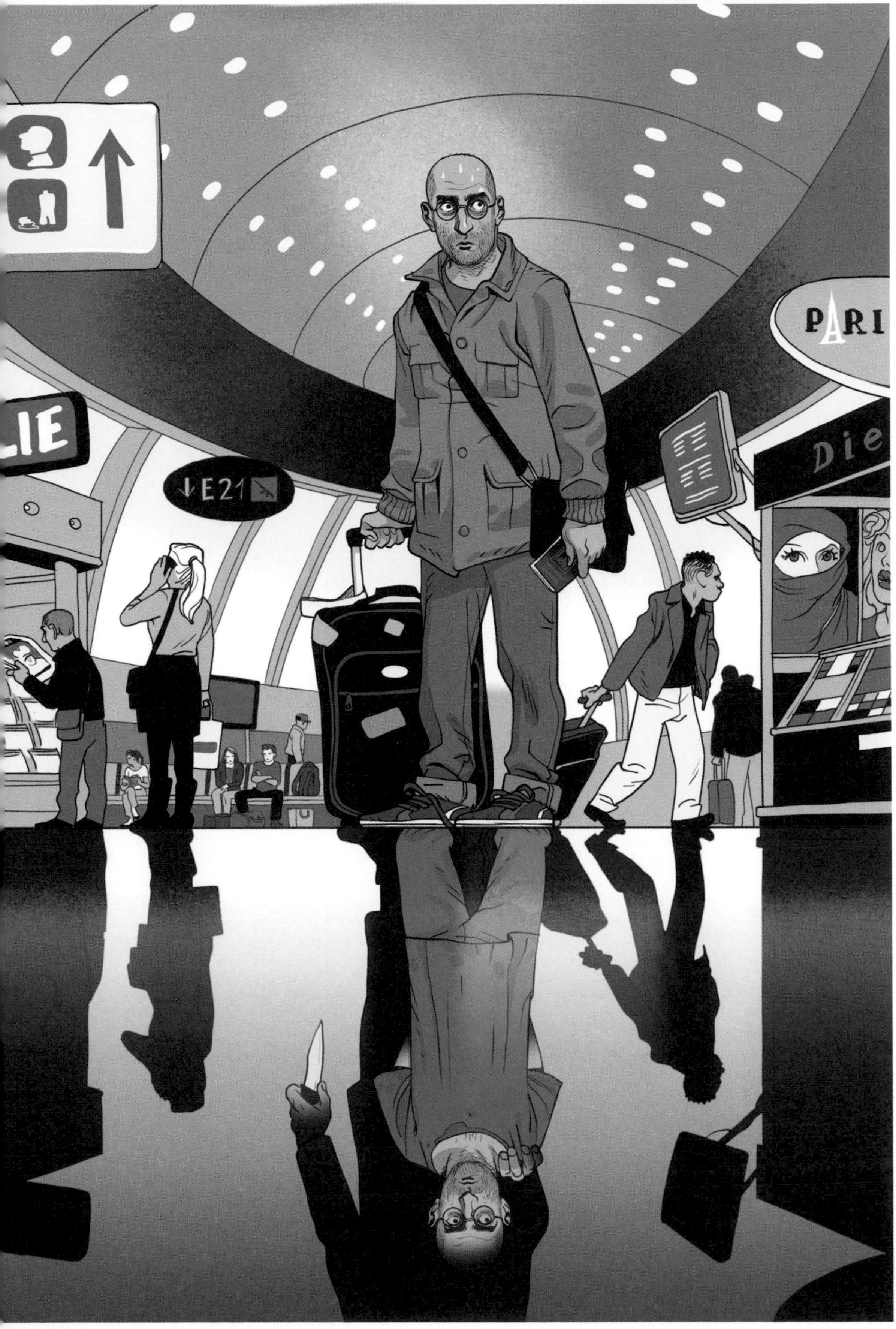
PARI
LIE
E21
Die

WORK TRIP

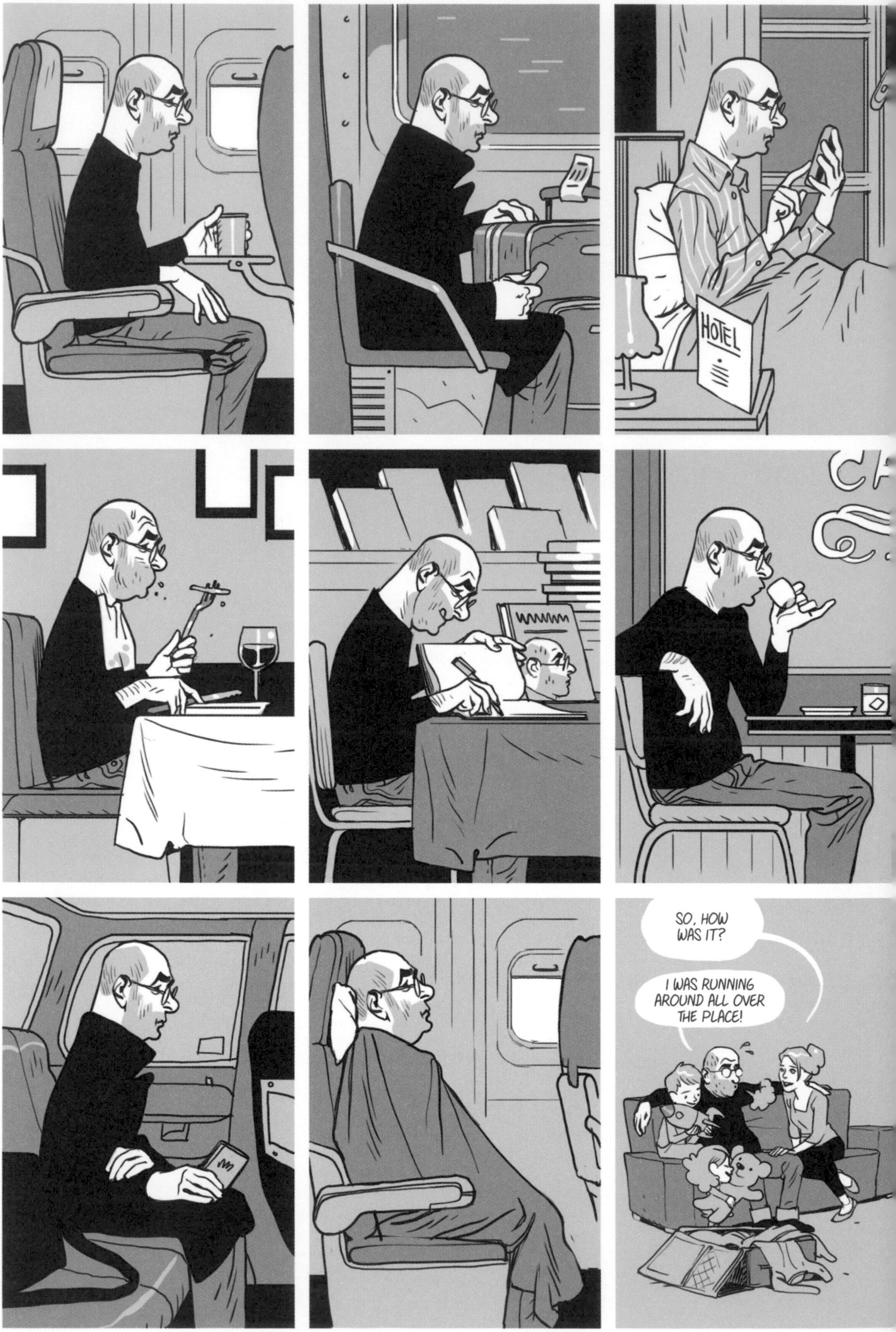
HOTEL
SO, HOW WAS IT?
I WAS RUNNING AROUND ALL OVER THE PLACE!

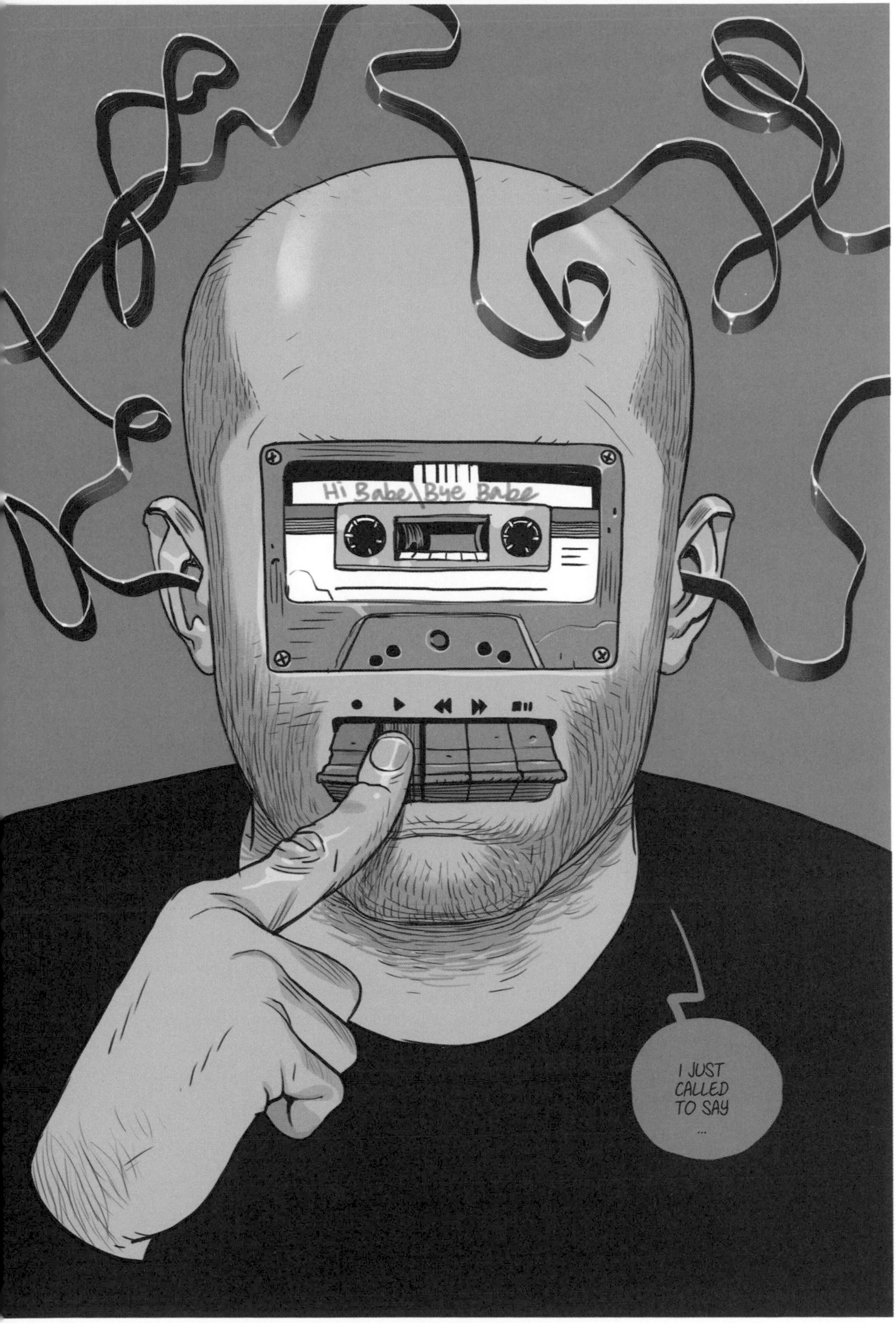
Hi Babe\Bye Babe
I JUST CALLED TO SAY ...

RICE SHOULD BE EATEN WITH A SPOON

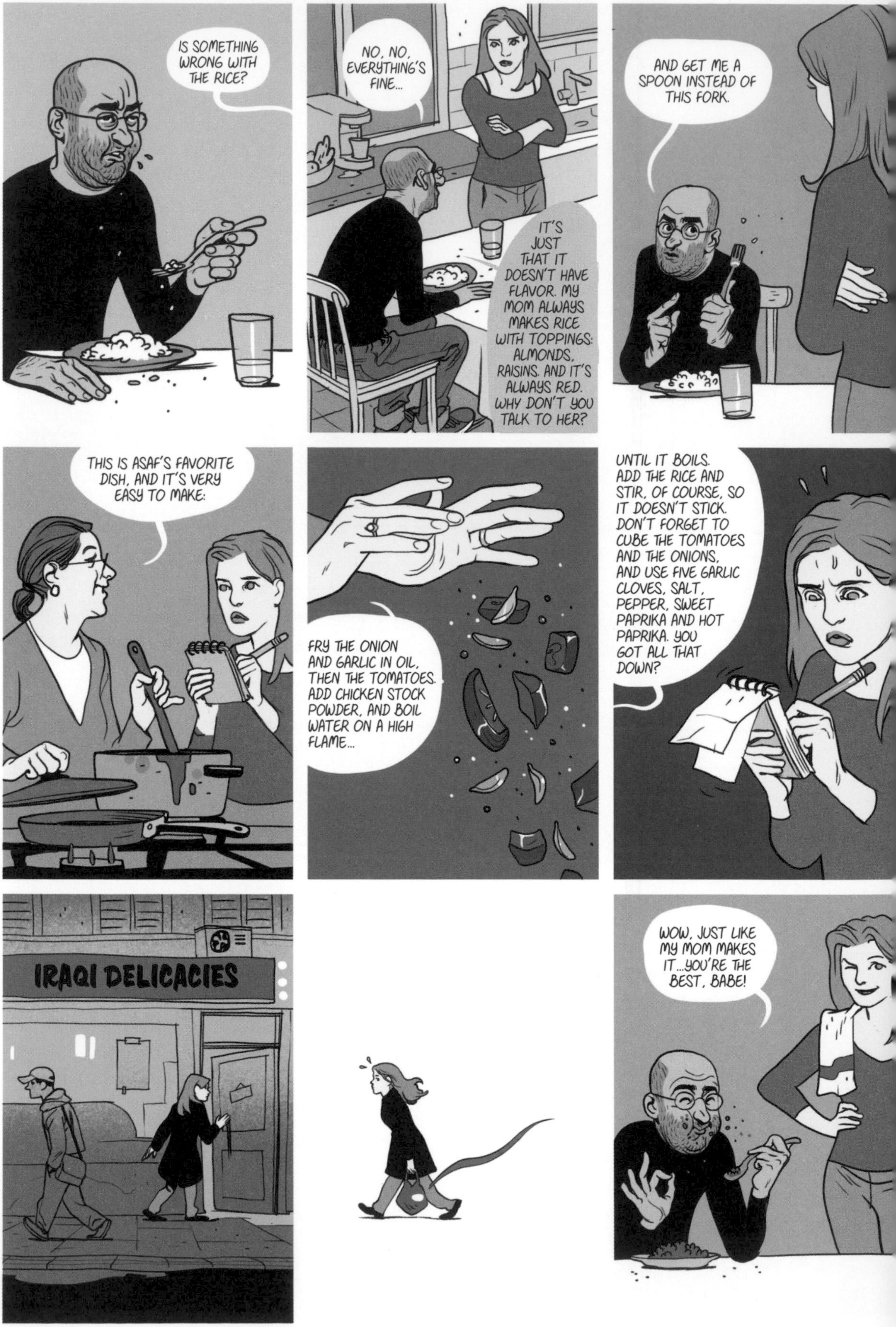

IS SOMETHING WRONG WITH THE RICE?
NO, NO, EVERYTHING'S FINE...
IT'S JUST THAT IT DOESN'T HAVE FLAVOR. MY MOM ALWAYS MAKES RICE WITH TOPPINGS: ALMONDS, RAISINS. AND IT'S ALWAYS RED. WHY DON'T YOU TALK TO HER?
AND GET ME A SPOON INSTEAD OF THIS FORK.
THIS IS ASAF'S FAVORITE DISH, AND IT'S VERY EASY TO MAKE:
FRY THE ONION AND GARLIC IN OIL, THEN THE TOMATOES. ADD CHICKEN STOCK POWDER, AND BOIL WATER ON A HIGH FLAME...
UNTIL IT BOILS. ADD THE RICE AND STIR, OF COURSE, SO IT DOESN'T STICK. DON'T FORGET TO CUBE THE TOMATOES AND THE ONIONS, AND USE FIVE GARLIC CLOVES, SALT, PEPPER, SWEET PAPRIKA AND HOT PAPRIKA. YOU GOT ALL THAT DOWN?
IRAQI DELICACIES
WOW, JUST LIKE MY MOM MAKES IT...YOU'RE THE BEST, BABE!

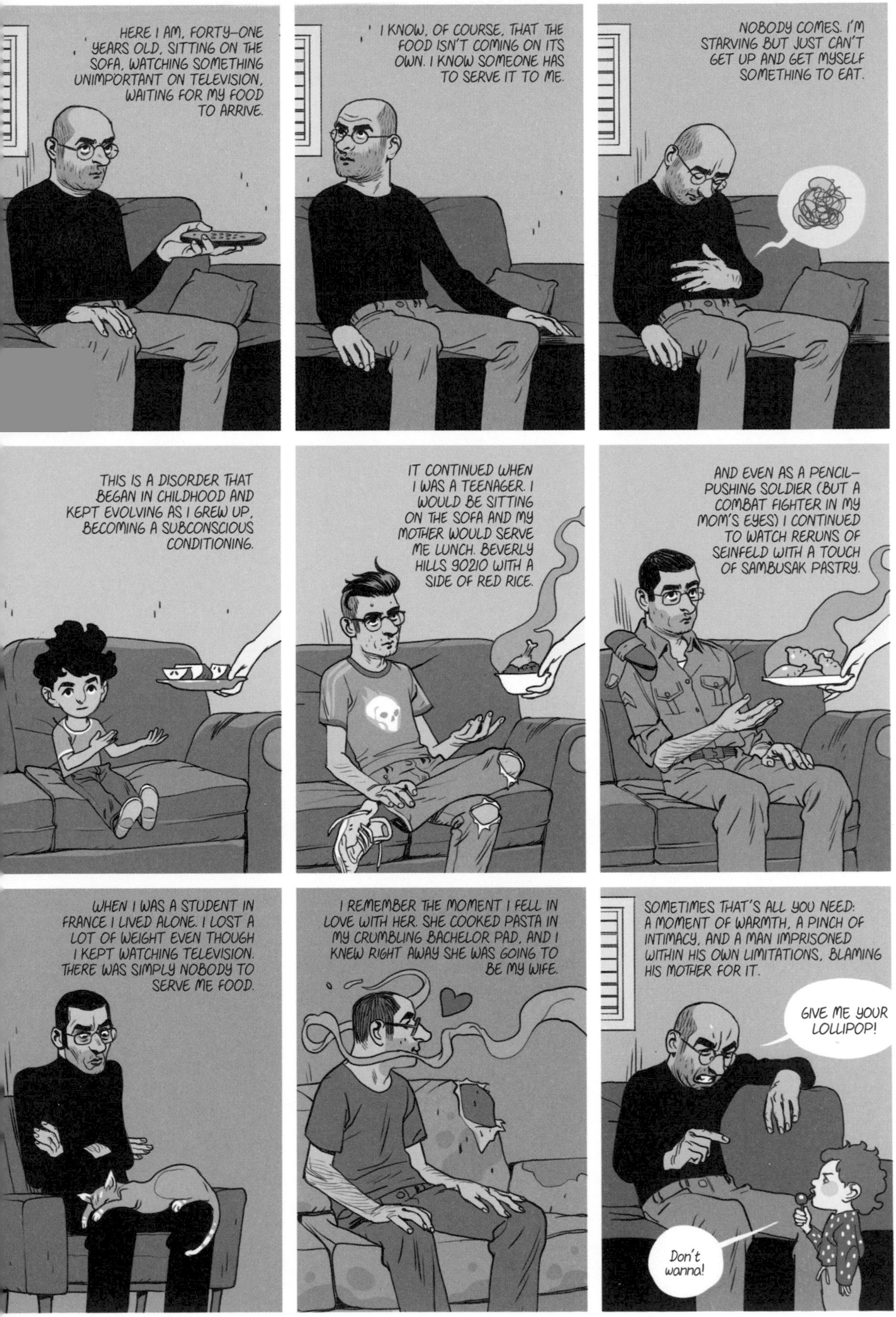
HERE I AM, FORTY-ONE YEARS OLD, SITTING ON THE SOFA, WATCHING SOMETHING UNIMPORTANT ON TELEVISION, WAITING FOR MY FOOD TO ARRIVE.
I KNOW, OF COURSE, THAT THE FOOD ISN'T COMING ON ITS OWN. I KNOW SOMEONE HAS TO SERVE IT TO ME.
NOBODY COMES. I'M STARVING BUT JUST CAN'T GET UP AND GET MYSELF SOMETHING TO EAT.
THIS IS A DISORDER THAT BEGAN IN CHILDHOOD AND KEPT EVOLVING AS I GREW UP, BECOMING A SUBCONSCIOUS CONDITIONING.
IT CONTINUED WHEN I WAS A TEENAGER. I WOULD BE SITTING ON THE SOFA AND MY MOTHER WOULD SERVE ME LUNCH. BEVERLY HILLS 90210 WITH A SIDE OF RED RICE.
AND EVEN AS A PENCIL-PUSHING SOLDIER (BUT A COMBAT FIGHTER IN MY MOM'S EYES) I CONTINUED TO WATCH RERUNS OF SEINFELD WITH A TOUCH OF SAMBUSAK PASTRY.
WHEN I WAS A STUDENT IN FRANCE I LIVED ALONE. I LOST A LOT OF WEIGHT EVEN THOUGH I KEPT WATCHING TELEVISION. THERE WAS SIMPLY NOBODY TO SERVE ME FOOD.
I REMEMBER THE MOMENT I FELL IN LOVE WITH HER. SHE COOKED PASTA IN MY CRUMBLING BACHELOR PAD, AND I KNEW RIGHT AWAY SHE WAS GOING TO BE MY WIFE.
SOMETIMES THAT'S ALL YOU NEED: A MOMENT OF WARMTH, A PINCH OF INTIMACY, AND A MAN IMPRISONED WITHIN HIS OWN LIMITATIONS, BLAMING HIS MOTHER FOR IT.
GIVE ME YOUR LOLLIPOP!
Don't wanna!

OUR JUNK

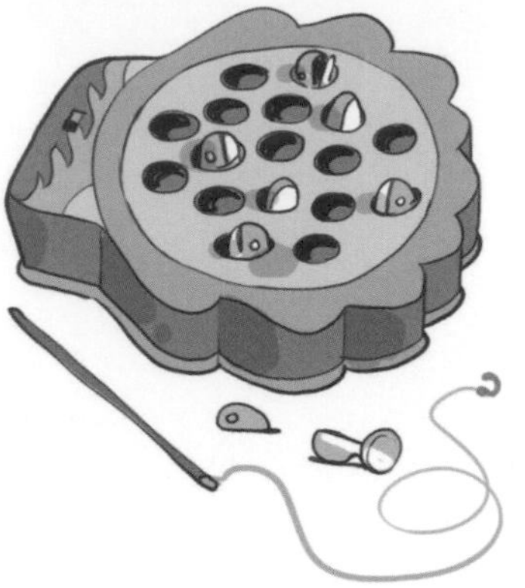

PASSOVER POSES MANY CHALLENGES: WHERE WILL WE HAVE THE SEDER? HOW WILL WE SURVIVE THE KIDS' LONG BREAK FROM SCHOOL?

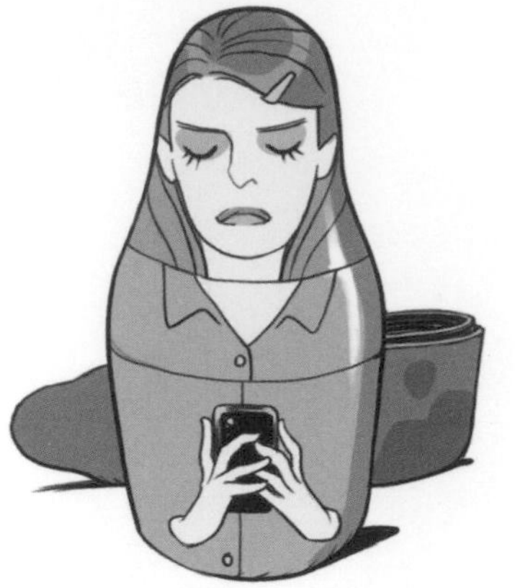

BUT THE BIGGEST CHALLENGE IS THE SPRING CLEANING, PULLING EVERYTHING OUT OF OUR CLOSETS AND DECIDING WHAT TO KEEP AND WHAT TO THROW OUT.

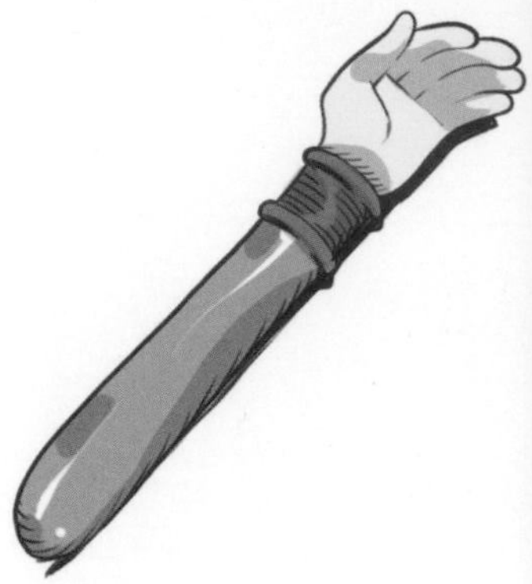

WE BUY WAY MORE THAN WE NEED. SHOPPING IS A KIND OF RELIGION, AND TRADITION BRINGS PEOPLE CLOSER TOGETHER.

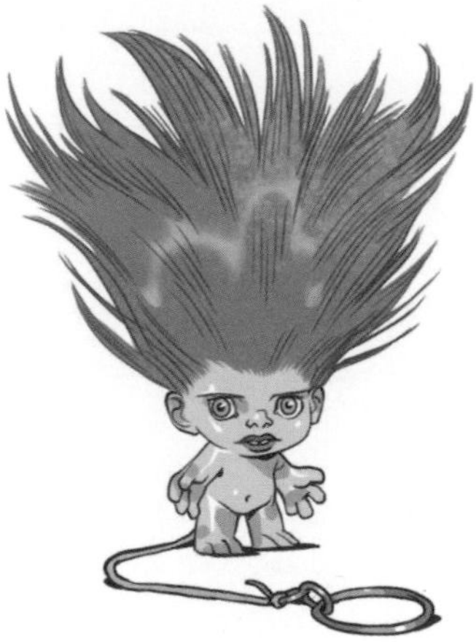

IT'S A CHANCE TO REEXAMINE THE PILE OF UNNECESSARY STUFF WE'VE ACCUMULATED IN THE PASSING YEAR. GETTING RID OF THESE THINGS IS HARD BECAUSE IT REQUIRES US TO ADMIT THEY EVEN EXIST.

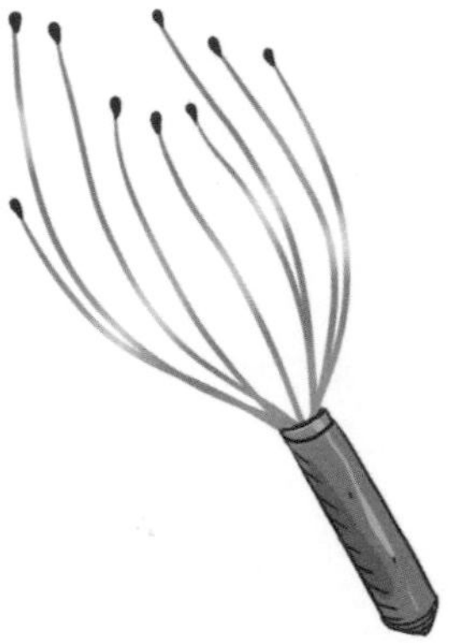

THESE ARE THINGS SO UNNECESSARY THAT A HIGHER POWER SHOVED THEM TO THE BACK OF THE DRAWER, THE PART YOU CAN'T SEE ANYMORE BECAUSE THE DRAWER WON'T OPEN ALL THE WAY.

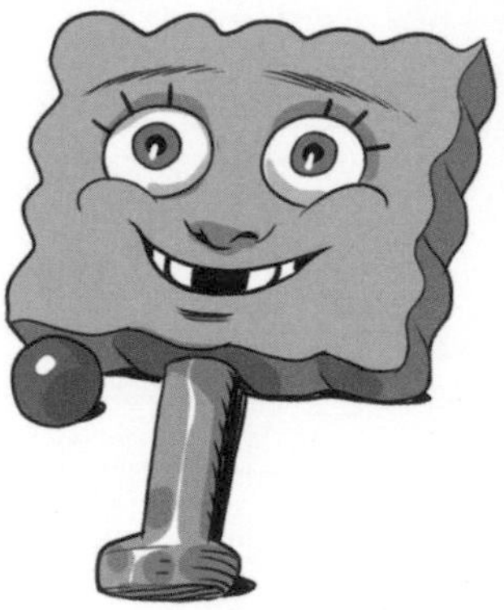

ENCOUNTERING THESE THINGS AGAIN RAISES SOME DIFFICULT QUESTIONS: ARE WE OURSELVES USELESS CONSUMER ITEMS PUSHE OVER TO THE DARK SIDE?

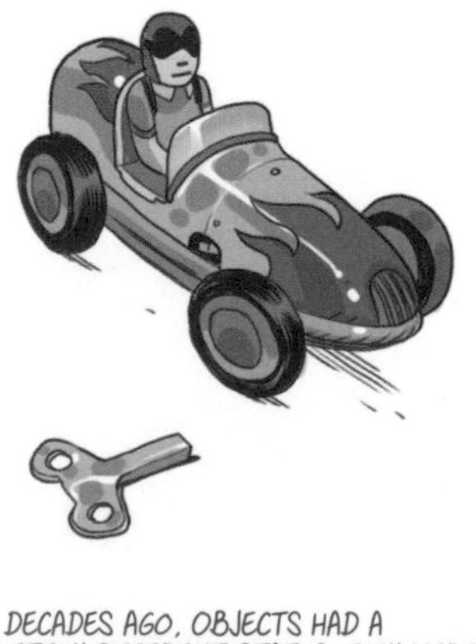

A FEW DECADES AGO, OBJECTS HAD A COMPLETELY DIFFERENT STATUS. THEY WERE TIME CAPSULES, SURVIVING WARS AND PASSED FROM ONE GENERATION TO THE NEXT.

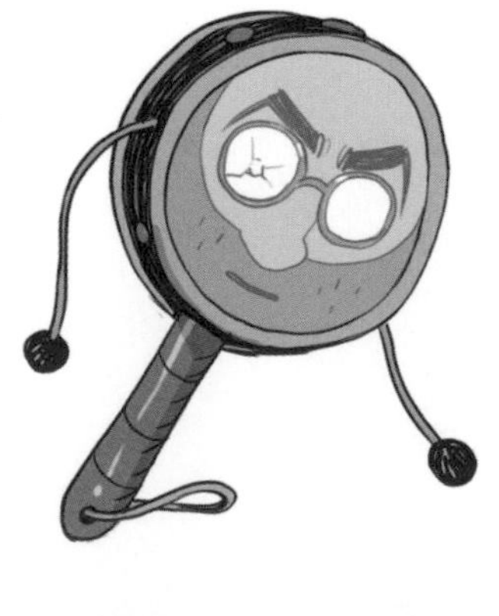

TODAY, AN OBJECT USUALLY GETS BURIED BENEATH A NEW ITEM AND DISAPPEARS. IN FACT, THE ONLY MEANINGFUL MOMENT IN THIS OBJECT'S LIFE IS THE MOMENT IT WAS PURCHASED.

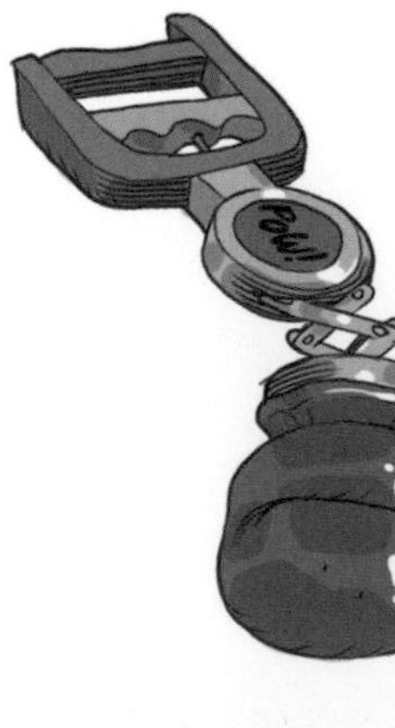
POW!

IT'S STILL SHINY ON THE STORE SHELF. THE CREDIT CARD PENETRATES THE SLOT IN A QUICK MOTION, AND THE CASH REGISTER EJECTS A PIECE OF WHITE PAPER. HERE'S YOU BAG. HAVE A GOOD ONE.

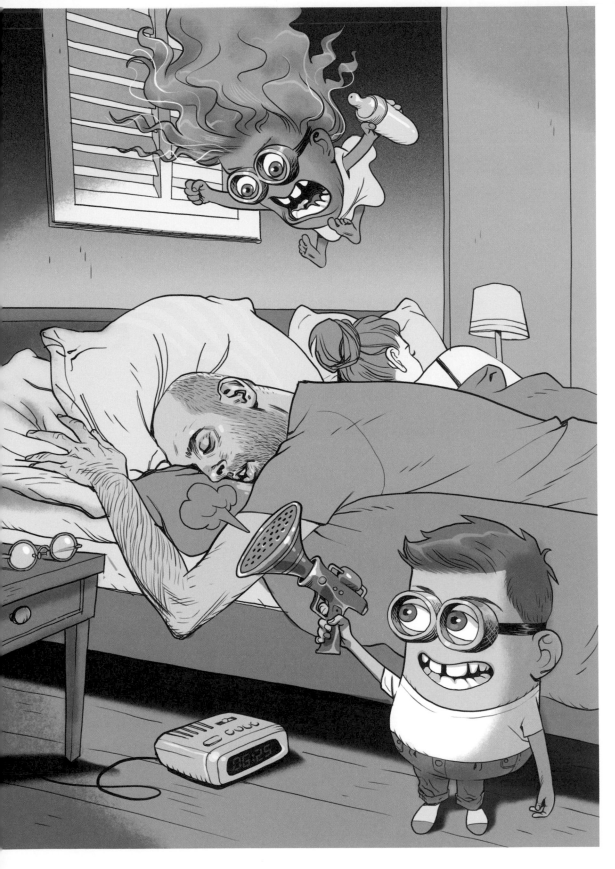

SECRETS FROM THE KITCHEN

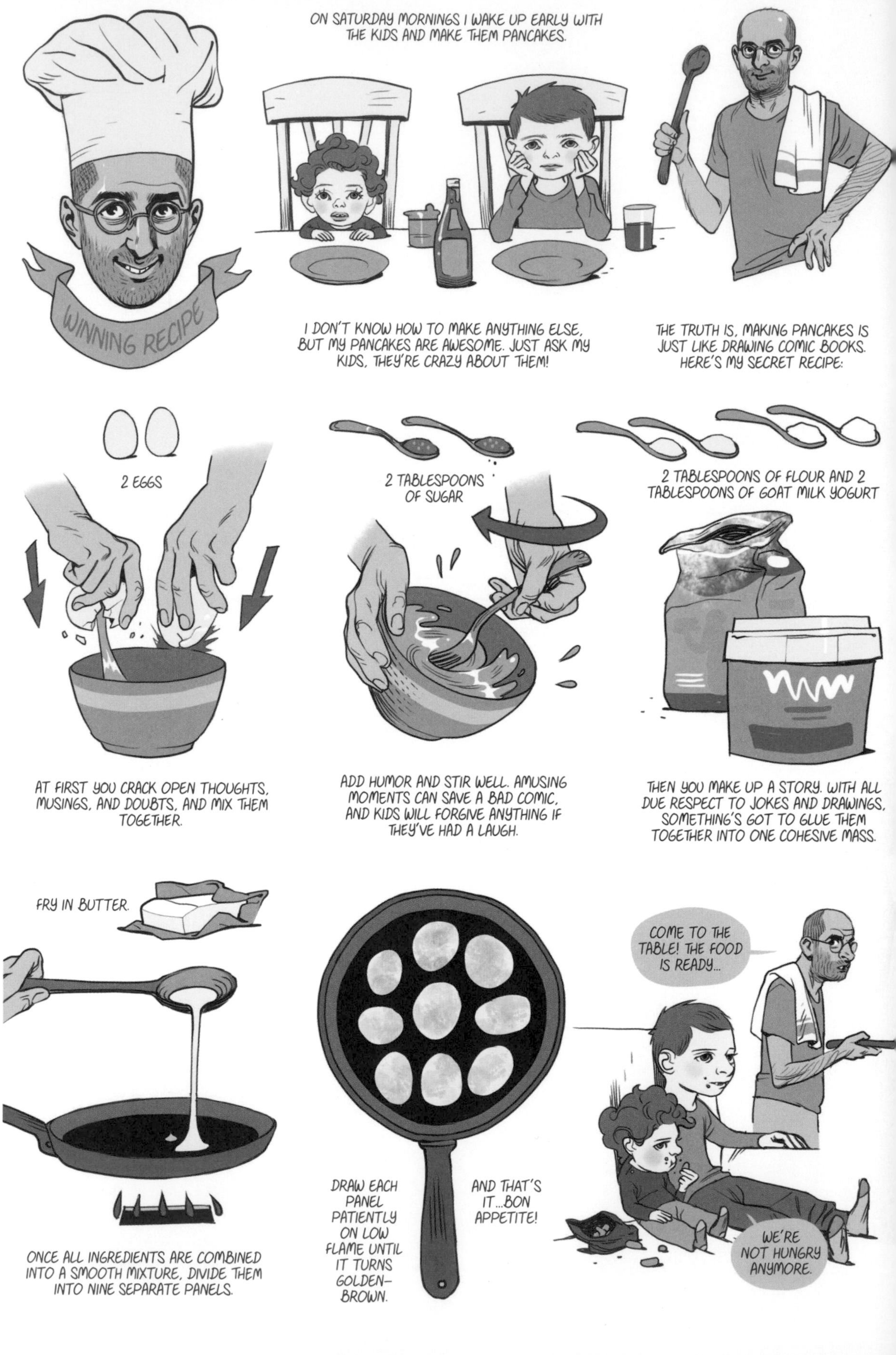
WINNING RECIPE
ON SATURDAY MORNINGS I WAKE UP EARLY WITH THE KIDS AND MAKE THEM PANCAKES.
I DON'T KNOW HOW TO MAKE ANYTHING ELSE, BUT MY PANCAKES ARE AWESOME. JUST ASK MY KIDS, THEY'RE CRAZY ABOUT THEM!
THE TRUTH IS, MAKING PANCAKES IS JUST LIKE DRAWING COMIC BOOKS. HERE'S MY SECRET RECIPE:
2 EGGS
AT FIRST YOU CRACK OPEN THOUGHTS, MUSINGS, AND DOUBTS, AND MIX THEM TOGETHER.
2 TABLESPOONS OF SUGAR
ADD HUMOR AND STIR WELL. AMUSING MOMENTS CAN SAVE A BAD COMIC, AND KIDS WILL FORGIVE ANYTHING IF THEY'VE HAD A LAUGH.
2 TABLESPOONS OF FLOUR AND 2 TABLESPOONS OF GOAT MILK YOGURT
THEN YOU MAKE UP A STORY. WITH ALL DUE RESPECT TO JOKES AND DRAWINGS, SOMETHING'S GOT TO GLUE THEM TOGETHER INTO ONE COHESIVE MASS.
FRY IN BUTTER.
ONCE ALL INGREDIENTS ARE COMBINED INTO A SMOOTH MIXTURE, DIVIDE THEM INTO NINE SEPARATE PANELS.
DRAW EACH PANEL PATIENTLY ON LOW FLAME UNTIL IT TURNS GOLDEN-BROWN.
AND THAT'S IT...BON APPETITE!
COME TO THE TABLE! THE FOOD IS READY...
WE'RE NOT HUNGRY ANYMORE.

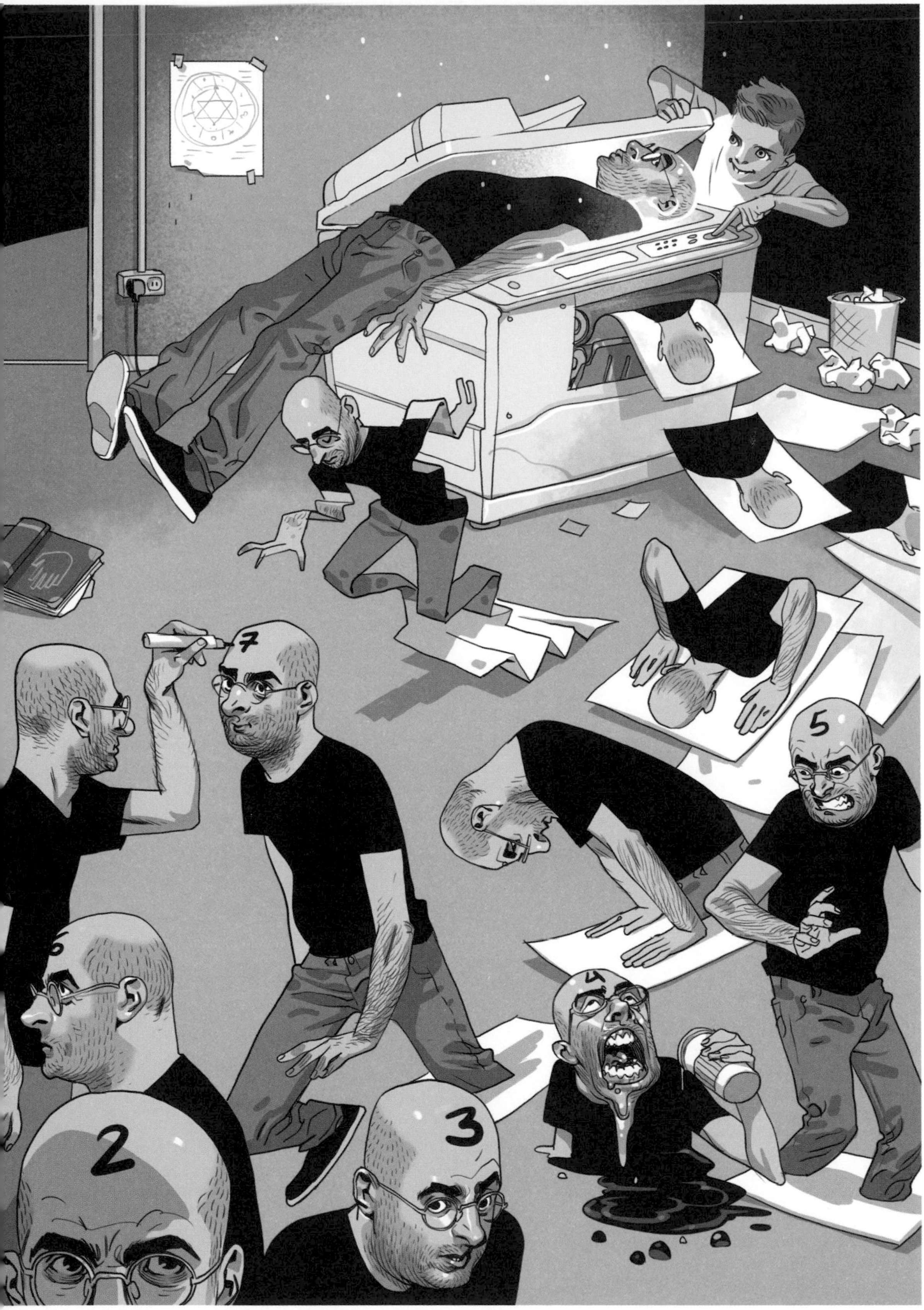
7
5
2
3

ARE YOU LISTENING?

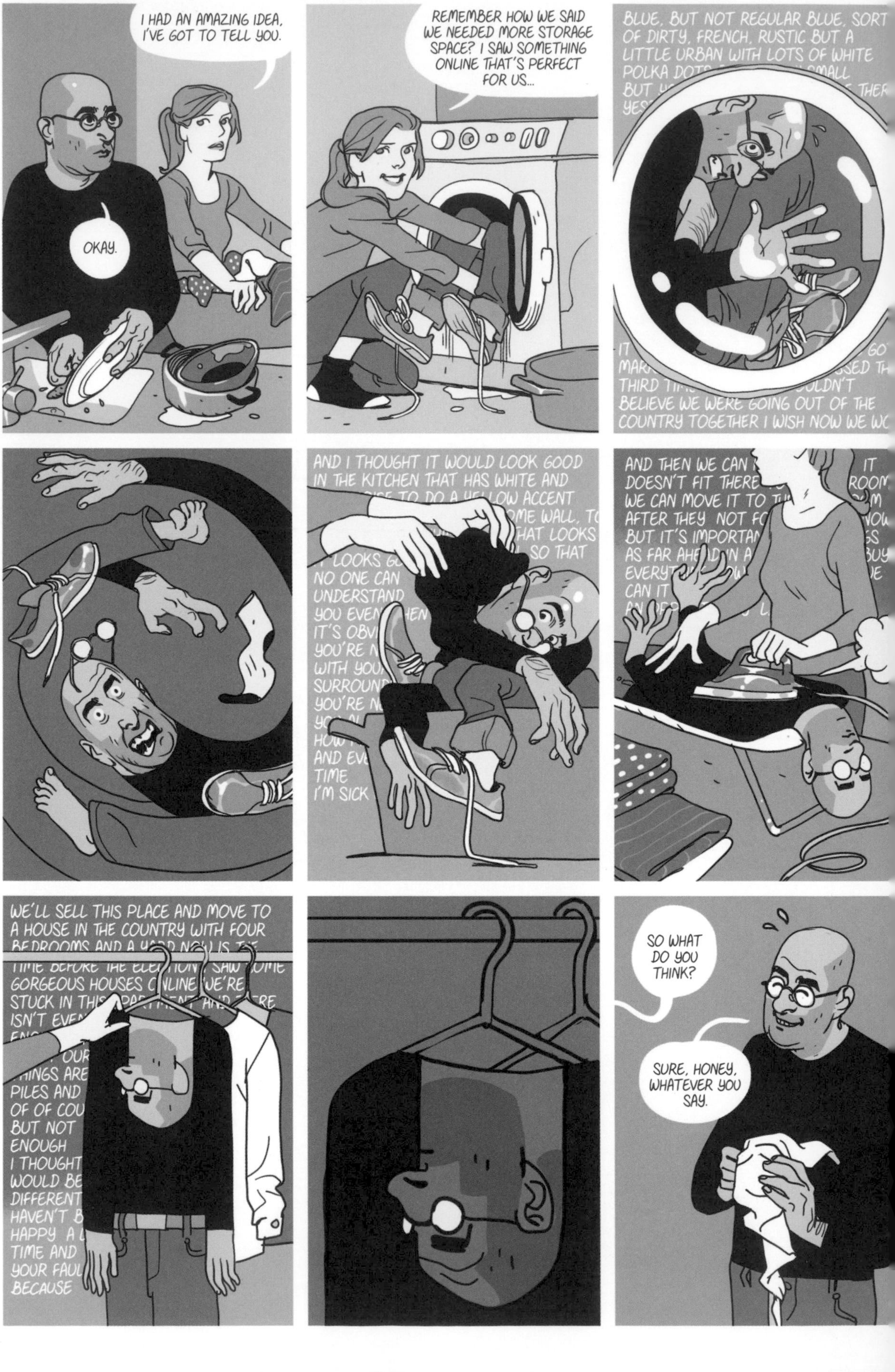
I HAD AN AMAZING IDEA, I'VE GOT TO TELL YOU.
OKAY.
REMEMBER HOW WE SAID WE NEEDED MORE STORAGE SPACE? I SAW SOMETHING ONLINE THAT'S PERFECT FOR US...
BLUE, BUT NOT REGULAR BLUE, SORT OF DIRTY, FRENCH, RUSTIC BUT A LITTLE URBAN WITH LOTS OF WHITE
BELIEVE WE WERE GOING OUT OF THE
AND I THOUGHT IT WOULD LOOK GOOD IN THE KITCHEN THAT HAS WHITE AND
NO ONE CAN
UNDERSTAND
AND THEN WE CAN
WE'LL SELL THIS PLACE AND MOVE TO A HOUSE IN THE COUNTRY WITH FOUR
SO WHAT DO YOU THINK?
SURE, HONEY, WHATEVER YOU SAY.

HAVE TO DO SOMETHING

MORNING, WE FOUND OUT THE FRIDGE HAD N LEAKING WATER ALL NIGHT LONG.

THE MOISTURE ON THE WOODEN COUNTER HAD BECOME A LIVING CREATURE.

AND THE EUROPEAN PANELS BID THE ISRAELI WALLS FAREWELL.

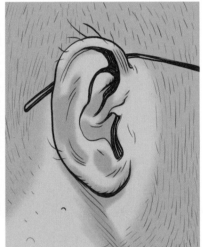

NTUALLY, I CAUGHT A FLU THAT FEATURED RY SINGLE TYPE OF COUGH AND SNEEZE.

MY IMMUNE SYSTEM ISN'T WHAT IT USED TO BE. THERE ARE ENTIRE AREAS IN MY BODY THAT I DON'T EVEN RECOGNIZE.

MY DISEASES, HER BACKACHES. THE SLEEP DEPRIVATION, THE T.V. ADDICTION.

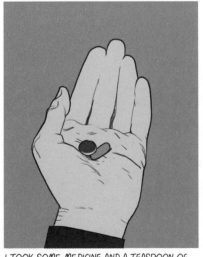

HAVE TO DO SOMETHING," SHE TEXTED AND SENT A LINK TO A FRIDGE ON SALE ONE OF THE ELECTRONICS WAREHOUSES.

I TOOK SOME MEDICINE AND A TEASPOON OF TURMERIC, AND GURGLED SOME SALTWATER.

WE TURNED OFF THE T.V., THE IPAD, AND THE LIGHT. THE NEXT MORNING, WE WOKE UP AS GOOD AS NEW.

I WOKE UP

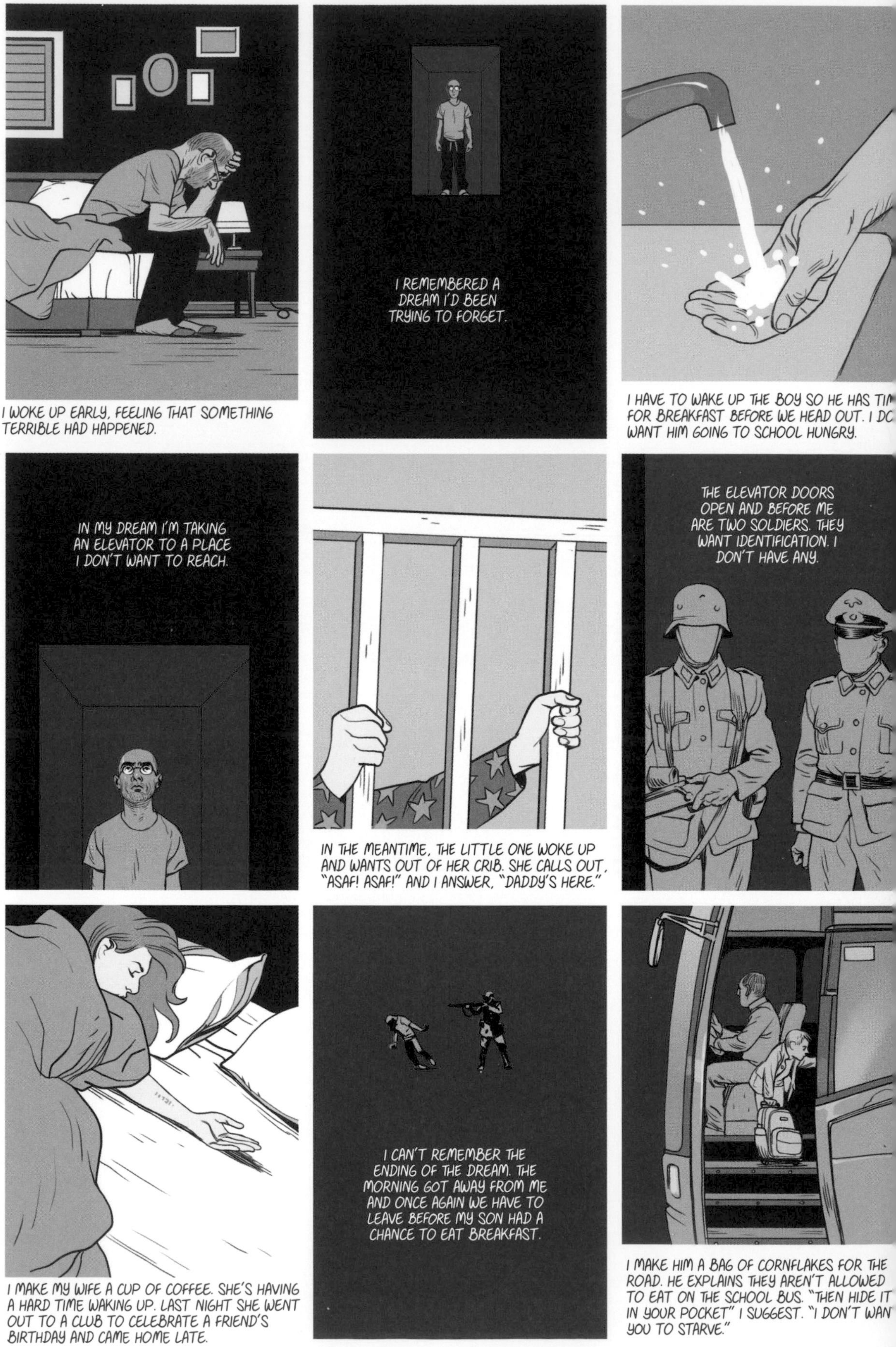
I WOKE UP EARLY, FEELING THAT SOMETHING TERRIBLE HAD HAPPENED.
I REMEMBERED A DREAM I'D BEEN TRYING TO FORGET.
I HAVE TO WAKE UP THE BOY SO HE HAS TI FOR BREAKFAST BEFORE WE HEAD OUT. I D WANT HIM GOING TO SCHOOL HUNGRY.
IN MY DREAM I'M TAKING AN ELEVATOR TO A PLACE I DON'T WANT TO REACH.
IN THE MEANTIME, THE LITTLE ONE WOKE UP AND WANTS OUT OF HER CRIB. SHE CALLS OUT, "ASAF! ASAF!" AND I ANSWER, "DADDY'S HERE."
THE ELEVATOR DOORS OPEN AND BEFORE ME ARE TWO SOLDIERS. THEY WANT IDENTIFICATION. I DON'T HAVE ANY.
I MAKE MY WIFE A CUP OF COFFEE. SHE'S HAVING A HARD TIME WAKING UP. LAST NIGHT SHE WENT OUT TO A CLUB TO CELEBRATE A FRIEND'S BIRTHDAY AND CAME HOME LATE.
I CAN'T REMEMBER THE ENDING OF THE DREAM. THE MORNING GOT AWAY FROM ME AND ONCE AGAIN WE HAVE TO LEAVE BEFORE MY SON HAD A CHANCE TO EAT BREAKFAST.
I MAKE HIM A BAG OF CORNFLAKES FOR THE ROAD. HE EXPLAINS THEY AREN'T ALLOWED TO EAT ON THE SCHOOL BUS. "THEN HIDE IT IN YOUR POCKET" I SUGGEST. "I DON'T WAN YOU TO STARVE."

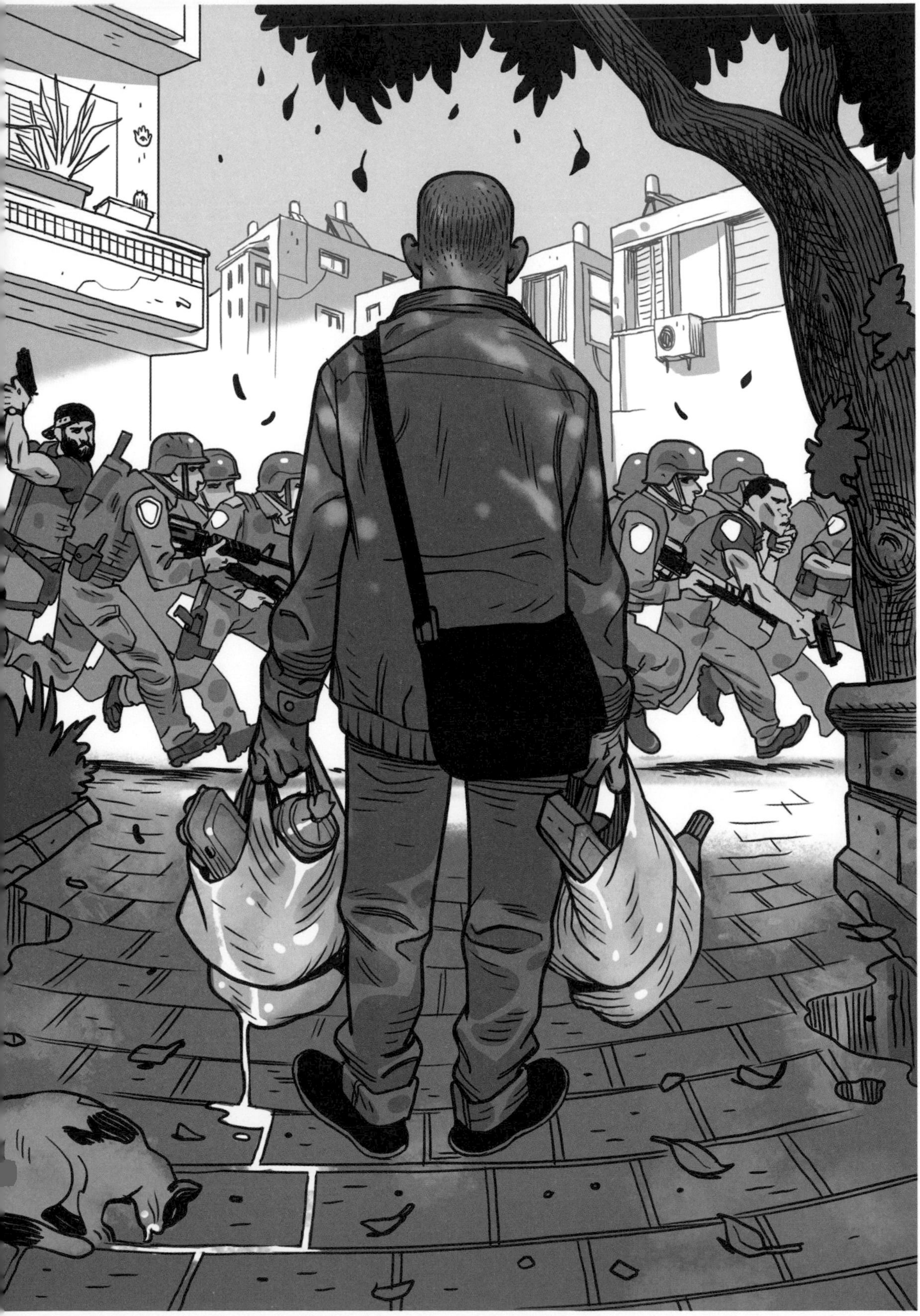

OWN GOAL

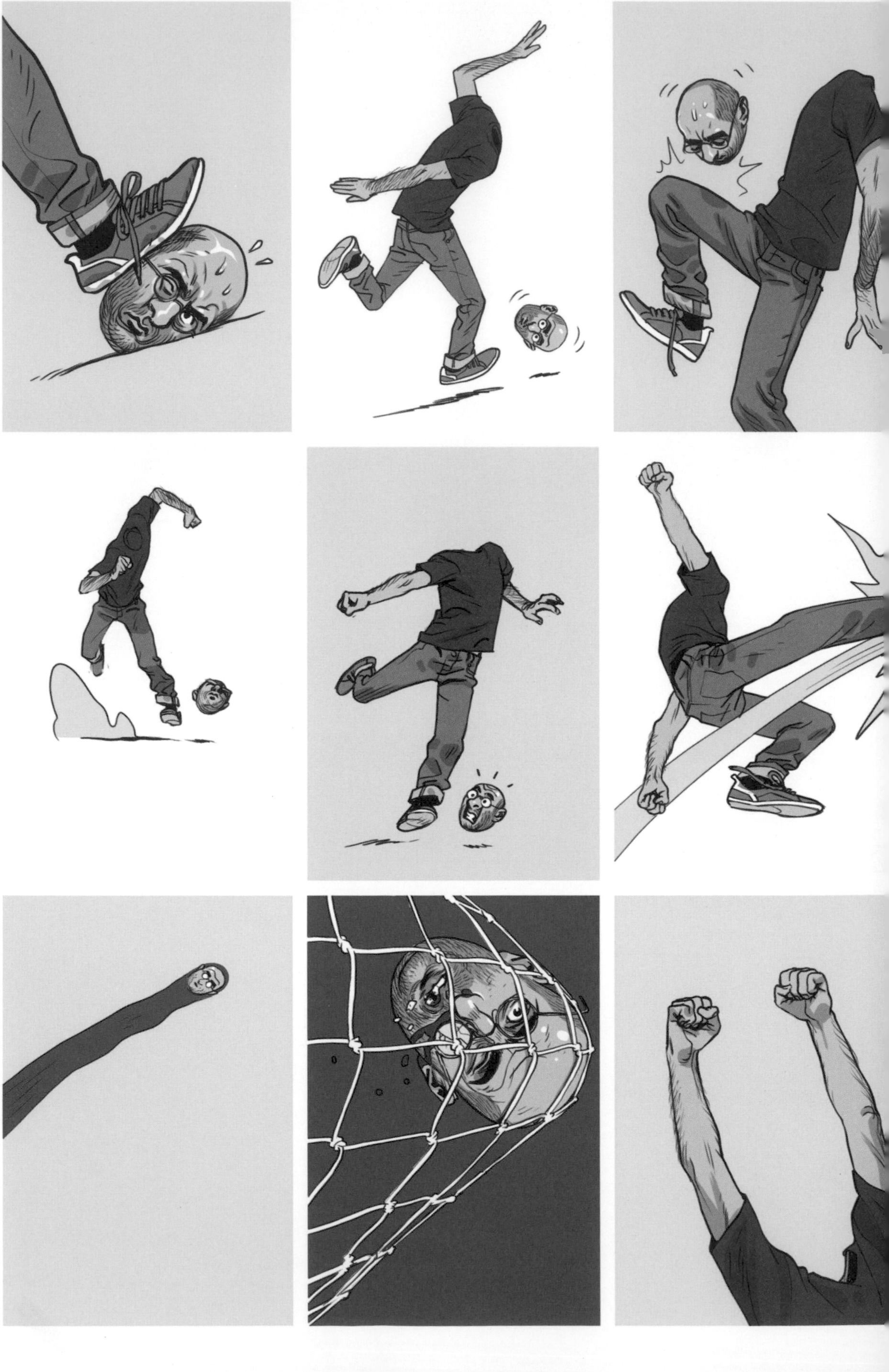

XTING TYPES

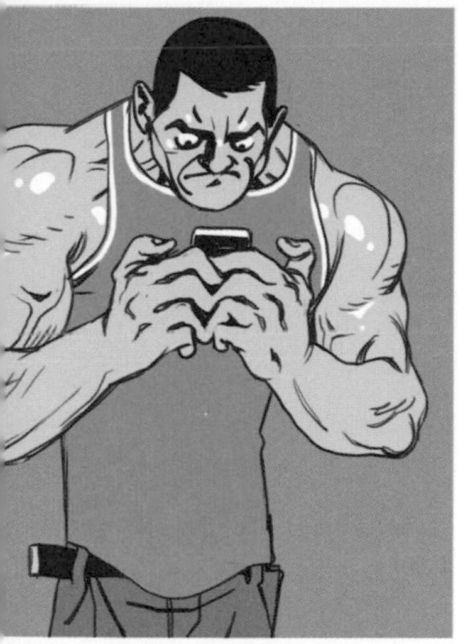

ANGRY-MAN: RIGID, GRACELESS TEXTING. IN
STANT CONFRONTATION. TENDENCY TOWARD
. FIGHTS.

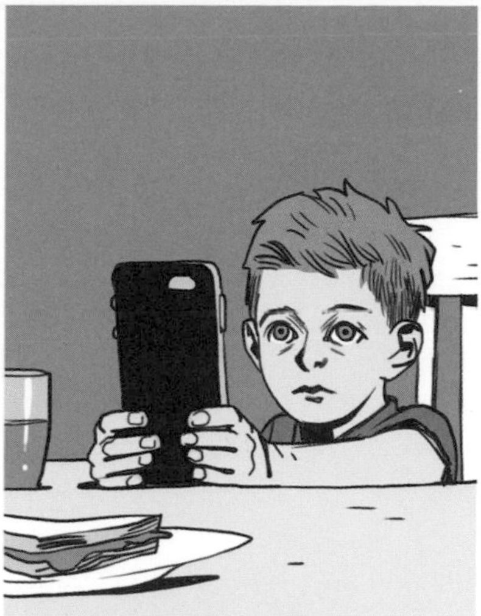

THE PRISONER: THE ACT OF TEXTING IS AUTOMATIC BUT THE MESSAGES HAVE NO MEANING. AT NIGHT, HE DREAMS IN EMOJIS.

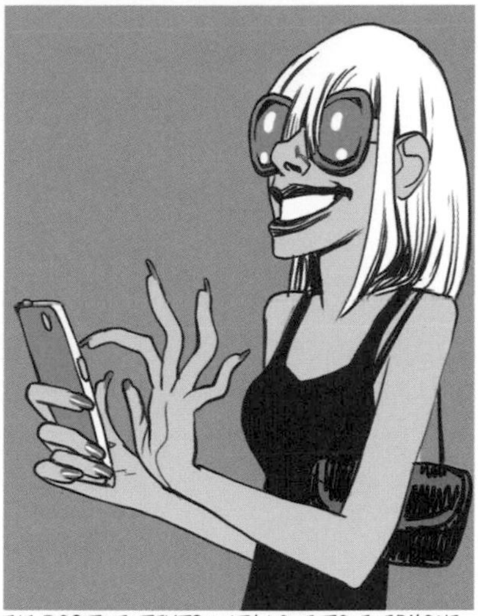

THE POSITIVE: TEXTS WITH LOVE TO EVERYONE, GOOD MORNING, HAPPY FRIDAY. SHARES JOKES IN AN ENDLESS THREAD. SHE CAN'T EVENNNNNNNN.

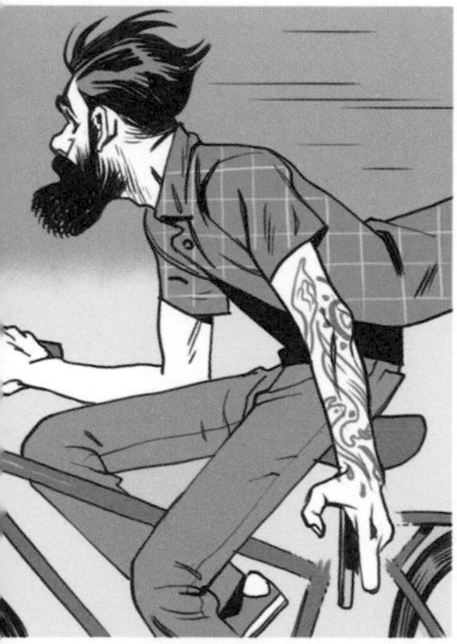

CASUAL: THE ACT OF TEXTING IS INCIDENTAL,
FORMED ON THE WAY TO A MUCH COOLER
CE WHERE EVERYONE TEXTS LIKE HIM.

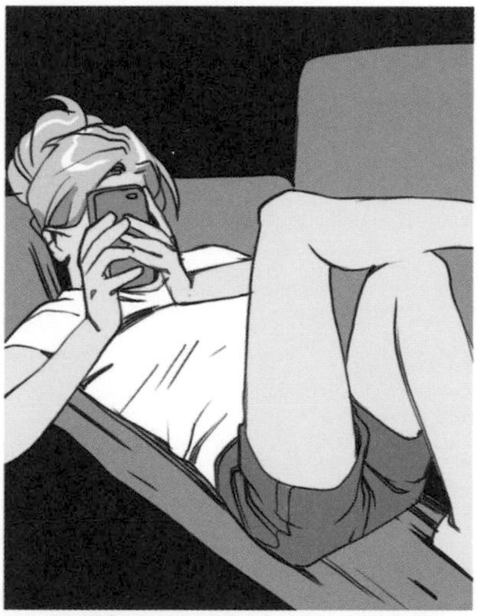

THE IRRITABLE: THE PROXIMITY OF THE PHONE TO HER FACE IS DONE IN DEFIANCE OF ANOTHER PERSON IN THE ROOM.

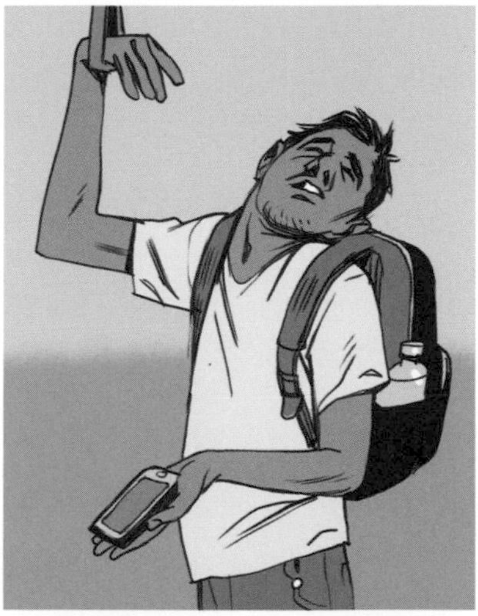

THE EXHAUSTED: TEXTS WITH THE LAST OF HIS ENERGY, USUALLY HALF-WORDS, COMPROMISING FOR THE RESULTS OF AUTOCORRECT.

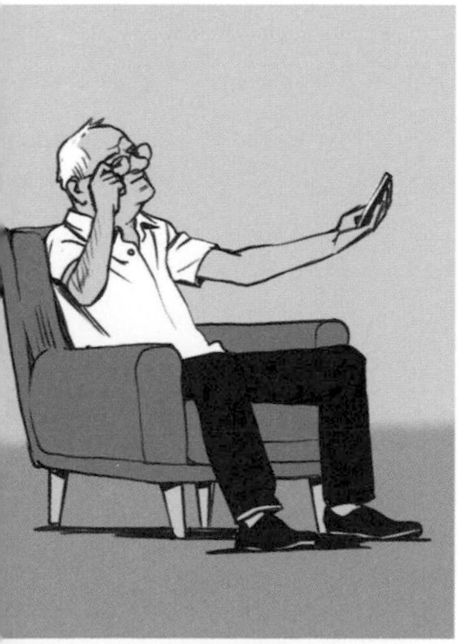

NEWBIE: USUALLY OVER AGE SIXTY, AND
L ADJUSTING TO NEW TECHNOLOGIES.
AYS SURPRISED WHEN HIS PHONE PINGS.

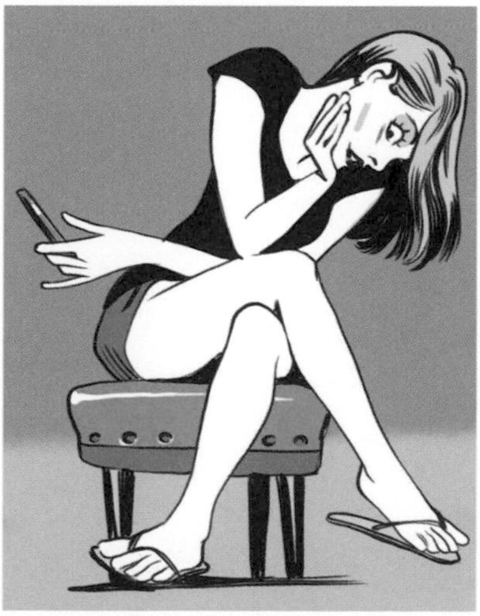

THE COMPLICATED: WAITING FOR A MESSAGE FROM THE RIGHT GUY. SHE WAS THE LAST ONE TO TEXT, NOW IT'S HIS TURN. PING!!

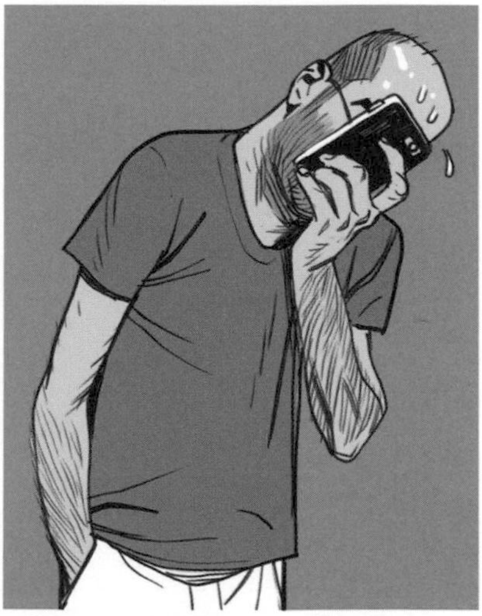

THE SOCIALLY AWKWARD: HE ISN'T REALLY TEXTING, HE'S HIDING.

CAN'T TOUCH

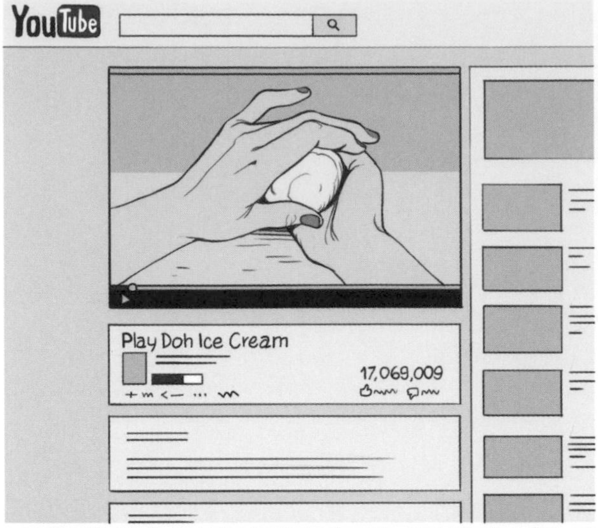
Play Doh Ice Cream
17,069,009

I CAN'T REMEMBER HOW WE FOUND THAT VIDEO, BUT MY DAUGHTER GOT VERY EXCITED ABOUT IT. IT'S JUST SOMEONE MAKING PLAY-DOH CANDY.

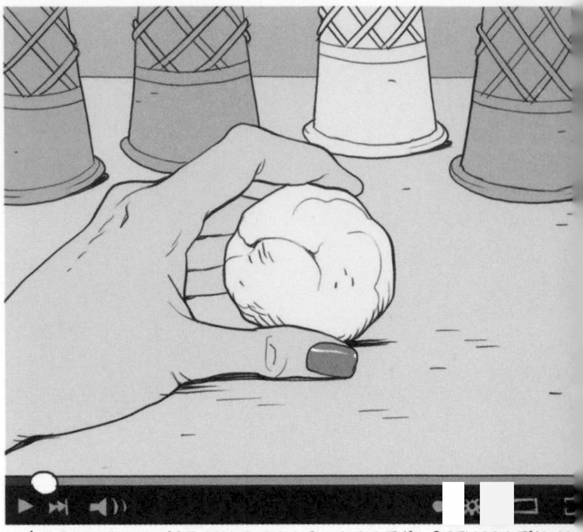

WE'VE SPENT THE LAST FEW EVENINGS, IN THE TIME BETWEEN TAKING BATH AND HAVING DINNER, WATCHING IT TOGETHER.

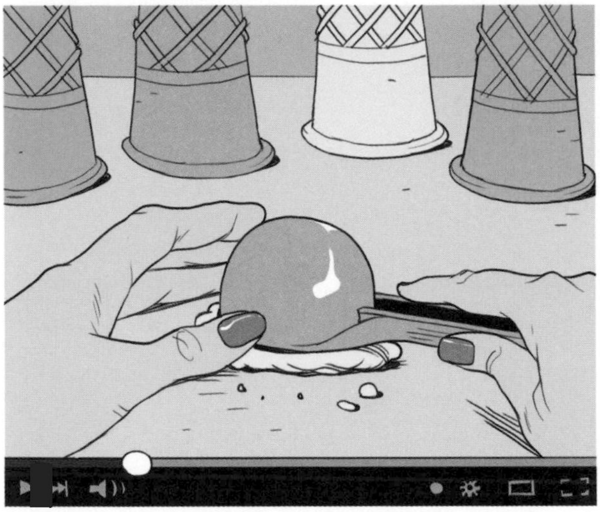

THERE'S AN ENTIRE INDUSTRY BUILT AROUND THIS IDEA IN AMERICA. THERE'S COLORFUL, FRAGRANT PLAY-DOH AND PLASTIC MOLDS FOR MAKING DIFFERENT KINDS OF CANDY.

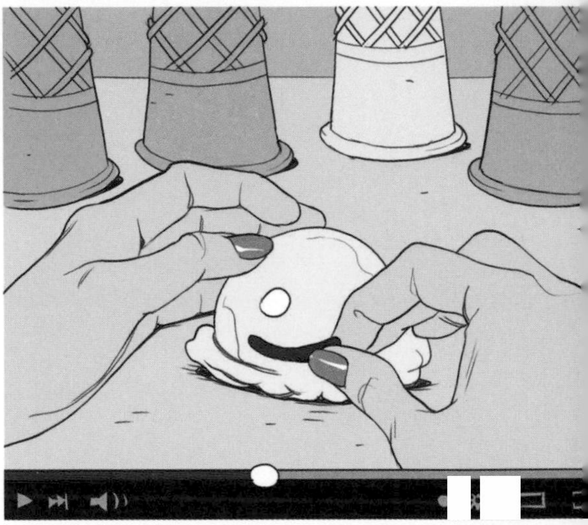

AMERICANS ARE FUNNY. THEY PUT SO MUCH EFFORT INTO SOMETHING THAT LOOKS LIKE FOOD BUT CAN'T BE EATEN.

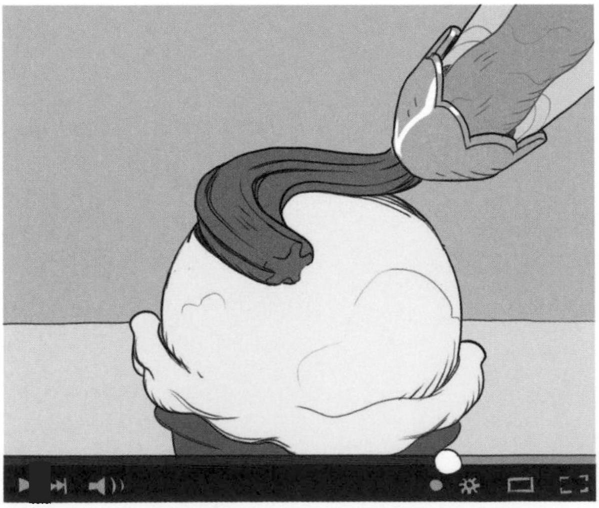

IT MIGHT BE FUN TO KNEAD THE STUFF, BUT I WOULDN'T KNOW, BECAUSE WE'VE ONLY WATCHED THE VIDEO. IN THE END SHE ALWAYS TRIES TO GRAB THE ICE CREAM.

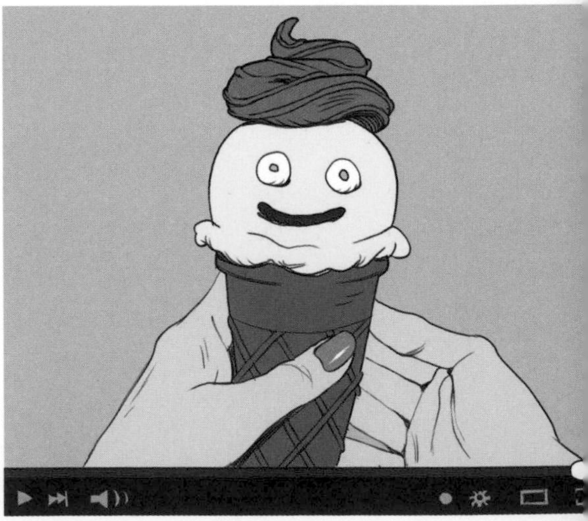

EVEN IF SHE COULD TOUCH THAT STUFF, IT ISN'T REALLY ICE CREAM. A THAT HOUR WE JUST ENJOYED TOGETHER? WE DIDN'T REALLY ENJOY AND WE WEREN'T REALLY TOGETHER.

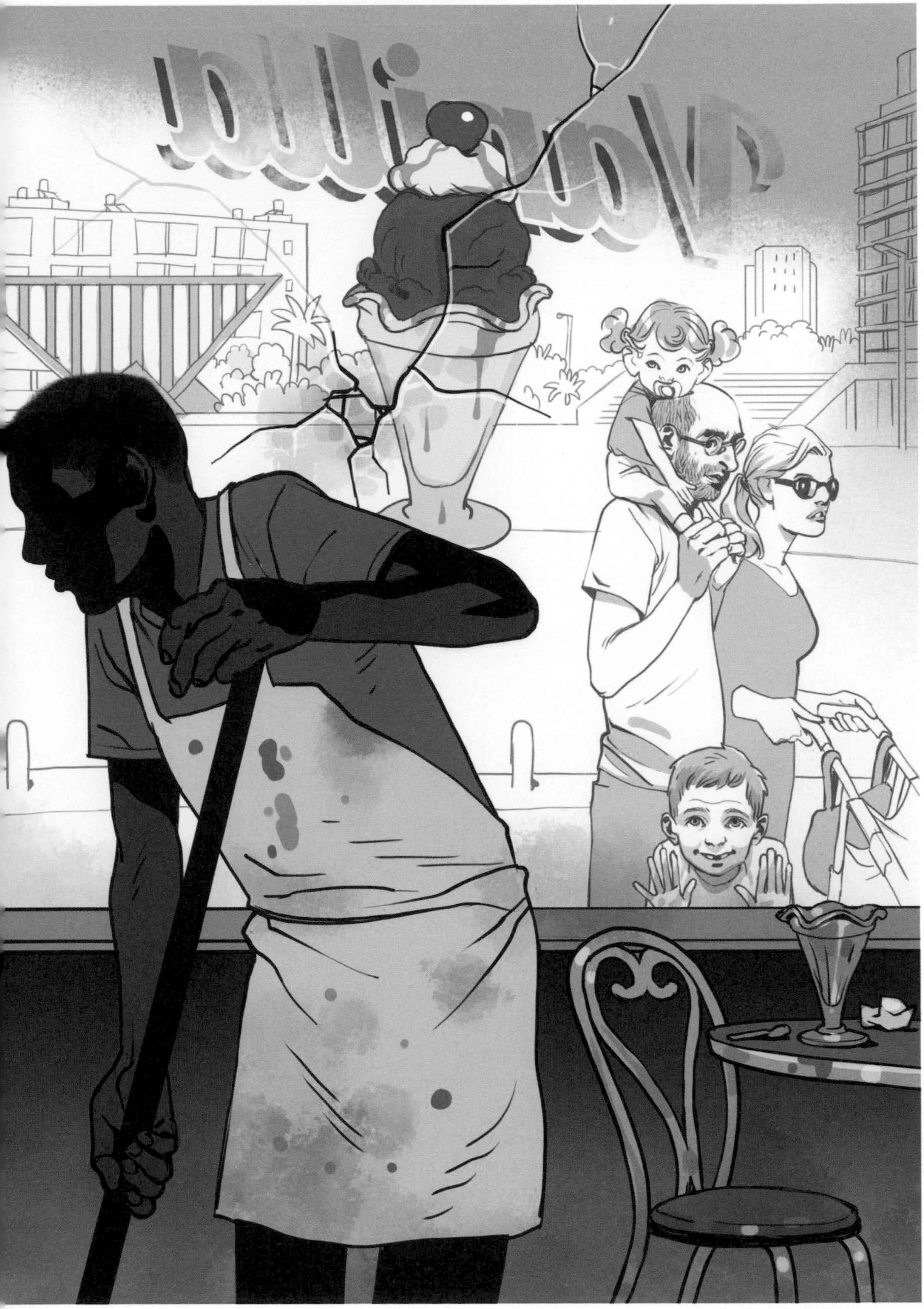

THE IN-HOUSE DESIGNER

CLARKS SHOES
PRICE: 350 SHEKELS
LOCATION: THE CLARKS STORE AT THE RAMAT AVIV MALL, TEL AVIV
PERSONAL TOUCH: A SPLASH OF MYSTERIOUS SUBSTANCE THAT HAD PROBABLY TRAVELED THROUGH THE DIGESTIVE TRACT BEFORE FINDING IT'S WAY TO THIS ITEM.

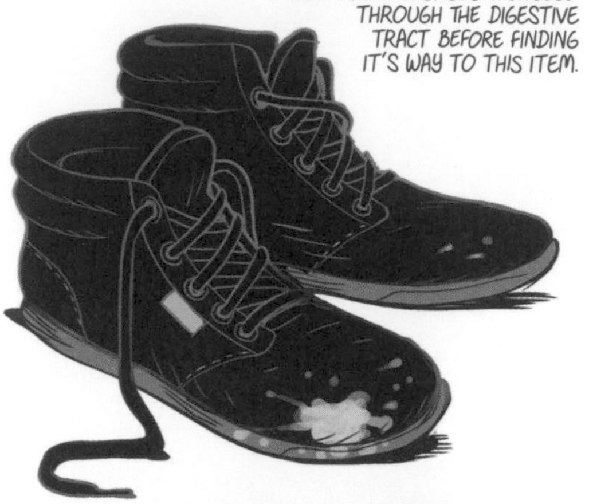

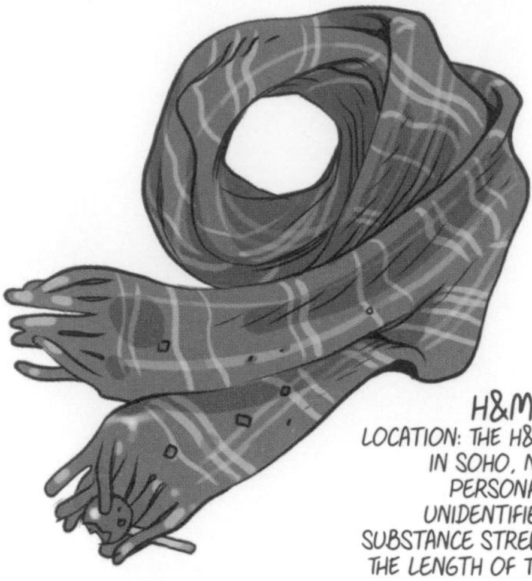

H&M SCARF
LOCATION: THE H&M STORE IN SOHO, NEW YORK
PERSONAL TOUCH: UNIDENTIFIED STICKY SUBSTANCE STREWN DOWN THE LENGTH OF THE SCARF.

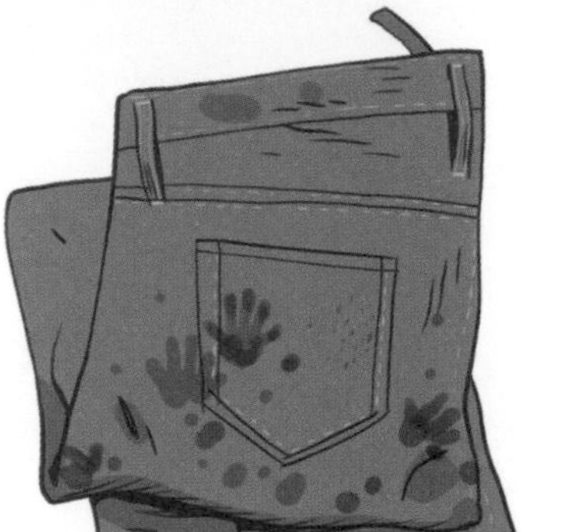

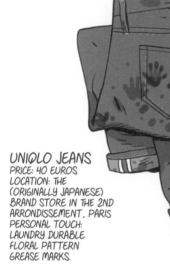

UNIQLO JEANS
PRICE: 40 EUROS
LOCATION: THE (ORIGINALLY JAPANESE) BRAND STORE IN THE 2ND ARRONDISSEMENT, PARIS
PERSONAL TOUCH: LAUNDRY DURABLE FLORAL PATTERN GREASE MARKS.

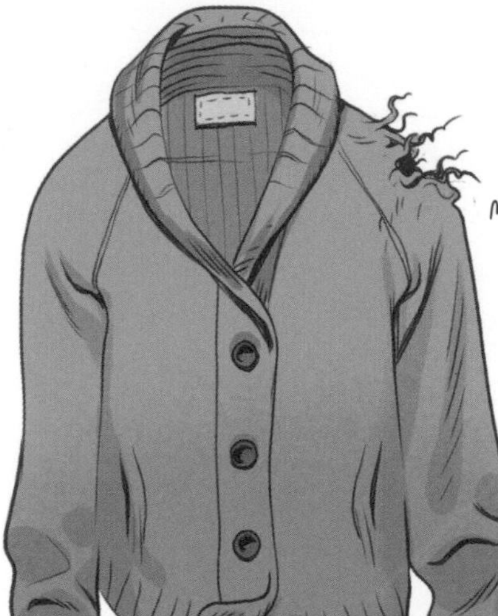

CELIO CARDIGA
PRICE: 30 EURO
LOCATION: TH
CELIO STORE AT TH
MONTPARNASSE METR
STATION IN PARI
PERSONAL TOUCH: TH
LEFT SHOULDER
COMPLETEL
UNRAVELE
TANTRUM STYL

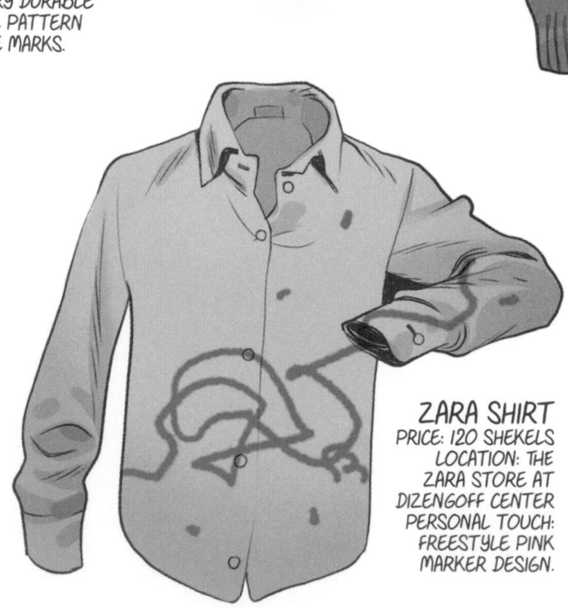

ZARA SHIRT
PRICE: 120 SHEKELS
LOCATION: THE ZARA STORE AT DIZENGOFF CENTER
PERSONAL TOUCH: FREESTYLE PINK MARKER DESIGN.

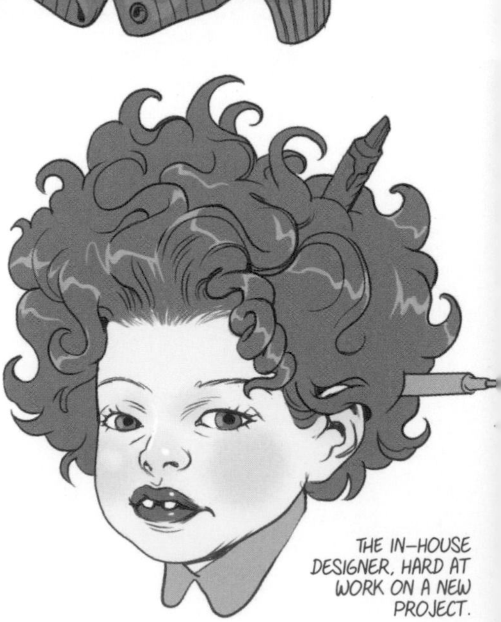

THE IN-HOUSE DESIGNER, HARD AT WORK ON A NEW PROJECT.

GOOD NIGHT SWEETHEARTS... SWEET DREAMS.

But Dad...

I want to go to the living room.

IT'S LATE. ONLY MOM AND DAD ARE ALLOWED TO BE IN THE LIVING ROOM NOW. AND YOU'RE GOING TO SLEEP.

SEE YOU TOMORROW MORNING. GOOD NIGHT.

You want to come with me to the living room?

BUT DAD SAID...

OKAY, I'LL COME!

BUT BE QUIET! WE CAN'T LET THEM HEAR US...

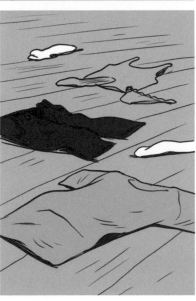

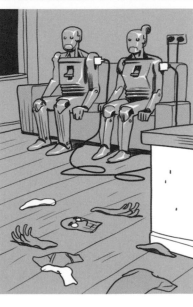

THE ART OF REPRESSION

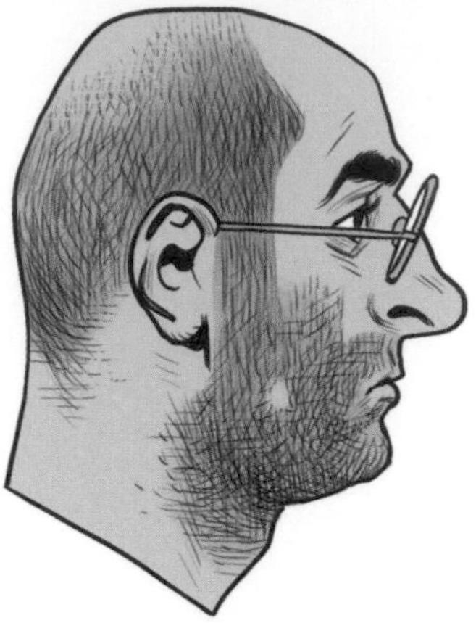

A STRANGE BALD SPOT APPEARED IN THE MIDDLE OF MY FACE, IN AN AREA THAT USED TO BE COVERED WITH STUBBLE.

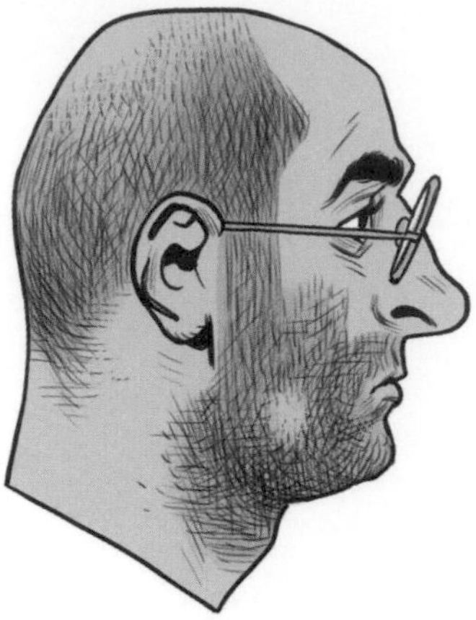

IT WAS BORN IN THE SHAPE OF A SMALL CIRCLE. MY DAUGHTER TRIED TO PEEL IT OFF, SAYING, "STICKER!" SINCE THEN THE BALD SPOT HAS GROWN AND CHANGED SHAPES.

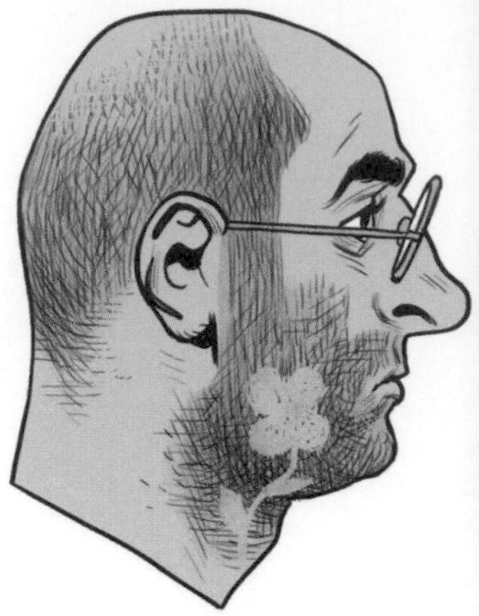

"IT'S NOT EXACTLY A DISEASE, IT'S JUST A CONDITION," THE DOCTOR ASSURED ME. AN UNSCIENTIFIC ASSESSMENT IS THAT IT IS CAUSED BY MENTAL STRESS.

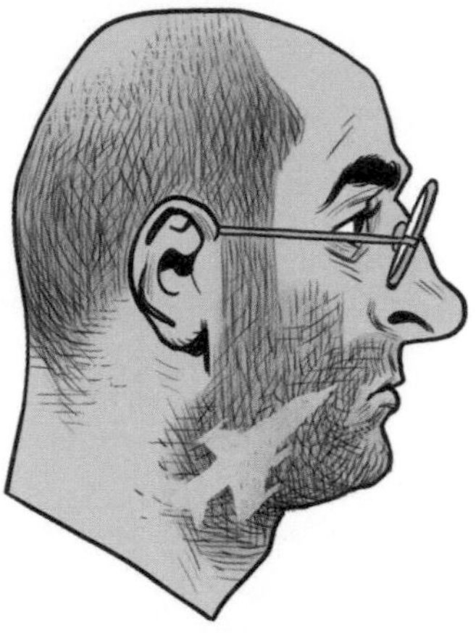

I ACTUALLY THOUGHT I WAS DOING PRETTY WELL. RELATIVELY SPEAKING. DOING ALL RIGHT. NOT CRAZY HAPPY, BUT NOT DEPRESSED, EITHER. NEITHER WAR NOR PEACE.

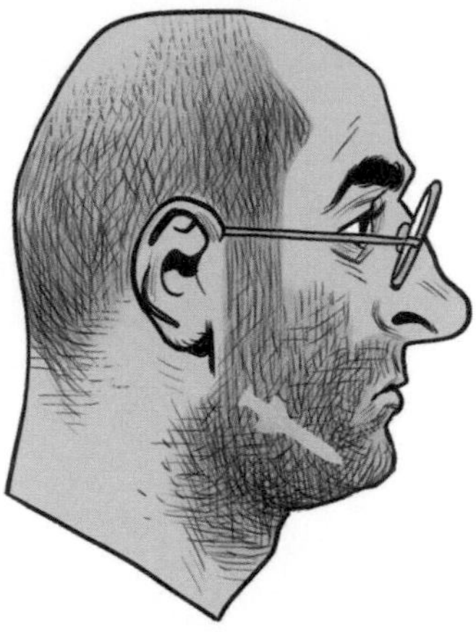

THE DOCTOR INJECTED ME WITH SOMETHING SHE SAID MIGHT HELP, BUT ADDED THAT THE MOST IMPORTANT THING IS THAT I TRY TO RELAX.

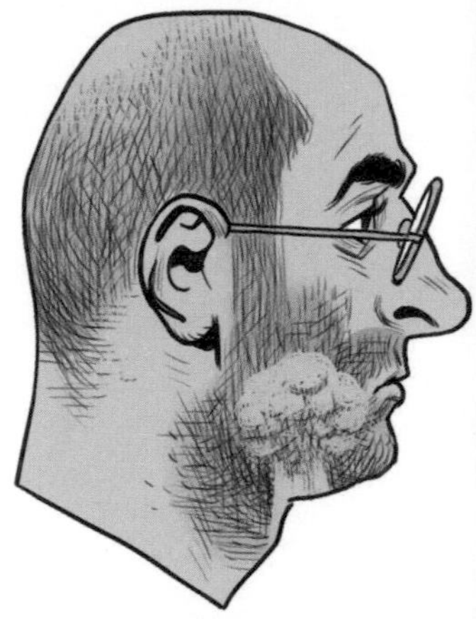

IN THE MEANTIME, THE BALD SPOT CONTINUE TO GROW, CHANGING SHAPE EVERY FEW DAYS, AS IF TRYING TO TELL ME SOMETHING. WHO COULD RELAX LIKE THAT?

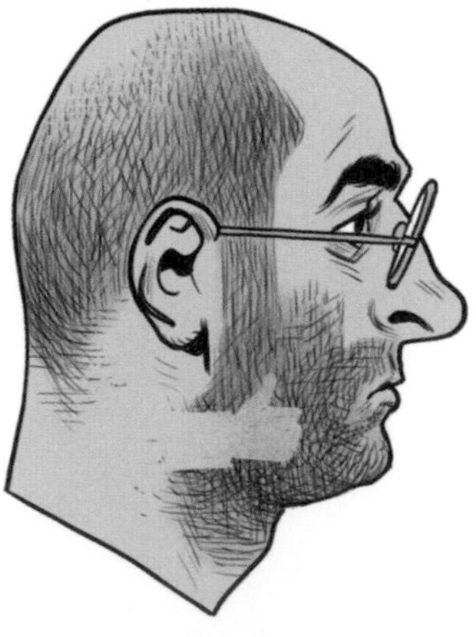

I REALIZED I HAD TO FACE MY ANXIETY HEAD ON, AND THAT THE RELATIVE QUIET I'D BEEN FEELING LATELY WAS A RESULT OF REPRESSION.

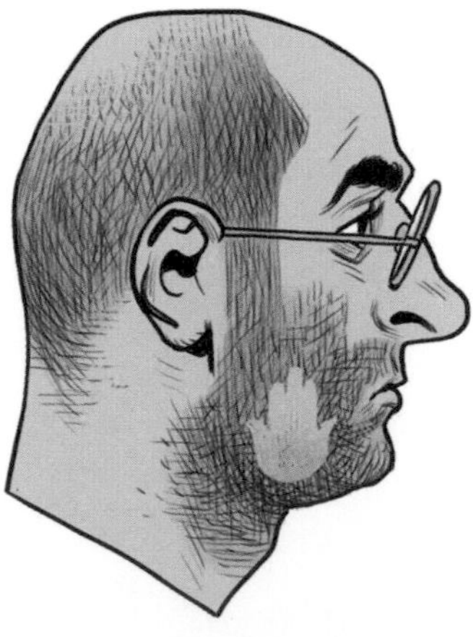

I WENT OVER ALL MY ANXIETIES AGAIN, TRYING TO SPOT SOMETHING I'D MISSED: THE KIDS' HEALTH, MY RELATIONSHIP WITH MY WIFE, THE OVERDRAFT IN THE BANK, THE NEXT WAR.

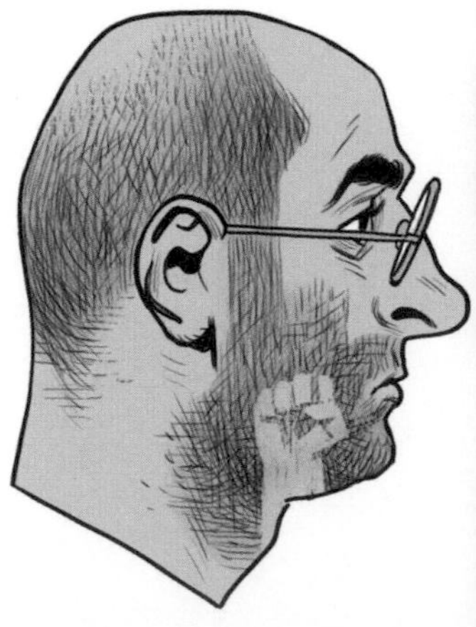

I'VE BEEN REPRESSING FOR YEARS AND I DON'T INTEND TO CHANGE NOW JUST BECAUSE OF SOME BIZARRE BALD SPOT. WHAT DOESN'T GET SOLVED BY REPRESSION GETS SOLVED BY MORE REPRESSION.

OOK LEFT, LOOK RIGHT, AND...

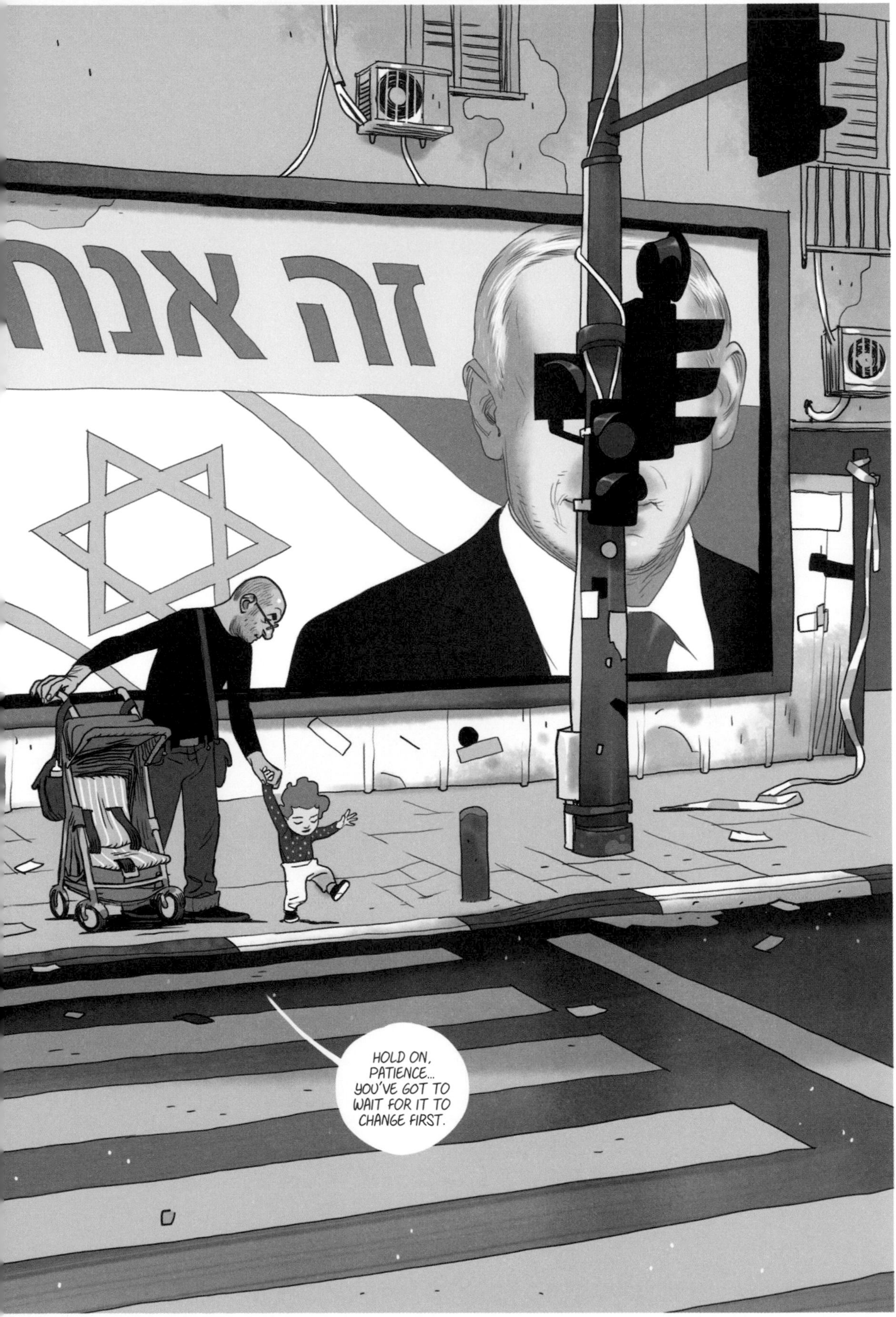
זה אנח
HOLD ON, PATIENCE... YOU'VE GOT TO WAIT FOR IT TO CHANGE FIRST.

HERITAGE OF PEACE

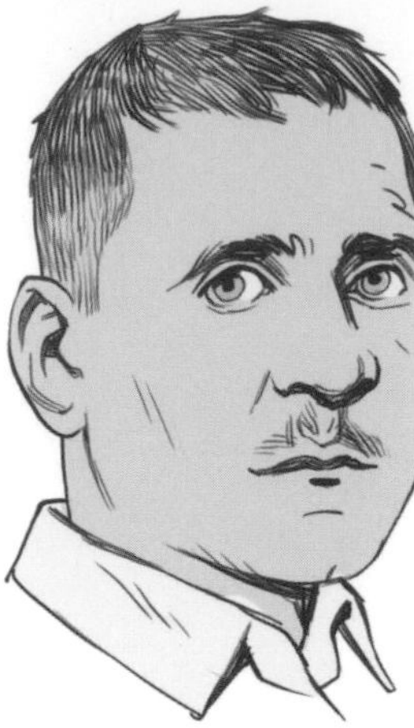

MY GRANDFATHER NEVER SPOKE MUCH. WHEN WE WERE LITTLE WE USED TO GO TO TIBERIAS ON FRIDAYS TO VISIT HIM AND GRANDMA. GRANDMA ALWAYS MADE FISH IN TOMATO SAUCE.

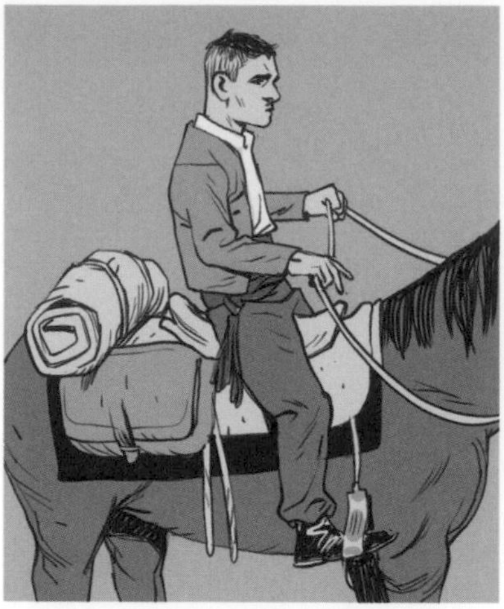

GRANDPA TRAVELED FROM KURDISTAN TO ISRAEL IN 1918. HE TRAVELED ON HORSEBACK ALL THE WAY TO TURKEY, AND FROM THERE TOOK TAXIES THROUGH LEBANON. HE WAS ONLY EIGHTEEN YEARS OLD.

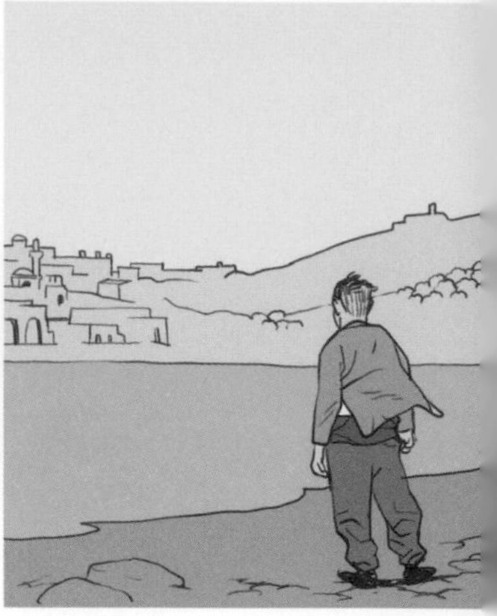

HE WAS RESOURCEFUL AND STREET SMART. HE SETTLED DOWN IN TIBERIAS, STARTED A FAMILY, AND MADE A LIVING IMPORTING FABRIC FROM DAMASCUS.

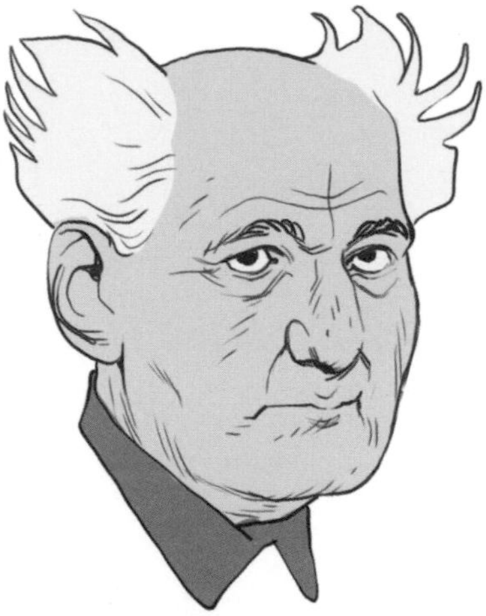

WHEN THE STATE OF ISRAEL WAS ESTABLISHED, PARTY OFFICIALS CHANGED HIS LAST NAME TO HANUKA-MIZRAHI AS A WAY OF MARKING HIM AS PART OF THE MIZRAHI JEWS.

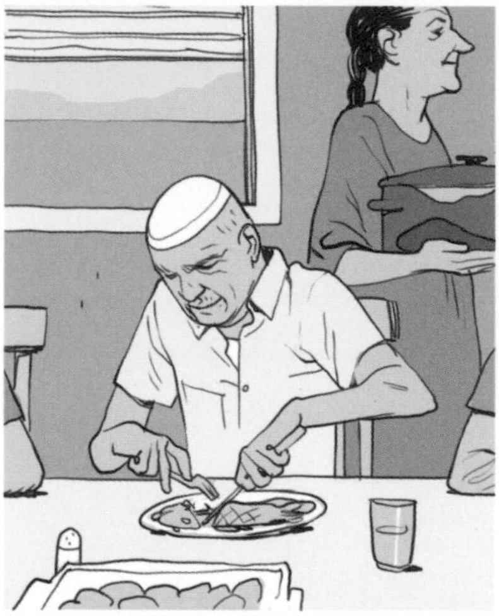

HE LIVED MODESTLY, FEEDING SEVEN CHILDREN. IN SPITE OF ALL HIS STRIFE, HE WASN'T LOOKING FOR ANY BATTLES. I REMEMBER HIM PATIENTLY FILETING HIS FISH, WATCHING OUT FOR BONES.

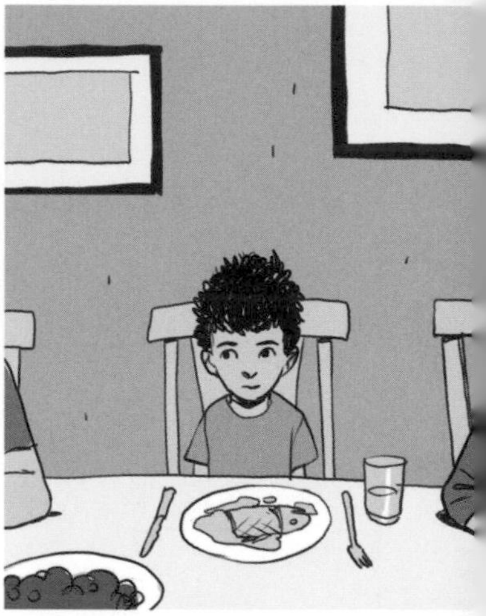

HE SPOKE FOUR LANGUAGES: ARABIC, HEBREW KURDISH, AND TURKISH, BUT HE ALMOST NEVE SPOKE TO ME.

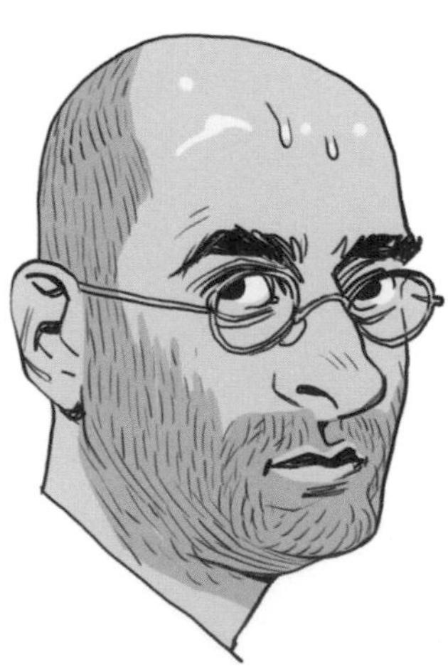

I TALK A LOT AND ONLY SMILE A LITTLE. I WAS BORN IN A SUBURB AND NOW I LIVE IN TEL AVIV. I TRAVELED HERE ON THE NO. 55 BUS.

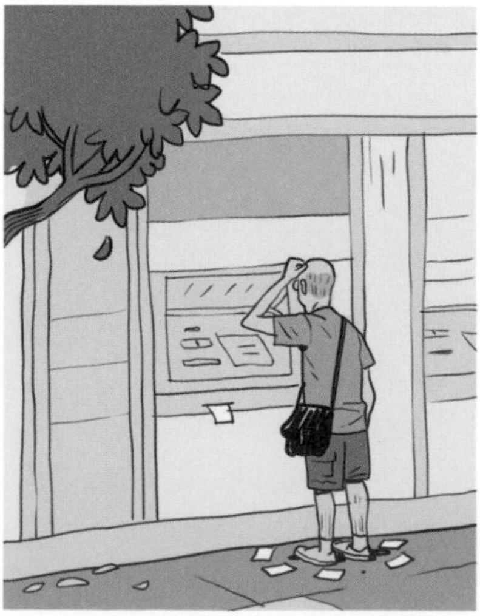

UNLIKE MY GRANDFATHER, I HAVE NO KNACK FOR SALES, AND MY LIFE ISN'T TOO COMPLICATED, BUT STILL, I BARELY MANAGE.

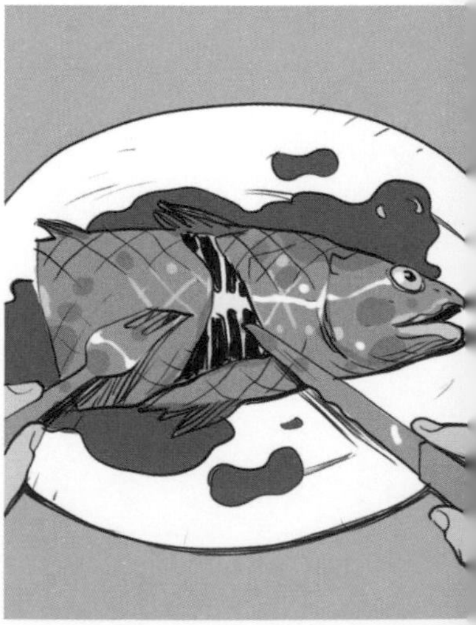

I GOT ALMOST NOTHING OF HIS, NOT EVEN THE BLUE EYES. BUT I LEARNED FROM HIM TO EAT FISH SLOWLY, AND WATCH OUT FOR BONES.

TATISTICAL DISTRIBUTION

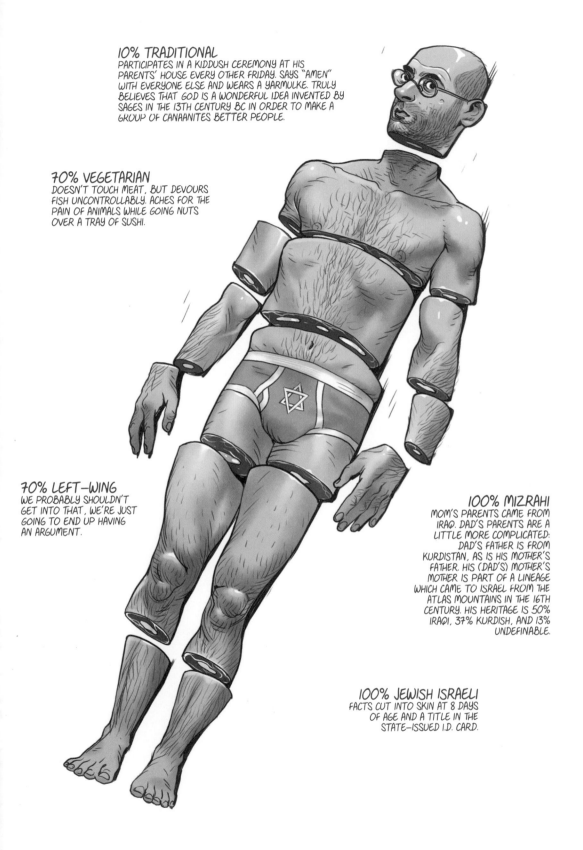

10% TRADITIONAL
PARTICIPATES IN A KIDDUSH CEREMONY AT HIS PARENTS' HOUSE EVERY OTHER FRIDAY. SAYS "AMEN" WITH EVERYONE ELSE AND WEARS A YARMULKE. TRULY BELIEVES THAT GOD IS A WONDERFUL IDEA INVENTED BY SAGES IN THE 13TH CENTURY BC IN ORDER TO MAKE A GROUP OF CANAANITES BETTER PEOPLE.

70% VEGETARIAN
DOESN'T TOUCH MEAT, BUT DEVOURS FISH UNCONTROLLABLY. ACHES FOR THE PAIN OF ANIMALS WHILE GOING NUTS OVER A TRAY OF SUSHI.

70% LEFT-WING
WE PROBABLY SHOULDN'T GET INTO THAT, WE'RE JUST GOING TO END UP HAVING AN ARGUMENT.

100% MIZRAHI
MOM'S PARENTS CAME FROM IRAQ. DAD'S PARENTS ARE A LITTLE MORE COMPLICATED: DAD'S FATHER IS FROM KURDISTAN, AS IS HIS MOTHER'S FATHER. HIS (DAD'S) MOTHER'S MOTHER IS PART OF A LINEAGE WHICH CAME TO ISRAEL FROM THE ATLAS MOUNTAINS IN THE 16TH CENTURY. HIS HERITAGE IS 50% IRAQI, 37% KURDISH, AND 13% UNDEFINABLE.

100% JEWISH ISRAELI
FACTS CUT INTO SKIN AT 8 DAYS OF AGE AND A TITLE IN THE STATE-ISSUED I.D. CARD.

HI HONEY,

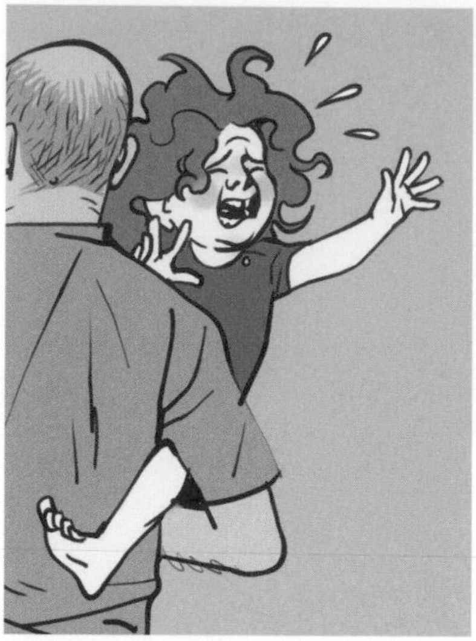

THE CHILDREN HAVE BEEN HAPPY AND HEALTHY SINCE YOU'VE BEEN GONE. THEY DON'T EVEN MISS YOU VERY MUCH.

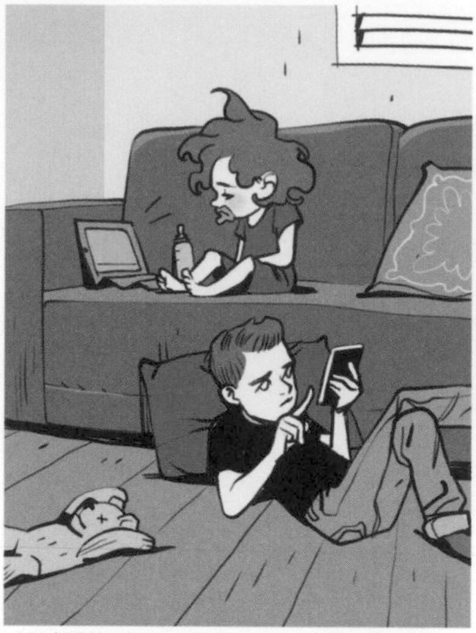

I DO JIGSAW PUZZLES AND LOGIC PROBLEMS WITH THE LITTLE ONE, AND THE BOY DOES HIS HOMEWORK EVERY DAY.

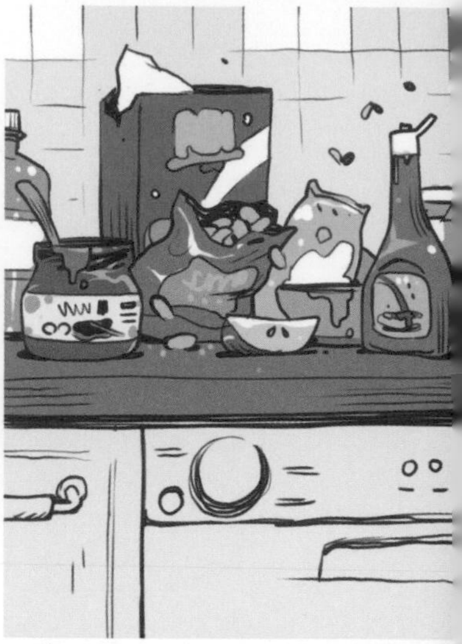

THEY'RE EATING HEALTHY, EXACTLY ACCORDING TO THE LIST YOU LEFT ME, AND LEAVE NOTHING ON THEIR PLATES.

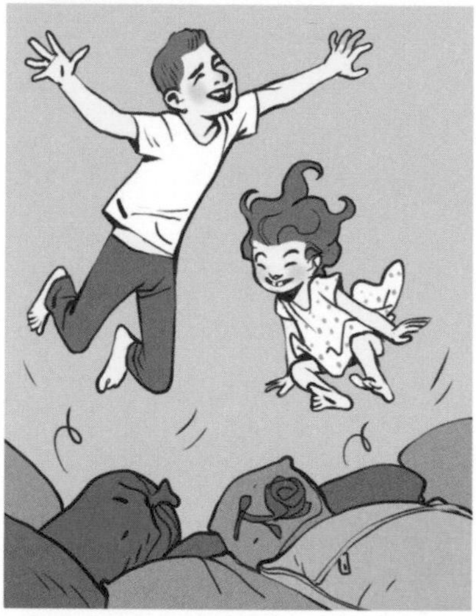

I MAKE SURE THEY BRUSH THEIR TEETH BEFORE BED, JUST LIKE I PROMISED YOU, AND I TELL THEM A BEDTIME STORY.

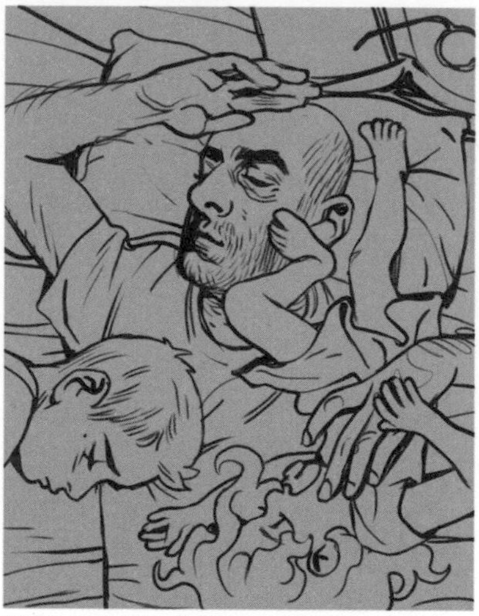

AFTER THEY FALL ASLEEP I CLEAN THE HOUSE AND EVEN READ A LITTLE BIT BEFORE BED.

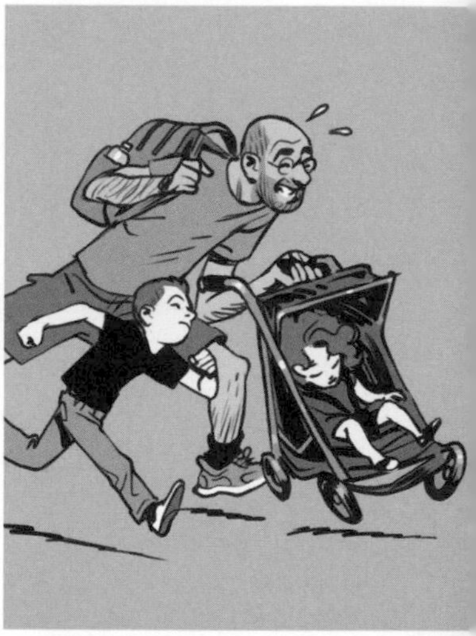

WE WAKE UP VERY EARLY, GET READY LIKE CLOCKWORK, AND ALWAYS MAKE THE SCHOOL BUS IN TIME.

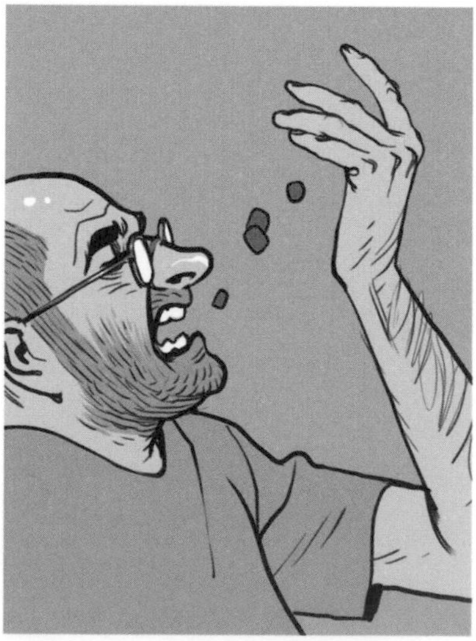

I HOPE YOU'RE HAVING A GREAT TIME IN LONDON, SHOPPING AND EATING OUT, AND NOT THINKING ABOUT US TOO MUCH.

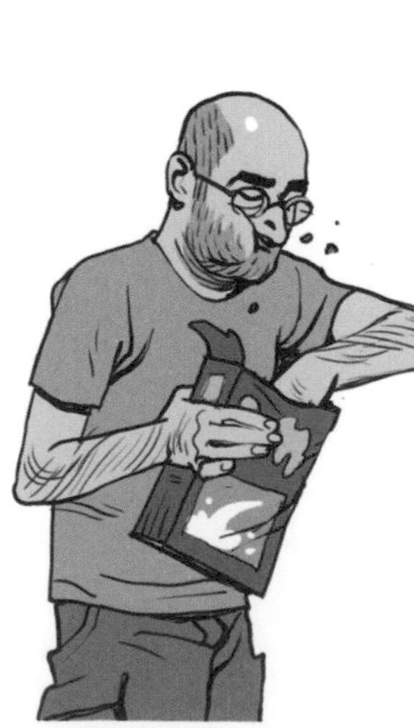

I THINK ABOUT YOU ALL THE TIME.

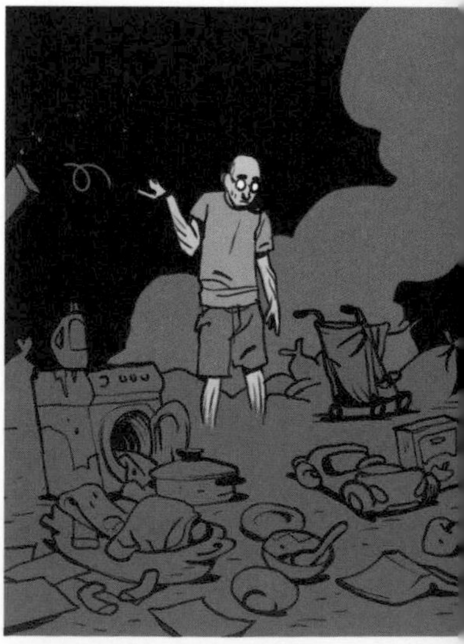

BEING A MOM IS PRETTY HARD.

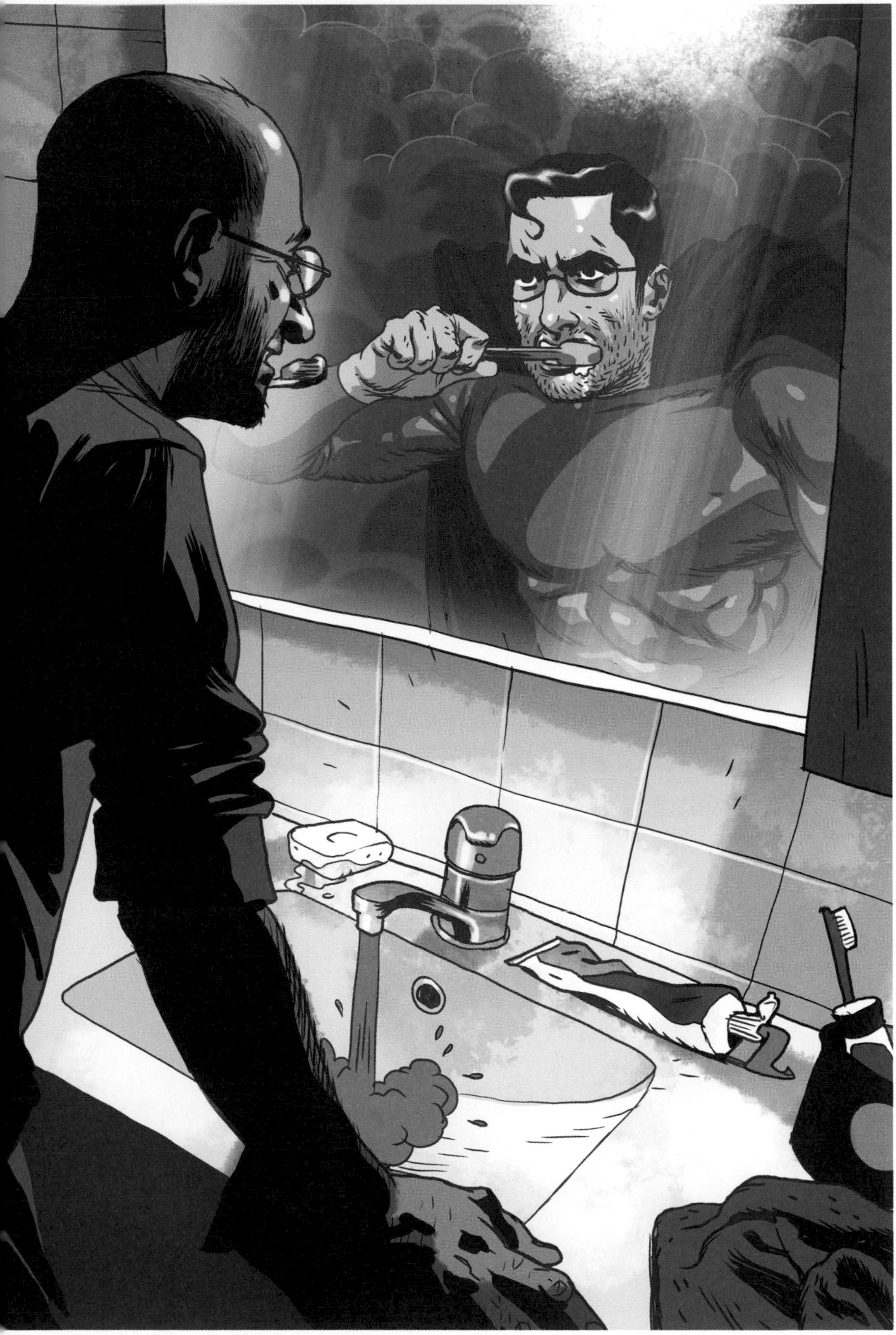

AMEN

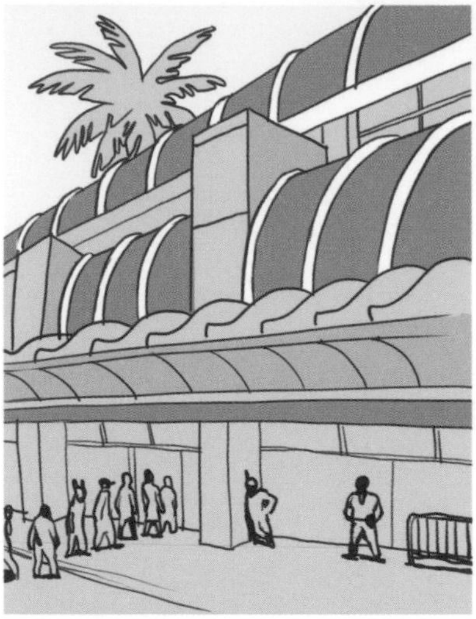

I WAS EXCITED ABOUT MY TRIP TO SAN DIEGO FOR COMIC CON.

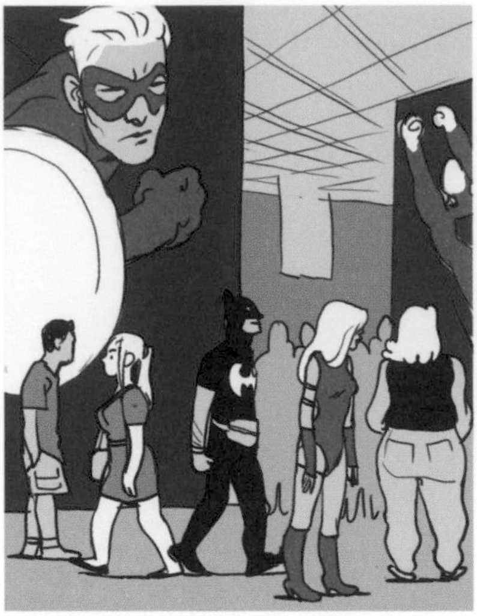

I WENT TO WALK AROUND THE STALLS, BUT INSTEAD OF LOOKING AT THE BOOKS, I LOOKED AT THE PEOPLE.

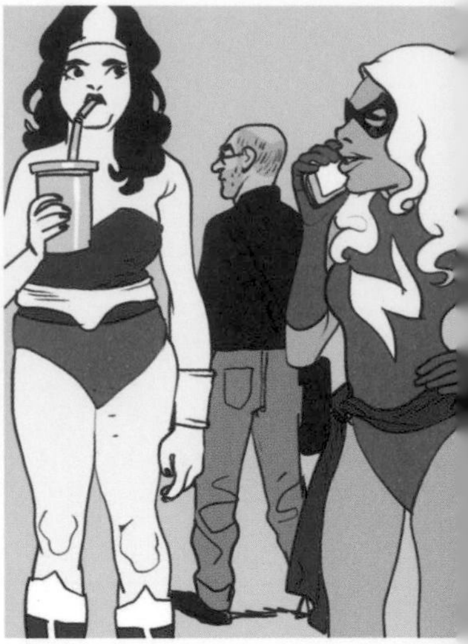

MANY OF THEM WERE DRESSED UP AS SUPER HEROES AND OTHER POPULAR CHARACTERS FROM COMIC BOOKS.

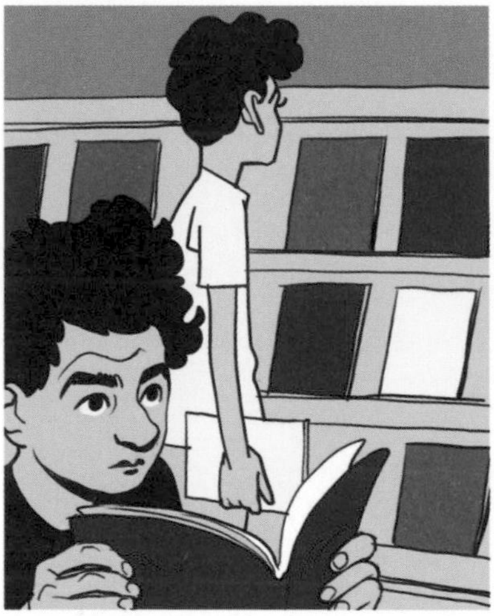

I FIRST FELL IN LOVE WITH COMIC BOOKS IN A SMALL SHOP IN CALIFORNIA. I BELIEVED THAT IF THE MUTANTS COULD BEAT THE BAD GUYS IN THE X-MEN SERIES, THEN I TOO HAD A CHANCE.

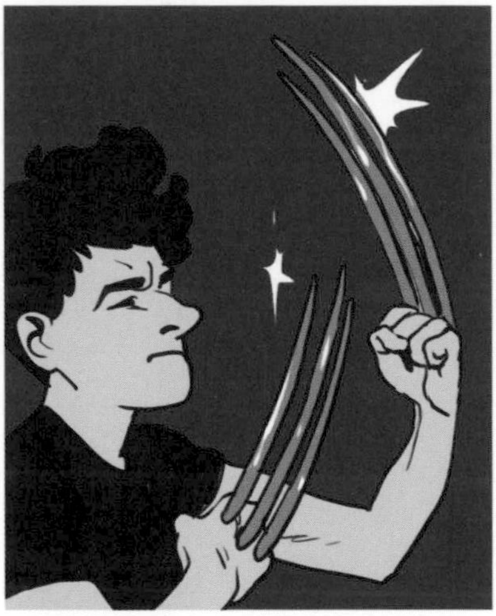

FOR YEARS LATER I WAS SURE IT'S JUST A MATTER OF TIME BEFORE I WOULD GROW CLAWS LIKE WOLVERINE.

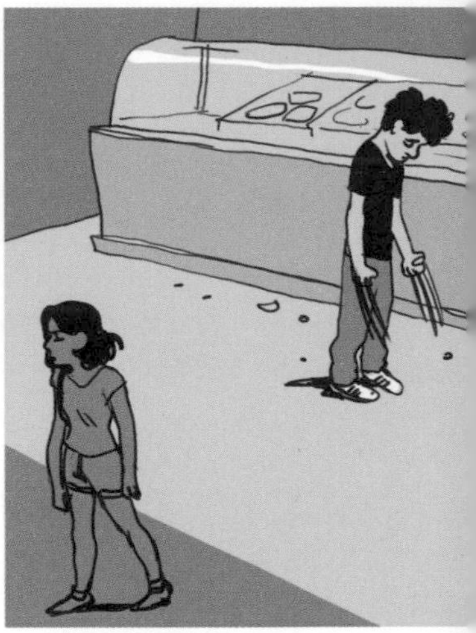

BUT ONE DAY MY GIRLFRIEND BROKE UP WIT ME. MY HEART WAS BROKEN. I GUESS IT WAS MADE OF ADAMANTIUM. I BECAME AN ADULT STOPPED BELIEVING IN SUPERHEROES.

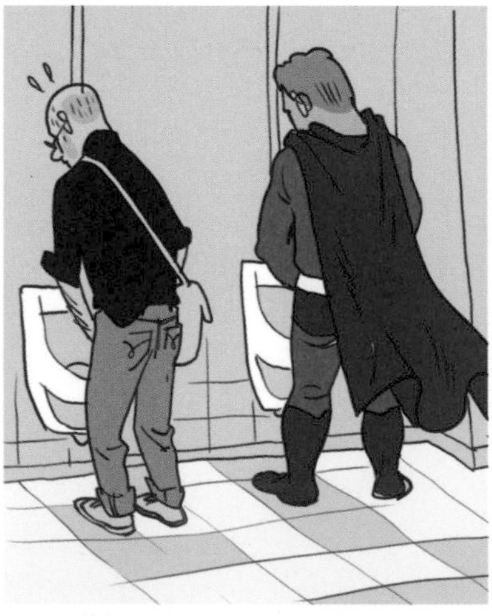

I ENVY RELIGIOUS PEOPLE, WHO BELIEVE THEY ARE PART OF A BIGGER STORY, PLAYERS IN A PRECONCEIVED PLOT, JUST LIKE AVID COMICS FANS.

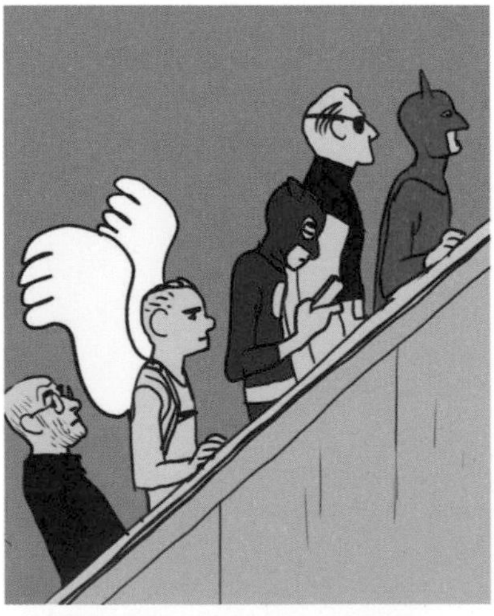

IT'S COMFORTING TO BELIEVE, WHETHER IT'S IN ONE GOD OR IN A PACK OF WEIRDOS IN COLORFUL UNDERWEAR. COMIC CON IS AN OPPORTUNITY FOR BELIEVERS TO BECOME GODS FOR A DAY.

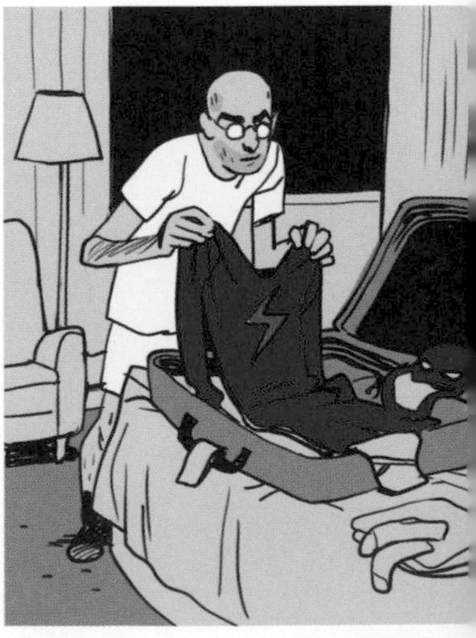

THAT NIGHT, I COULDN'T SLEEP. IT MIGHT HAVE BEEN THE JETLAG, BUT I THINK IT WAS SOMETHING MUCH BIGGER. SOMETHING THAT WOULD SAVE THE FUTURE OF HUMANKIND.

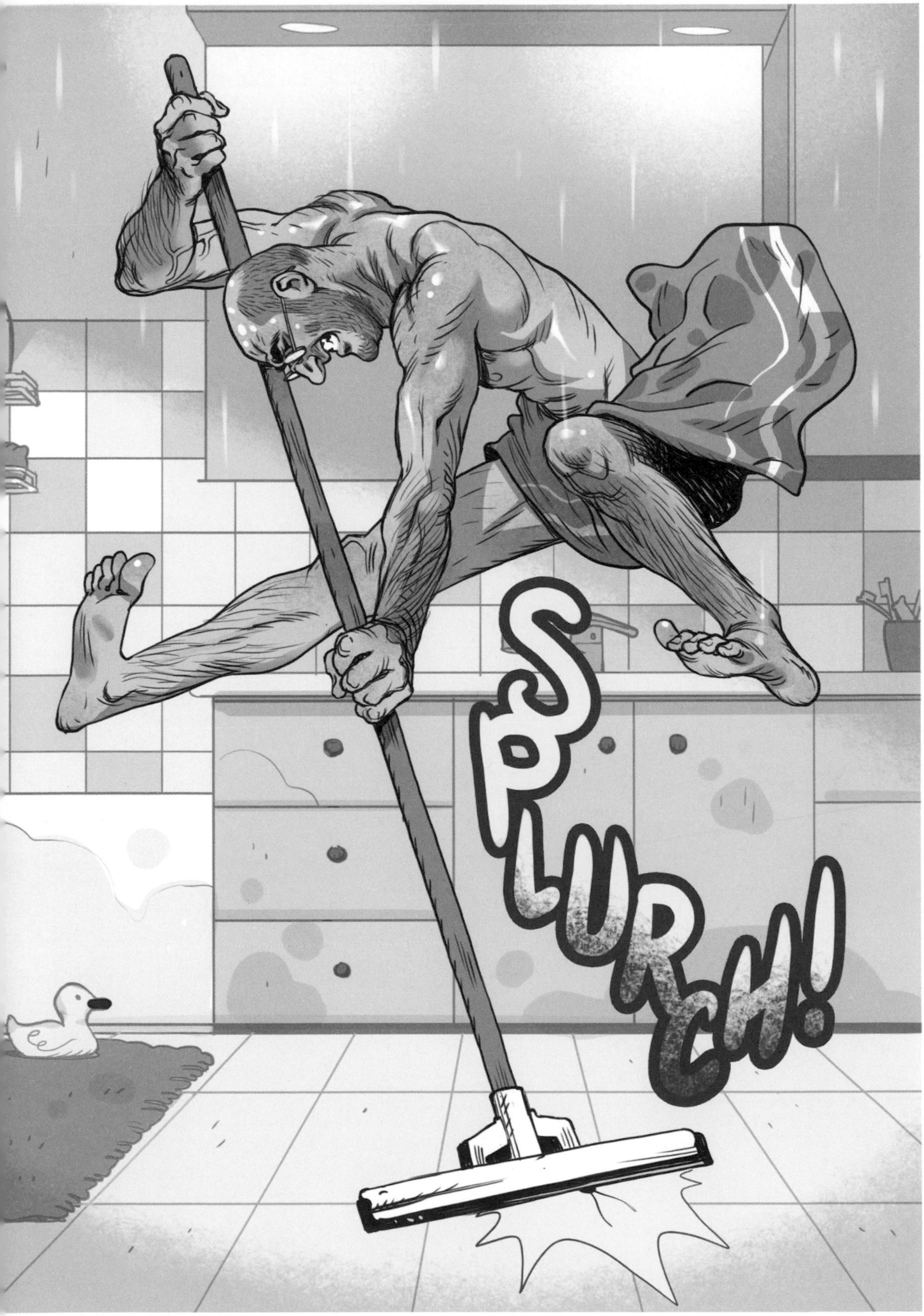
SPLURCH!

BE FRUITFUL AND MULTIPLY

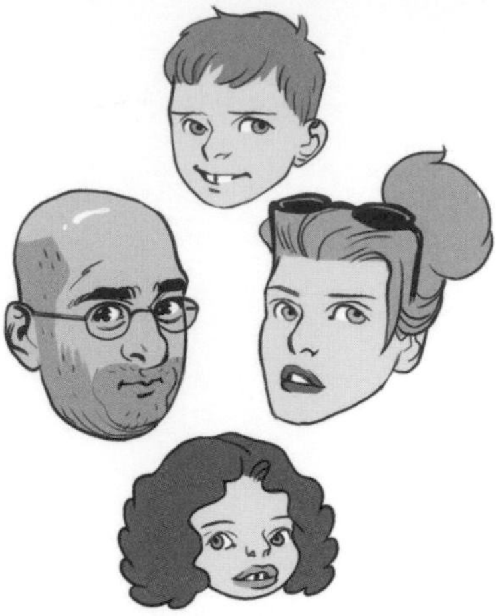

WE HAVE TWO KIDS AND ZERO CHANCE OF HAVING ANOTHER ONE.

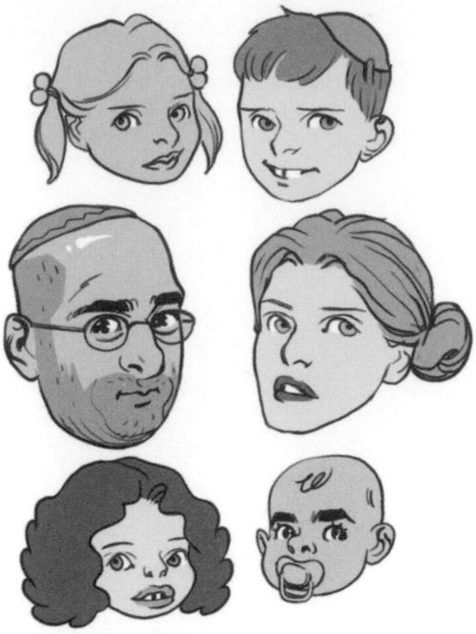

IF WE WERE RELIGIOUS ZIONISTS WE'D PROBABLY HAVE FOUR KIDS. IT'S EASIER FOR THEM BECAUSE THEY SEND ALL THEIR CHILDREN TO RELIGIOUS BOARDING SCHOOLS.

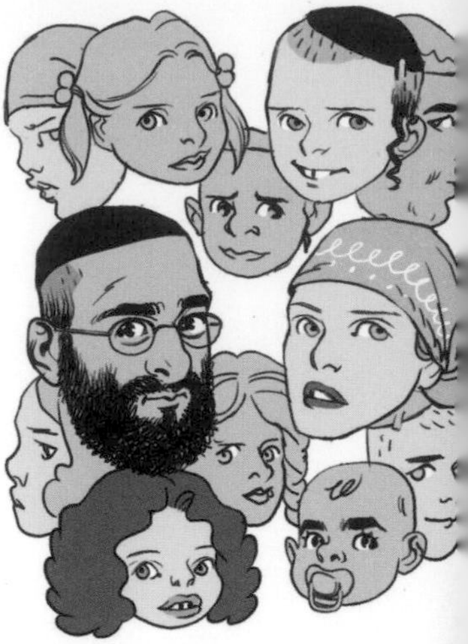

IF WE WERE ORTHODOX WE'D PROBABLY HAV TEN KIDS. THEY HAVE AN ARRANGEMENT TOO WHEN THERE ARE SO MANY CHILDREN IN A FAMILY, THEY ALL RAISE EACH OTHER.

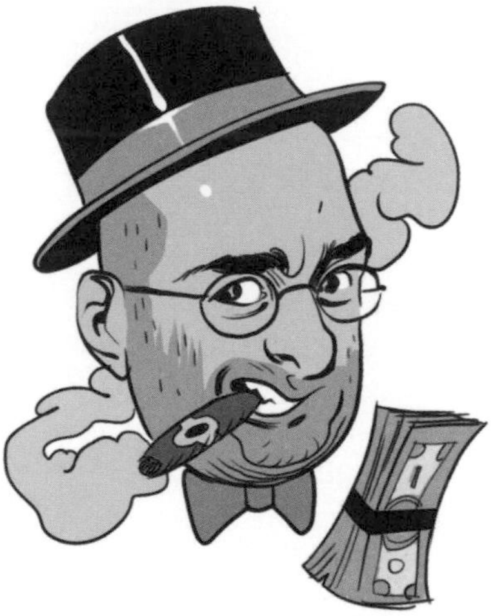

BUT WE'RE SECULAR CAPITALISTS. OUR RELIGION IS SHOPPING, WHICH IS WHY WE'RE WORKAHOLICS.

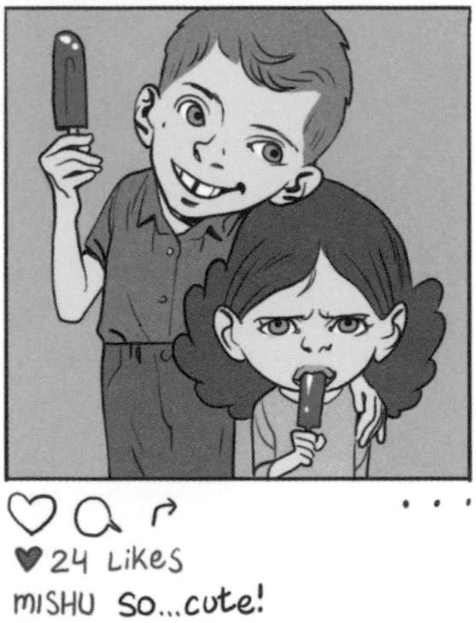
24 Likes
MISHU So...cute!

THE TEN COMMANDMENTS OF THE CAPITALIST FAITH ARE THE TENETS OF BRANDING, AND OUR CHILDREN REFLECT THE VALUE OF THE FAMILY BRAND. THAT'S WHY WE DEVOTE SO MUCH TIME AND ATTENTION TO THEM.

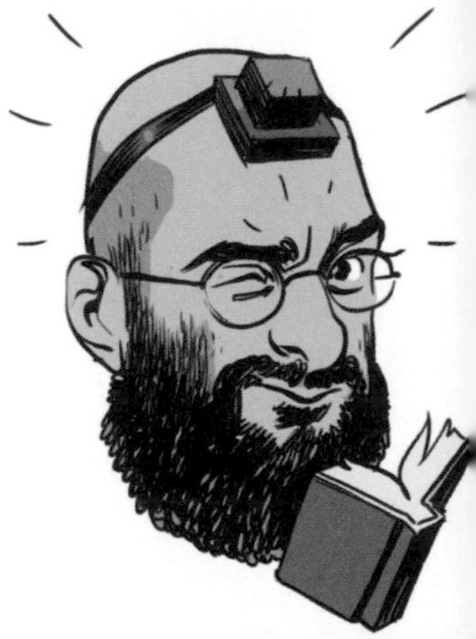

A THIRD CHILD WOULD LEAD TO A DECLINE IN INVESTMENT AND A DECREASE IN THE VALUE OF THE FAMILY BRAND. SOMETIMES I THINK SHOULD BECOME RELIGIOUS ONLY SO WE CO HAVE LOTS OF CHILDREN.

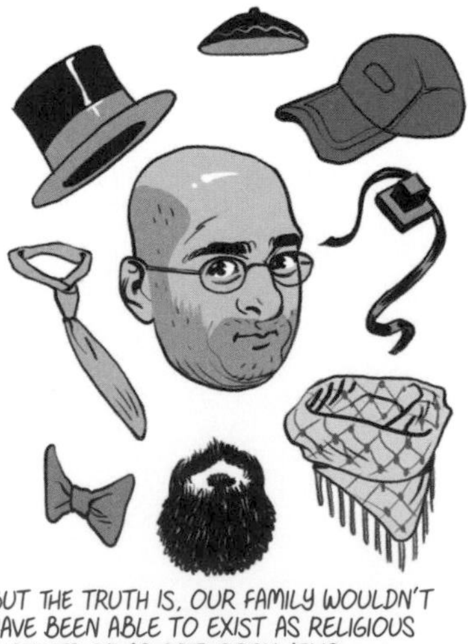

BUT THE TRUTH IS, OUR FAMILY WOULDN'T HAVE BEEN ABLE TO EXIST AS RELIGIOUS ZIONISTS OR AS ORTHODOX JEWS, BECAUSE THOSE FAITHS HARDLY ALLOW MIXED MARRIAGES BETWEEN MIZRAHIS AND ASHKENAZIS.

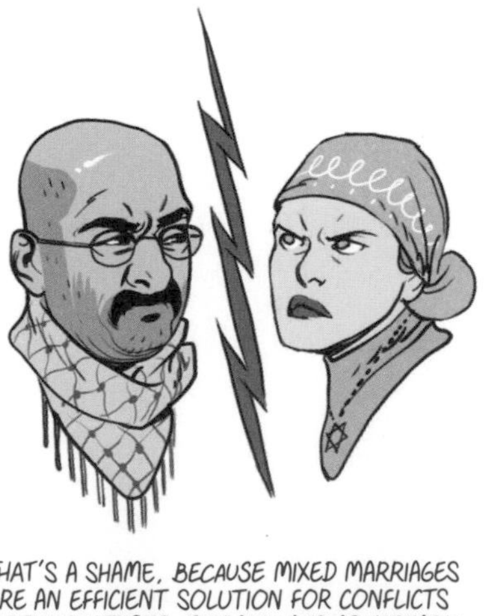

THAT'S A SHAME, BECAUSE MIXED MARRIAGES ARE AN EFFICIENT SOLUTION FOR CONFLICTS BETWEEN TRIBES: MIZRAHIS AND ASHKENAZIS, RELIGIOUS AND SECULAR, JEWS AND ARABS.

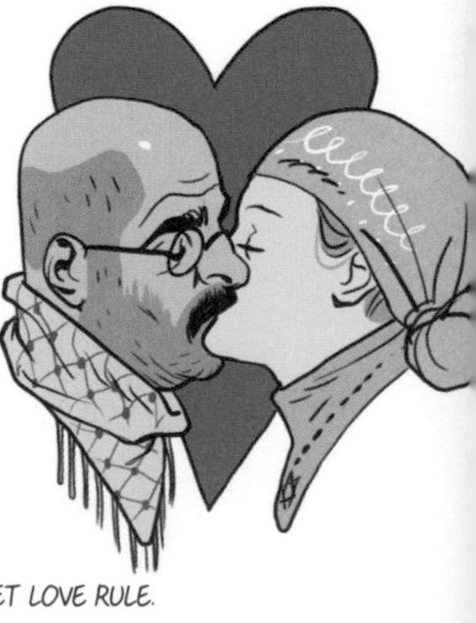

LET LOVE RULE.

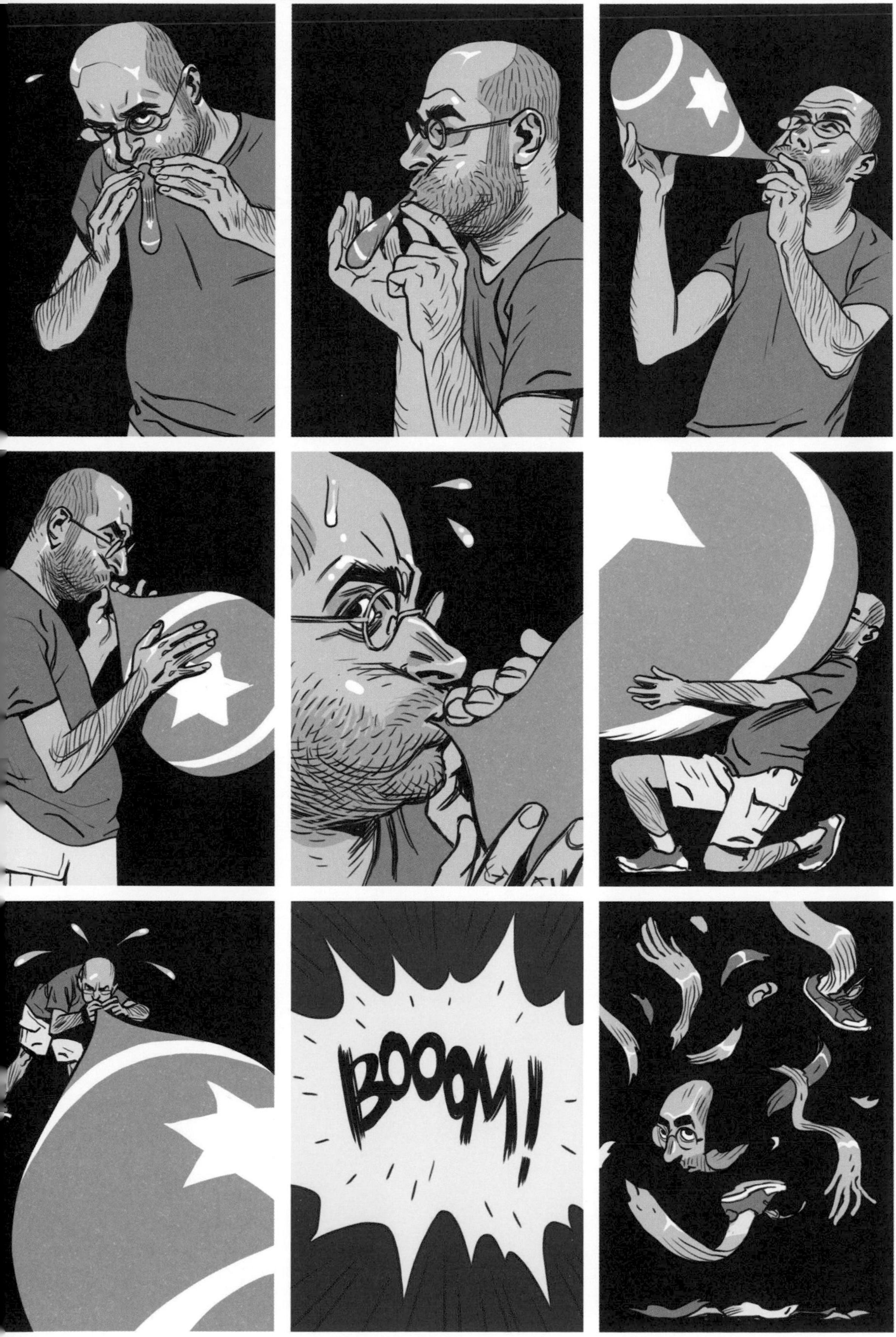
BOOOM!

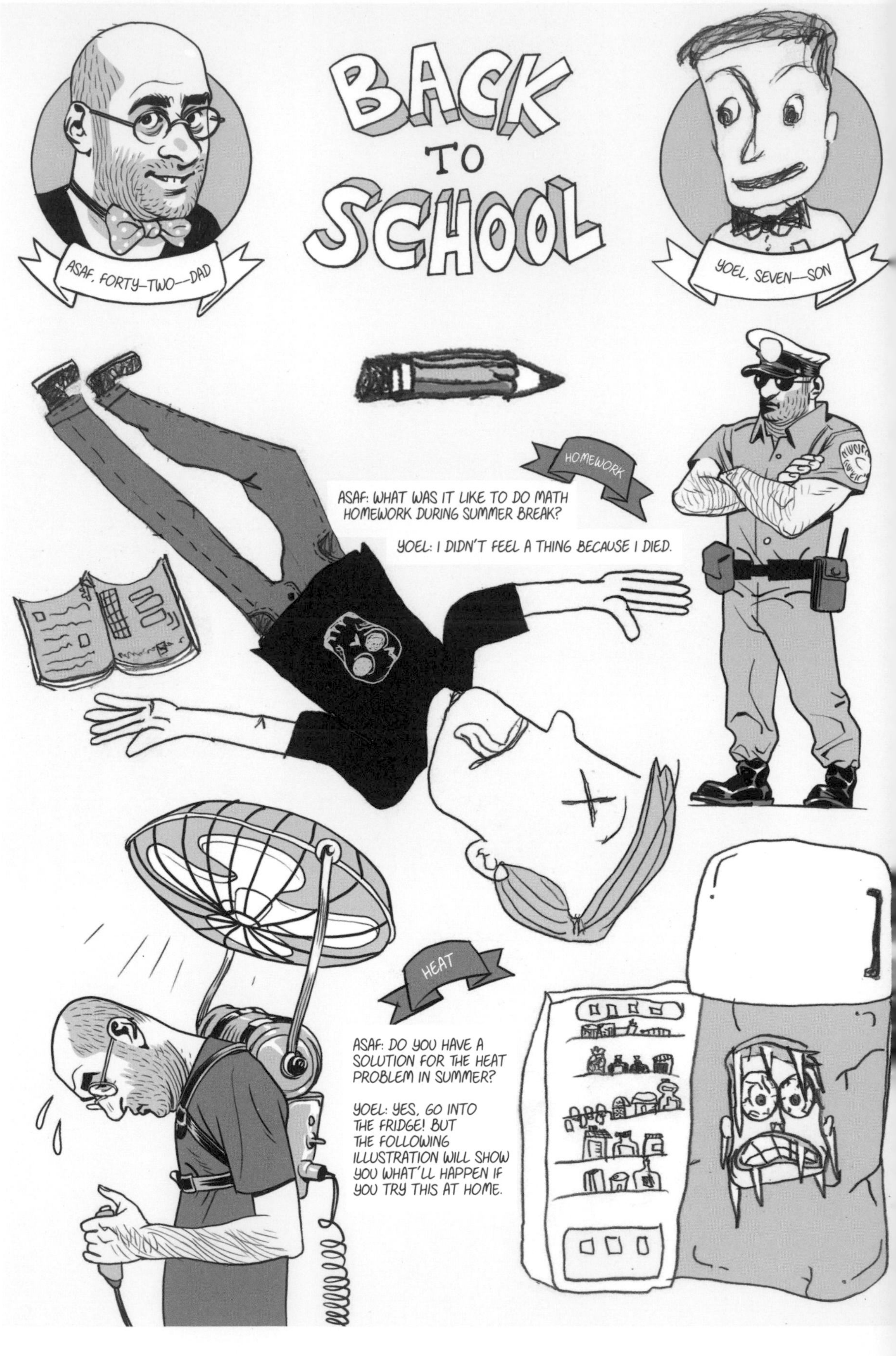
BACK TO SCHOOL
ASAF, FORTY-TWO—DAD
YOEL, SEVEN—SON
HOMEWORK
ASAF: WHAT WAS IT LIKE TO DO MATH HOMEWORK DURING SUMMER BREAK?
YOEL: I DIDN'T FEEL A THING BECAUSE I DIED.
HEAT
ASAF: DO YOU HAVE A SOLUTION FOR THE HEAT PROBLEM IN SUMMER?
YOEL: YES, GO INTO THE FRIDGE! BUT THE FOLLOWING ILLUSTRATION WILL SHOW YOU WHAT'LL HAPPEN IF YOU TRY THIS AT HOME.

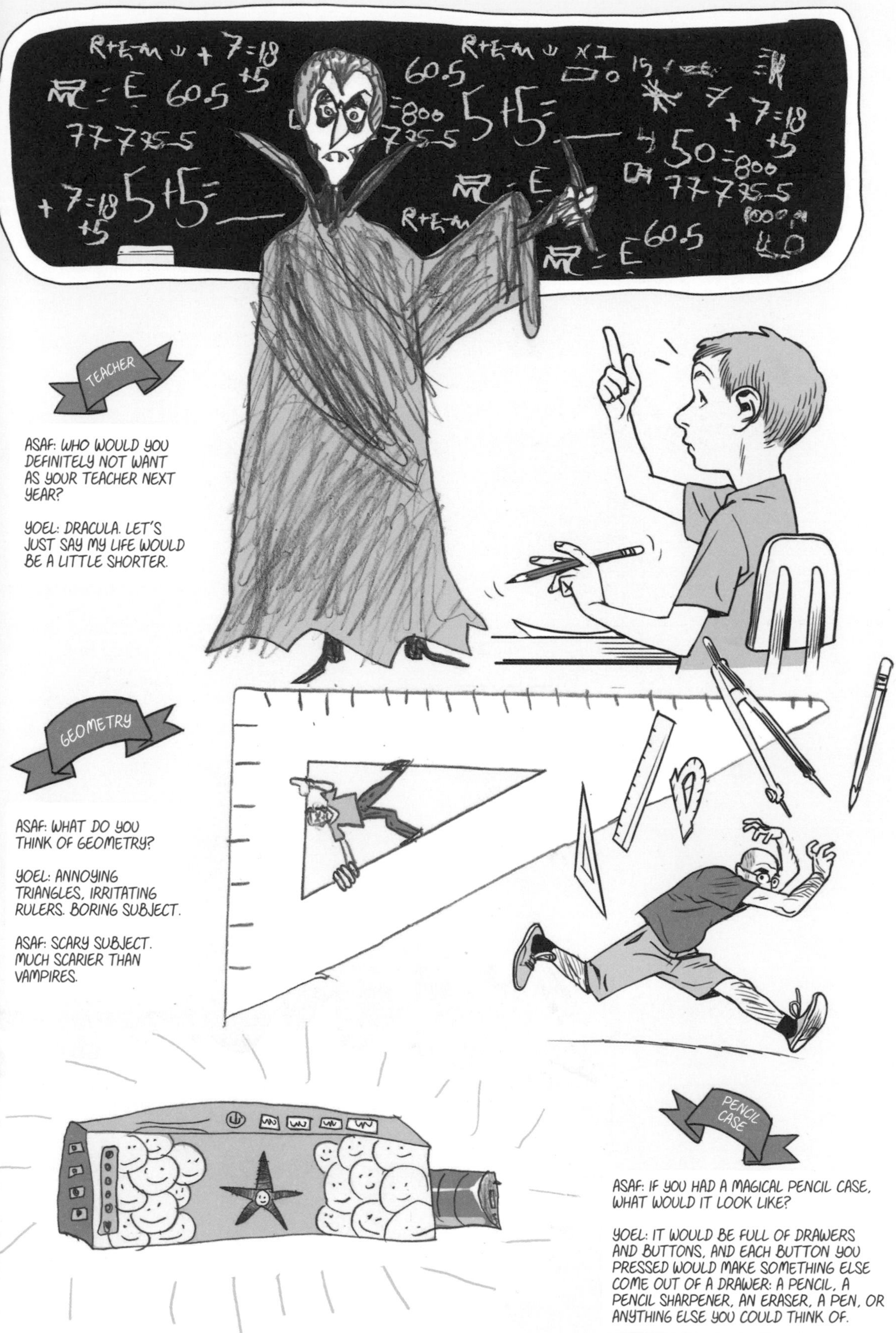
TEACHER
ASAF: WHO WOULD YOU DEFINITELY NOT WANT AS YOUR TEACHER NEXT YEAR?
YOEL: DRACULA. LET'S JUST SAY MY LIFE WOULD BE A LITTLE SHORTER.
GEOMETRY
ASAF: WHAT DO YOU THINK OF GEOMETRY?
YOEL: ANNOYING TRIANGLES, IRRITATING RULERS. BORING SUBJECT.
ASAF: SCARY SUBJECT. MUCH SCARIER THAN VAMPIRES.
PENCIL CASE
ASAF: IF YOU HAD A MAGICAL PENCIL CASE, WHAT WOULD IT LOOK LIKE?
YOEL: IT WOULD BE FULL OF DRAWERS AND BUTTONS, AND EACH BUTTON YOU PRESSED WOULD MAKE SOMETHING ELSE COME OUT OF A DRAWER: A PENCIL, A PENCIL SHARPENER, AN ERASER, A PEN, OR ANYTHING ELSE YOU COULD THINK OF.

THE FUTURE OF OUR RELATIONSHIP

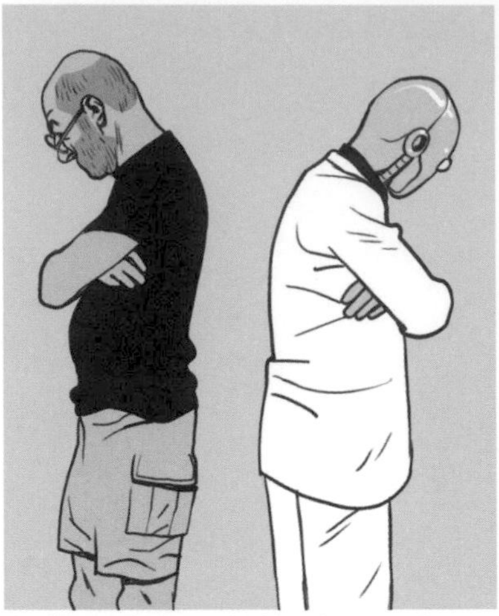

THAT'S IT. IT'S OVER. MY BANK ACCOUNT AND I ARE NO LONGER AN ITEM.

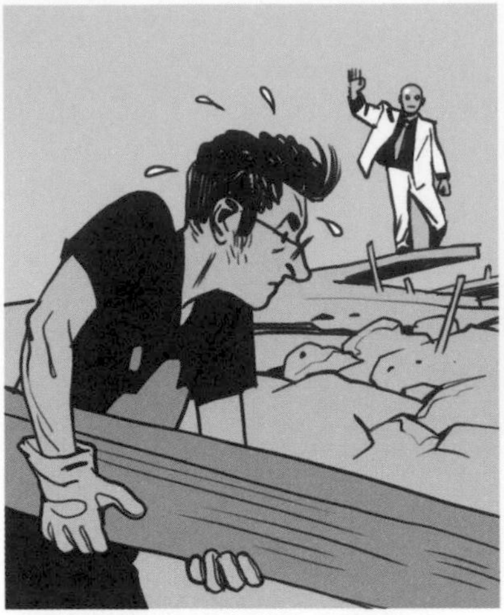

WE HAD A PROMISING START. I OPENED IT WHEN I WAS SIXTEEN YEARS OLD, TO DEPOSIT THE MONEY I EARNED WORKING CONSTRUCTION OVER THE SUMMER BREAK. I WAS SAVING UP FOR DRIVING LESSONS.

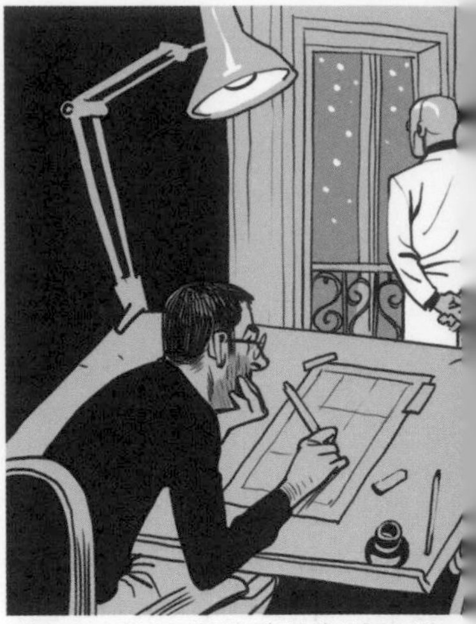

WE HIT LOTS OF IMPORTANT MILESTONES, FROM THE MODEST SALARY OF A SOLDIER TO THE ENORMOUS OVERDRAFT OF A COLLEGE STUDENT, AND THEN THE INCOME FROM A SMALL FREELANCE BUSINESS.

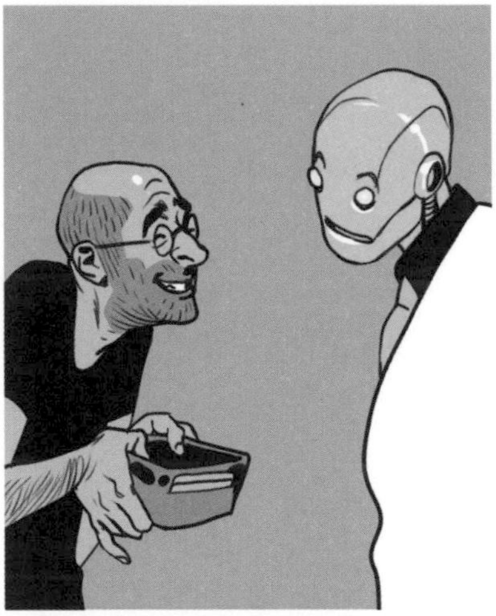

I HAVE THE BASIC SKILLS NECESSARY TO UNDERSTAND MY BANK ACCOUNT. I HAVE A 4-UNIT MATH G.E.D. AND I HATE SHOPPING. I LIKE LISTS. I'M PARANOID AND ANXIOUS.

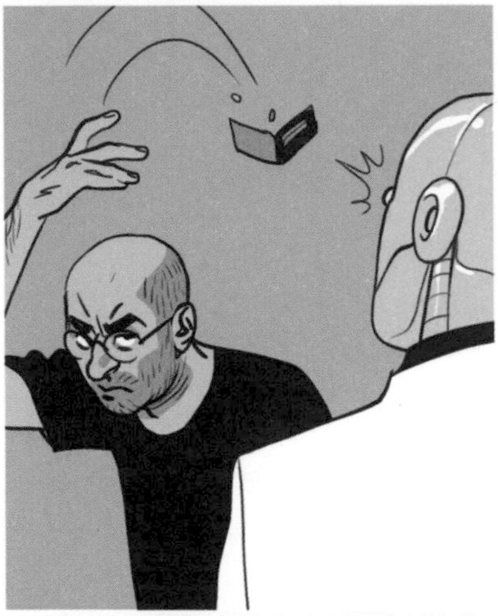

ON PAPER, OUR RELATIONSHIP LOOKS LIKE IT SHOULD BE PERFECT. SO, HOW DID WE GET HERE? WHEN DID I STOP UNDERSTANDING IT AND GIVE IN TO CHAOS?

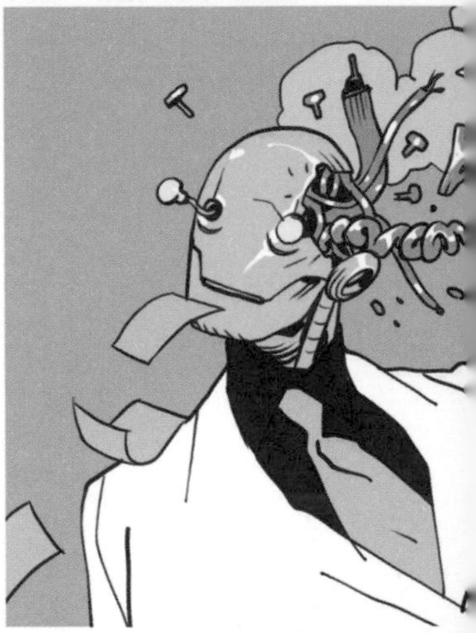

WE USED TO HAVE INTIMACY. I FELT LIKE I REALLY KNEW IT. NOW, WITH AN ENDLESS L OF CHARGES, I MOSTLY FEEL ESTRANGED.

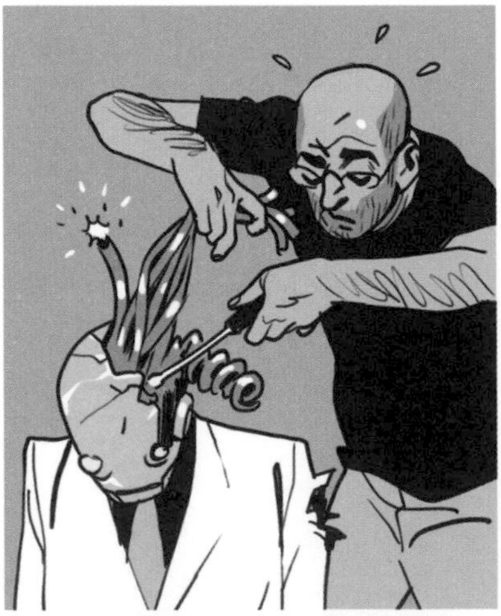

THIS RELATIONSHIP IS ASKING ME FOR TOO MUCH: BECOMING FAMILIAR WITH EVERY SINGLE CHARGE AND FINANCIAL DECISIONS, WHICH IS A EUPHEMISM FOR BEING THRIFTY.

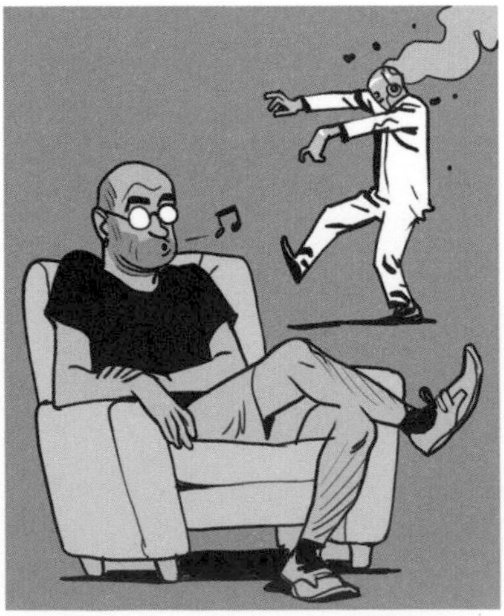

THE PROBLEM IS THAT WHEN I STOPPED UNDERSTANDING IT I BEGAN TO FEAR IT AND PREFERRED TO KNOW AS LITTLE AS POSSIBLE. LET IT MANAGE BY ITSELF.

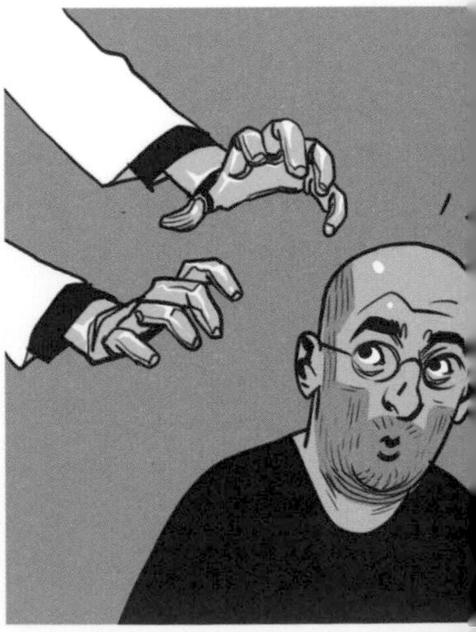

SO I JUST GIVE EVERYTHING I CAN AND HOPE TO TAKE AS LITTLE AS POSSIBLE. FAITH AN HOPE CAN TAKE YOU VERY FAR, AT LEAST UNTIL YOU CRASH INTO REALITY.

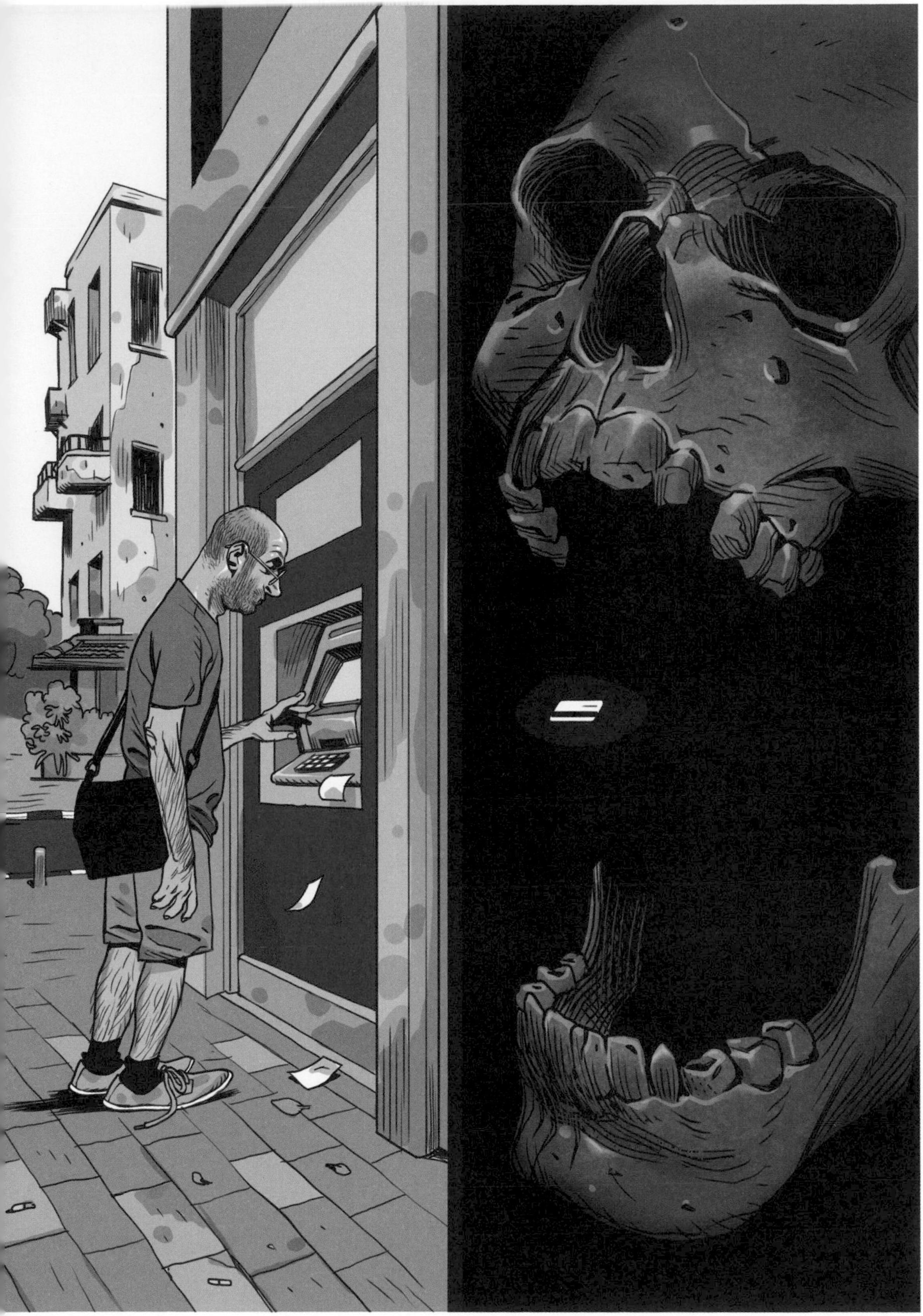

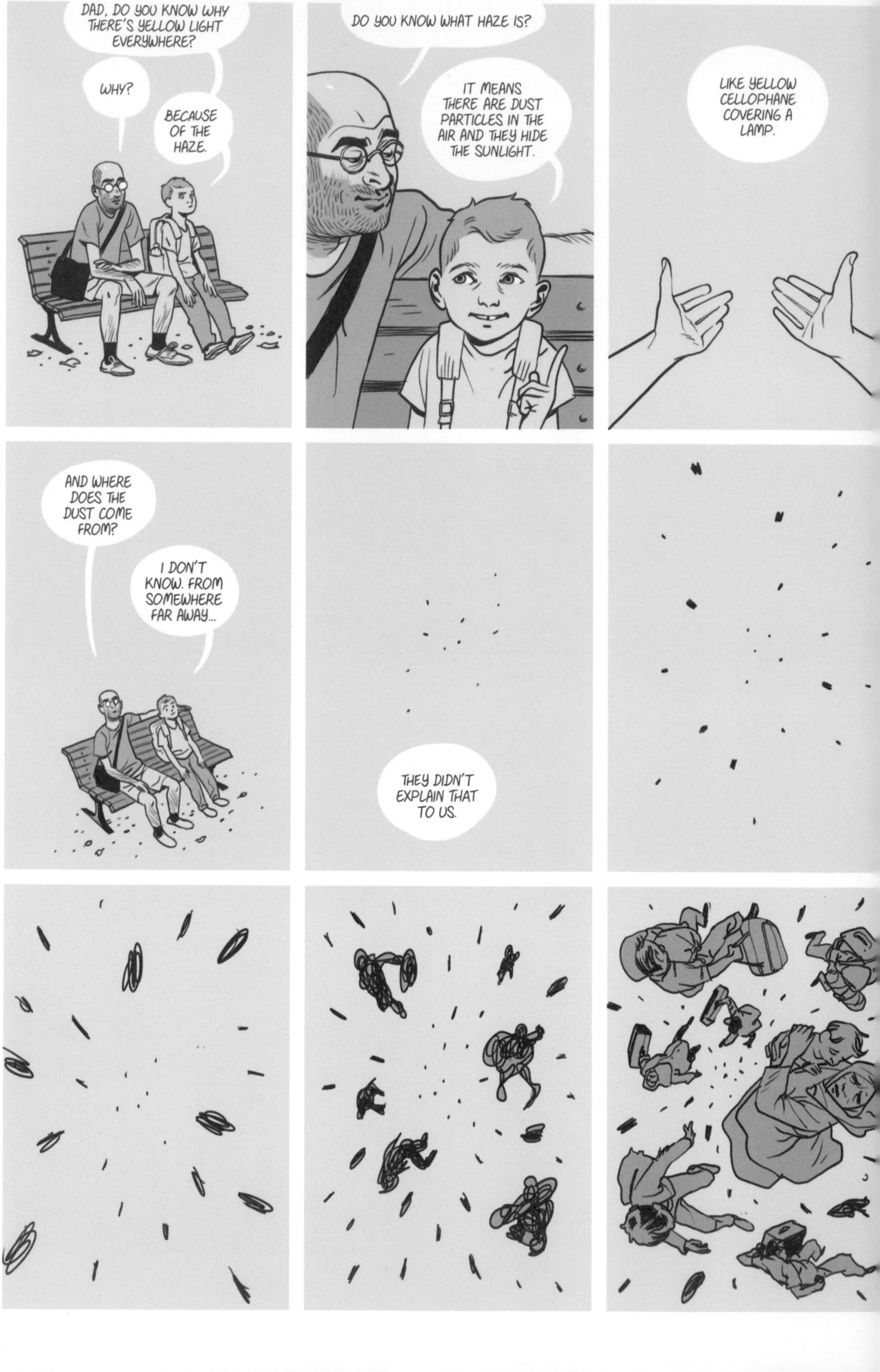
DAD, DO YOU KNOW WHY THERE'S YELLOW LIGHT EVERYWHERE?
WHY?
BECAUSE OF THE HAZE.
DO YOU KNOW WHAT HAZE IS?
IT MEANS THERE ARE DUST PARTICLES IN THE AIR AND THEY HIDE THE SUNLIGHT.
LIKE YELLOW CELLOPHANE COVERING A LAMP.
AND WHERE DOES THE DUST COME FROM?
I DON'T KNOW. FROM SOMEWHERE FAR AWAY...
THEY DIDN'T EXPLAIN THAT TO US.

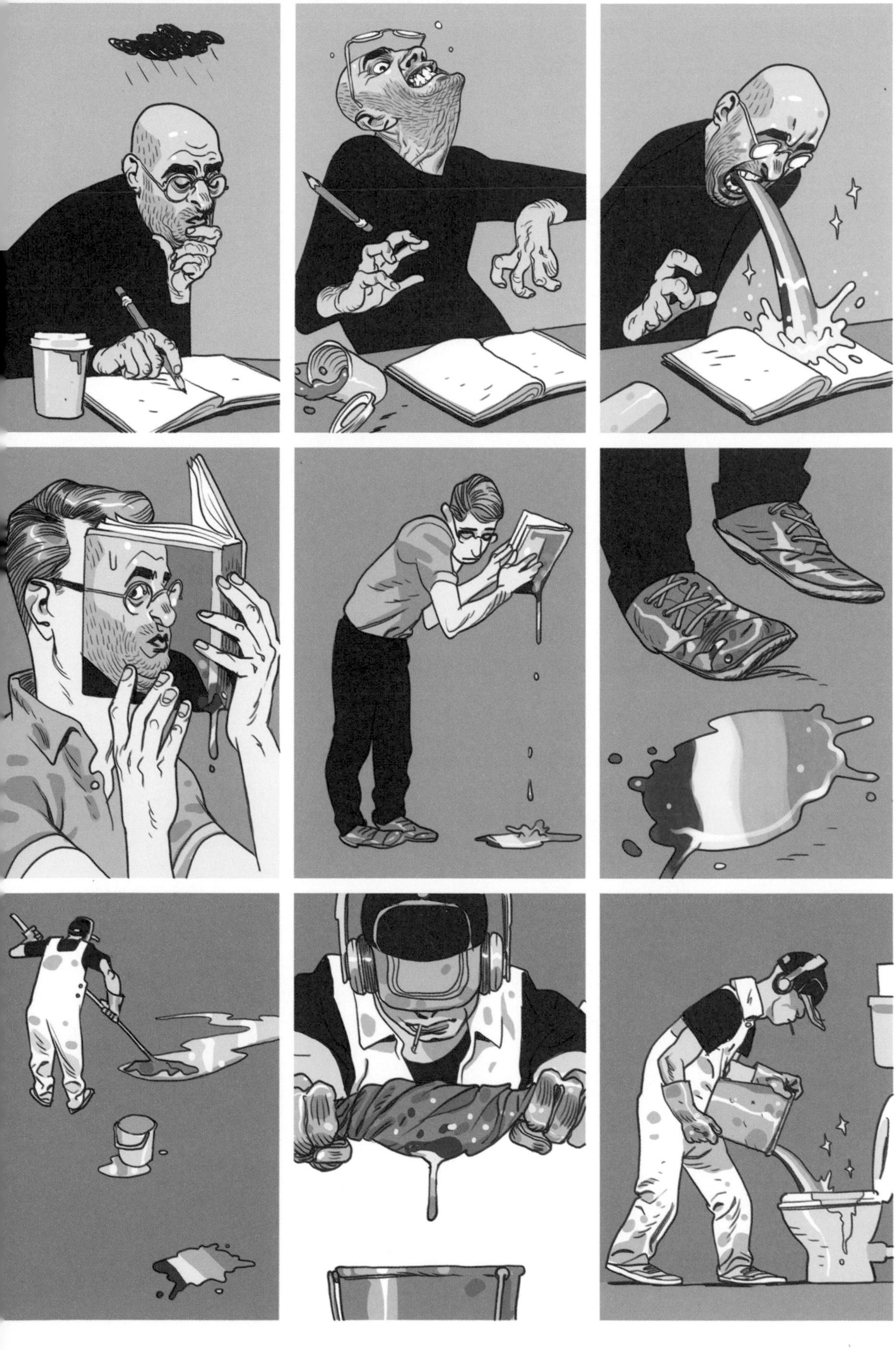

SELF EXAMINATION

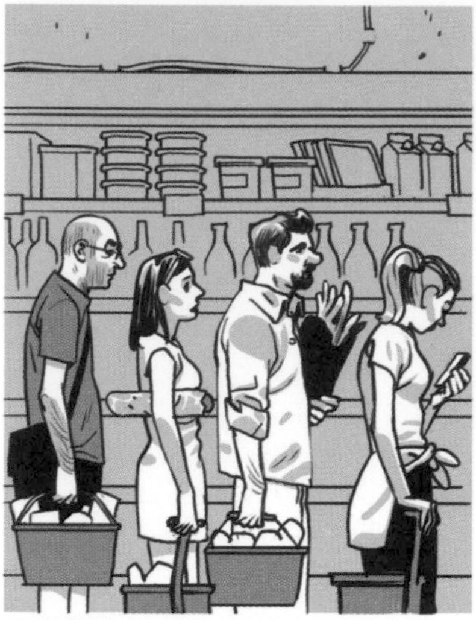

ON YOM KIPPUR EVE, I GOT STUCK IN AN ENDLESS CHECKOUT LINE AT THE SUPERMARKET.

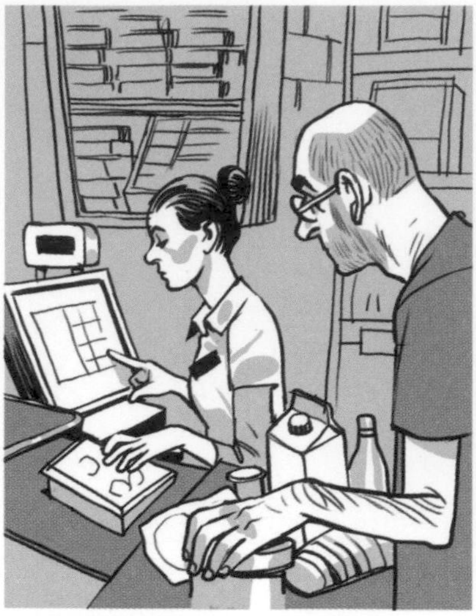

PEOPLE SHOPPED AS IF THE END OF THE WORLD HAD ARRIVED, ONLY BECAUSE THE STORE WOULD BE CLOSED THE NEXT DAY.

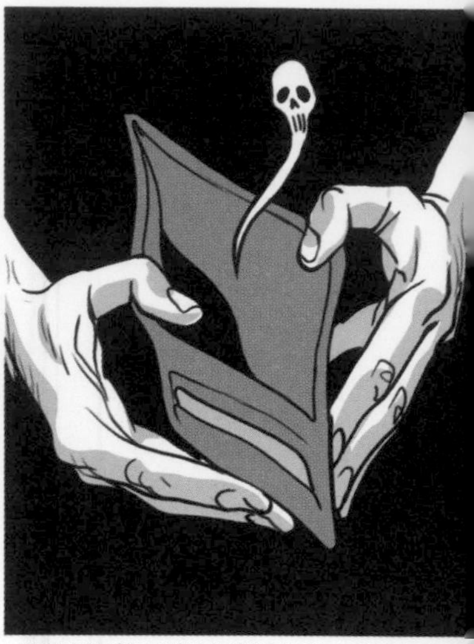

WHEN IT WAS FINALLY MY TURN, I DISCOVERE THAT MY CREDIT CARD WAS GONE. I HAD NO CASH, EITHER.

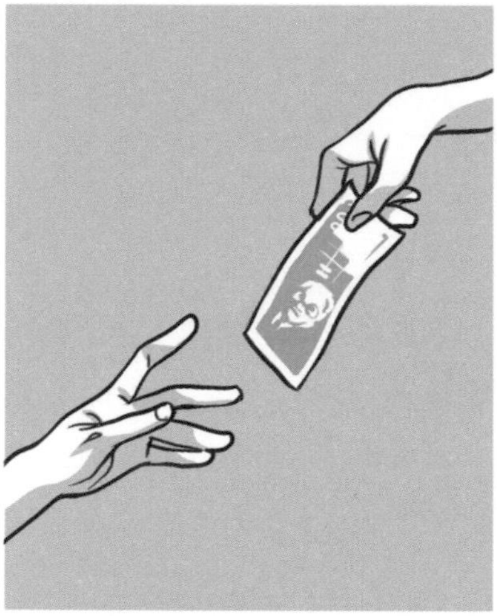

THE WOMAN BEHIND ME SAID SHE'D PAY MY BILL. I REFUSED, BUT SHE INSISTED AND I DIDN'T WANT TO GO HOME WITHOUT ANY FOOD ON YOM KIPPUR EVE.

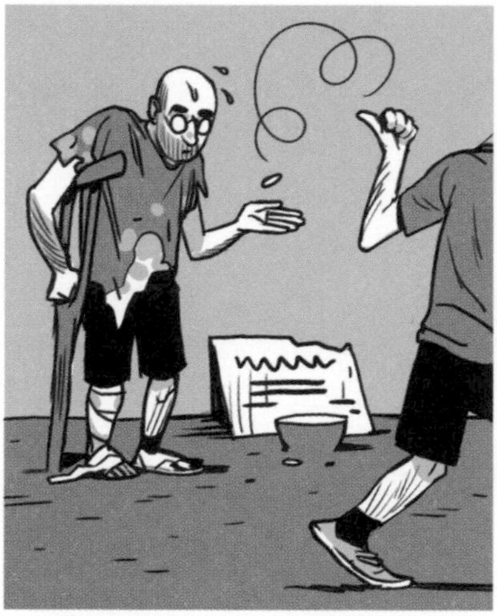

I ASKED FOR HER PHONE NUMBER SO I COULD PAY HER BACK. SHE ANSWERED POLITELY, "IT'S ONLY MONEY."

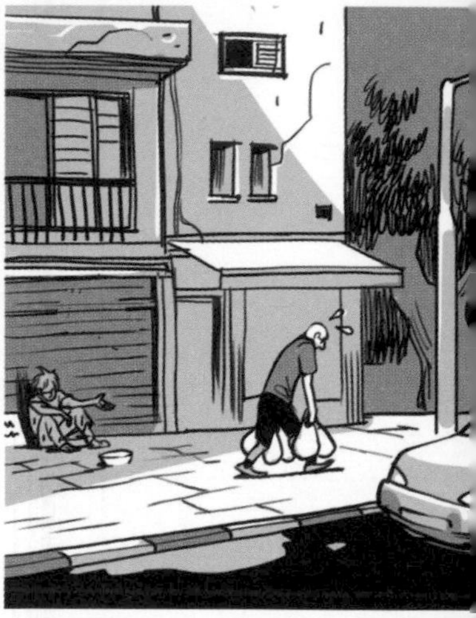

ALL THROUGH THE HOLY DAY, I WAS BOTHERE BY A QUESTION: WOULD I SETTLE SOMEONE ELSE'S GROCERY BILL? WOULD ANYONE I KNO DO THAT KIND OF THING?

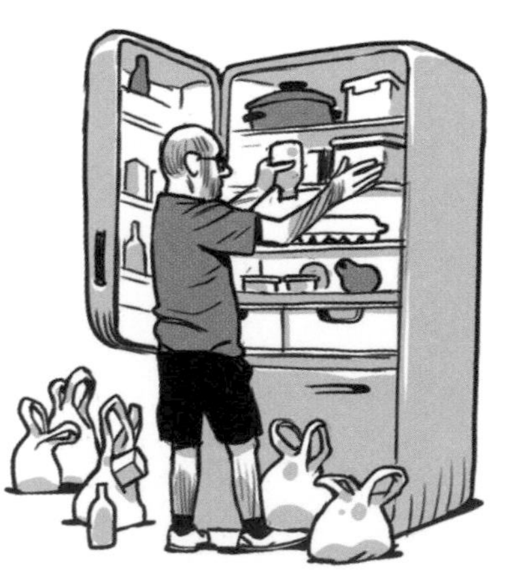

MY CONCLUSION WAS: NO. I DON'T REALLY CARE ABOUT ANYTHING BEYOND THE LIMITED CIRCLE OF FAMILY AND A VERY SMALL NUMBER OF FRIENDS.

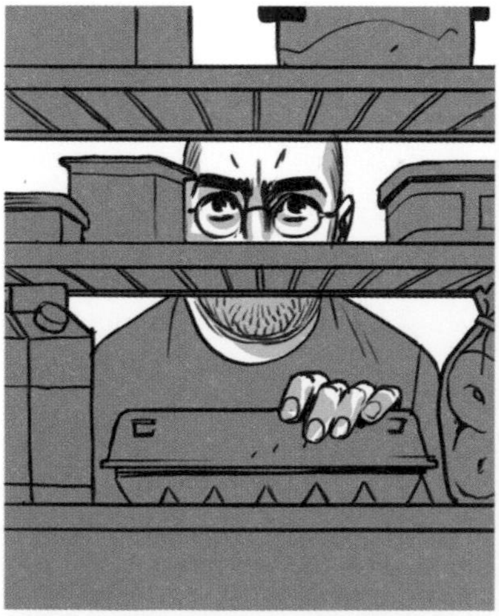

EATING, FASTING, ATONING, RIDING BICYCLES. WE ALL DO THE SAME THING SO WE CAN FEEL LIKE WE'RE TOGETHER, BUT THE TRUTH IS, WE LIVE COMPLETELY APART FROM EACH OTHER.

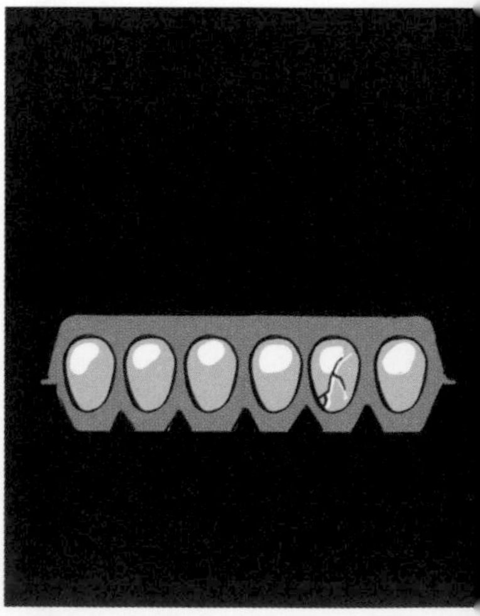

SOMETHING EXTREME NEEDS TO HAPPEN FOR US TO STEP OUT OF OUR CIRCLE: THE APOCALYPSE, A ZOMBIE ATTACK, OR AN INEXPLICABLE ACT OF KINDNESS BY A COMPLETE STRANGER.

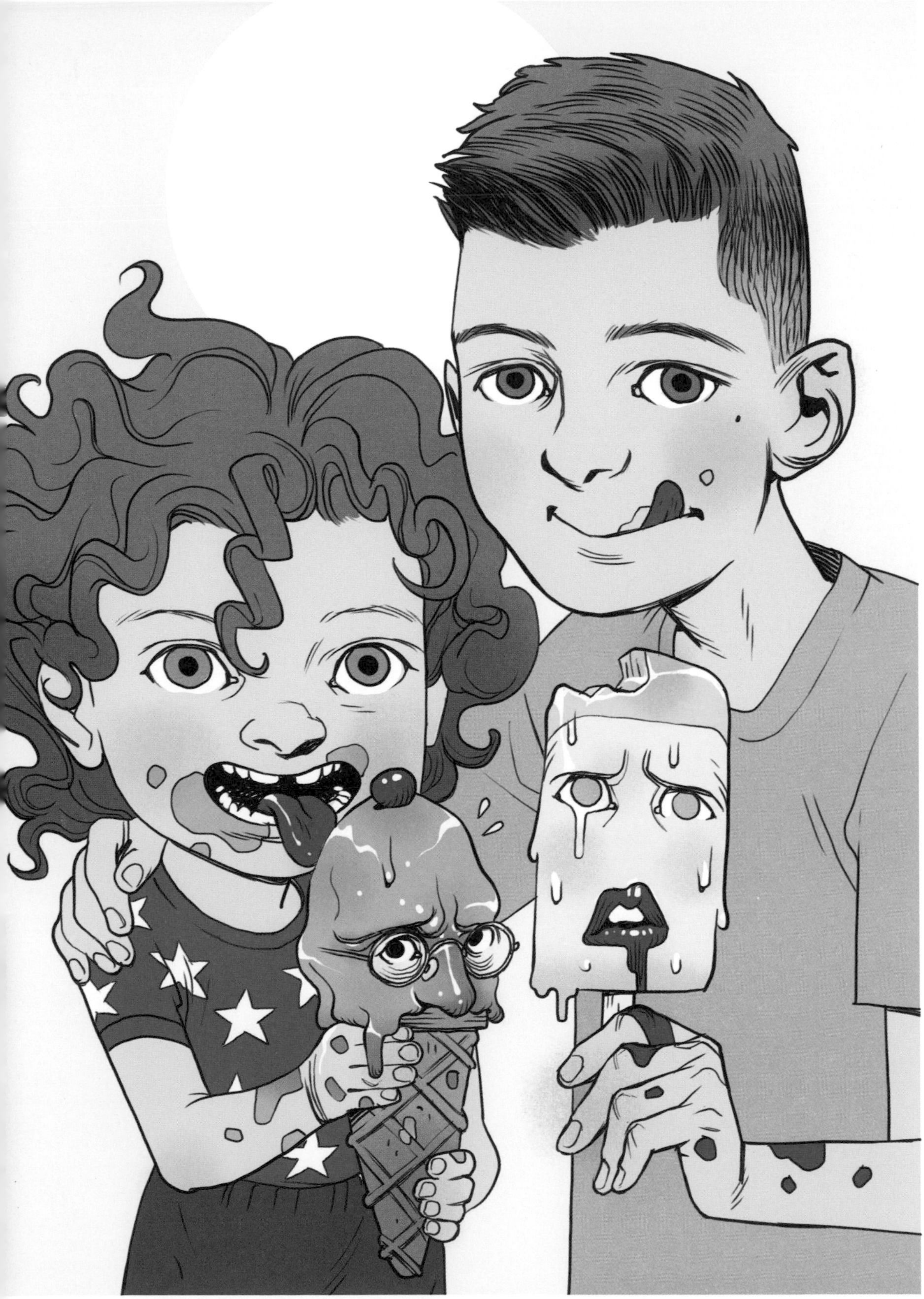

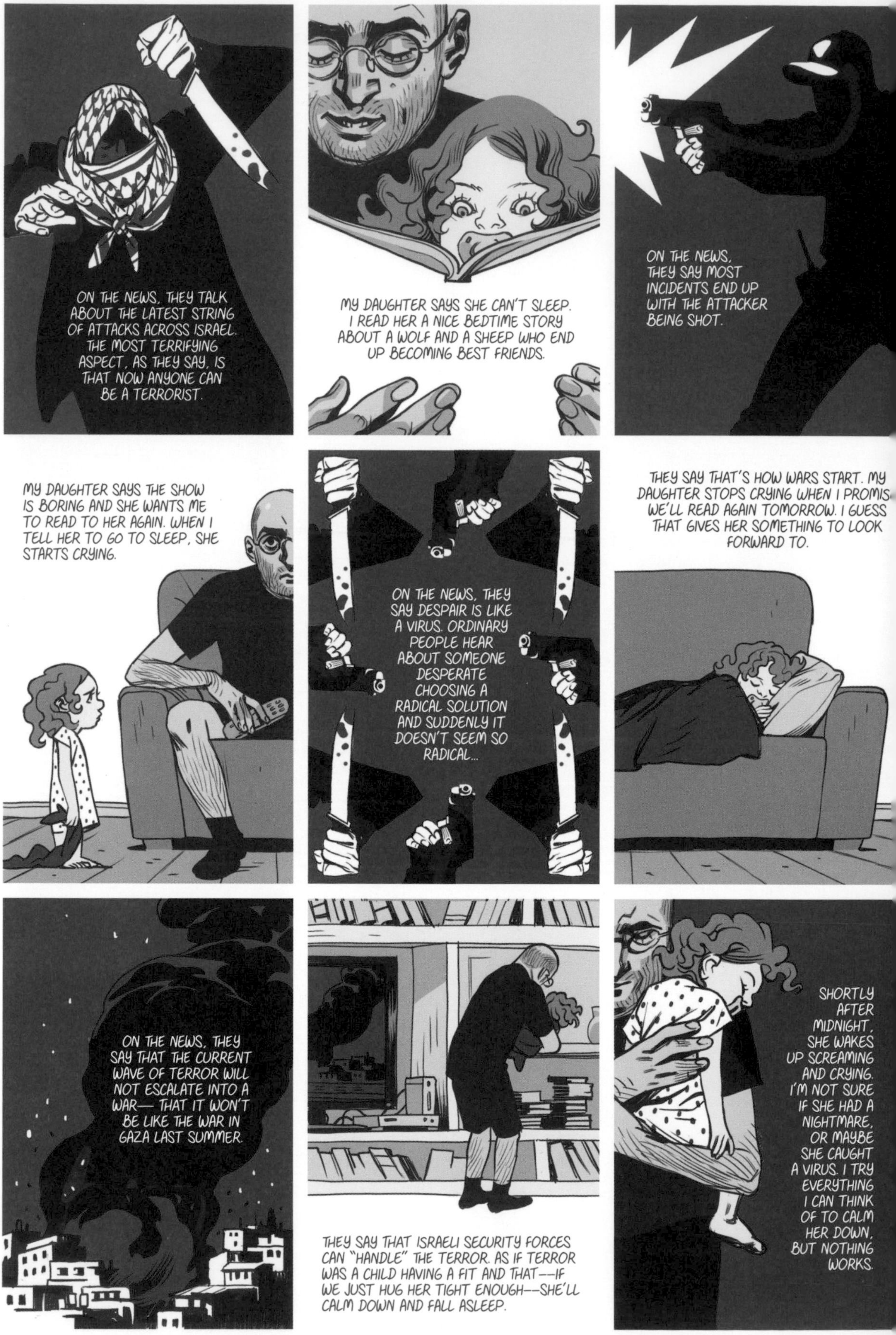
ON THE NEWS, THEY TALK ABOUT THE LATEST STRING OF ATTACKS ACROSS ISRAEL. THE MOST TERRIFYING ASPECT, AS THEY SAY, IS THAT NOW ANYONE CAN BE A TERRORIST.
MY DAUGHTER SAYS SHE CAN'T SLEEP. I READ HER A NICE BEDTIME STORY ABOUT A WOLF AND A SHEEP WHO END UP BECOMING BEST FRIENDS.
ON THE NEWS, THEY SAY MOST INCIDENTS END UP WITH THE ATTACKER BEING SHOT.
MY DAUGHTER SAYS THE SHOW IS BORING AND SHE WANTS ME TO READ TO HER AGAIN. WHEN I TELL HER TO GO TO SLEEP, SHE STARTS CRYING.
ON THE NEWS, THEY SAY DESPAIR IS LIKE A VIRUS. ORDINARY PEOPLE HEAR ABOUT SOMEONE DESPERATE CHOOSING A RADICAL SOLUTION AND SUDDENLY IT DOESN'T SEEM SO RADICAL...
THEY SAY THAT'S HOW WARS START. MY DAUGHTER STOPS CRYING WHEN I PROMIS WE'LL READ AGAIN TOMORROW. I GUESS THAT GIVES HER SOMETHING TO LOOK FORWARD TO.
ON THE NEWS, THEY SAY THAT THE CURRENT WAVE OF TERROR WILL NOT ESCALATE INTO A WAR— THAT IT WON'T BE LIKE THE WAR IN GAZA LAST SUMMER.
THEY SAY THAT ISRAELI SECURITY FORCES CAN "HANDLE" THE TERROR. AS IF TERROR WAS A CHILD HAVING A FIT AND THAT––IF WE JUST HUG HER TIGHT ENOUGH––SHE'LL CALM DOWN AND FALL ASLEEP.
SHORTLY AFTER MIDNIGHT, SHE WAKES UP SCREAMING AND CRYING. I'M NOT SURE IF SHE HAD A NIGHTMARE, OR MAYBE SHE CAUGHT A VIRUS. I TRY EVERYTHING I CAN THINK OF TO CALM HER DOWN, BUT NOTHING WORKS.

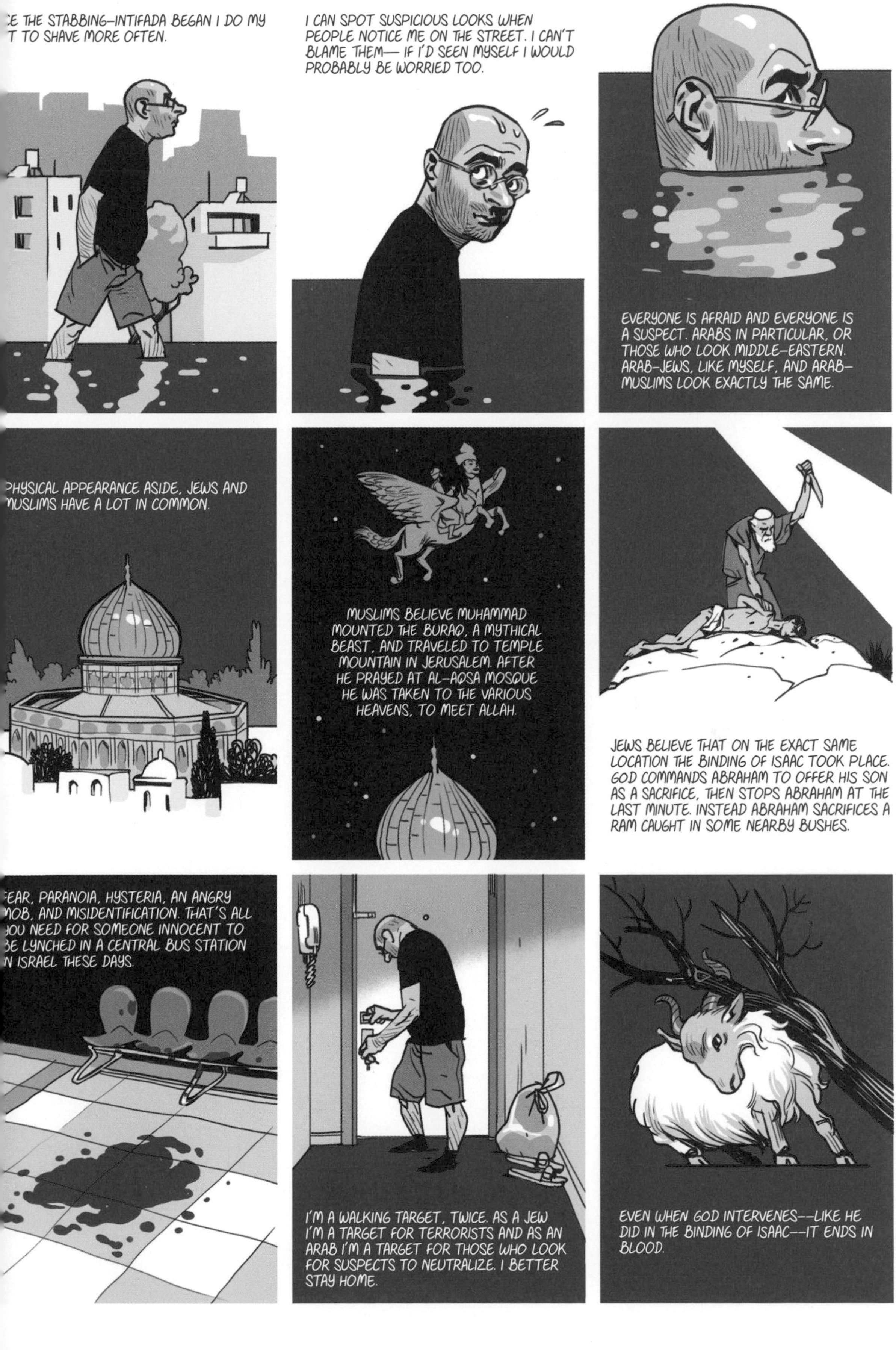
E THE STABBING–INTIFADA BEGAN I DO MY
T TO SHAVE MORE OFTEN.
I CAN SPOT SUSPICIOUS LOOKS WHEN PEOPLE NOTICE ME ON THE STREET. I CAN'T BLAME THEM— IF I'D SEEN MYSELF I WOULD PROBABLY BE WORRIED TOO.
EVERYONE IS AFRAID AND EVERYONE IS A SUSPECT. ARABS IN PARTICULAR, OR THOSE WHO LOOK MIDDLE–EASTERN. ARAB–JEWS, LIKE MYSELF, AND ARAB–MUSLIMS LOOK EXACTLY THE SAME.
PHYSICAL APPEARANCE ASIDE, JEWS AND
MUSLIMS HAVE A LOT IN COMMON.
MUSLIMS BELIEVE MUHAMMAD MOUNTED THE BURAQ, A MYTHICAL BEAST, AND TRAVELED TO TEMPLE MOUNTAIN IN JERUSALEM. AFTER HE PRAYED AT AL–AQSA MOSQUE HE WAS TAKEN TO THE VARIOUS HEAVENS, TO MEET ALLAH.
JEWS BELIEVE THAT ON THE EXACT SAME LOCATION THE BINDING OF ISAAC TOOK PLACE. GOD COMMANDS ABRAHAM TO OFFER HIS SON AS A SACRIFICE, THEN STOPS ABRAHAM AT THE LAST MINUTE. INSTEAD ABRAHAM SACRIFICES A RAM CAUGHT IN SOME NEARBY BUSHES.
FEAR, PARANOIA, HYSTERIA, AN ANGRY
MOB, AND MISIDENTIFICATION. THAT'S ALL
OU NEED FOR SOMEONE INNOCENT TO
E LYNCHED IN A CENTRAL BUS STATION
N ISRAEL THESE DAYS.
I'M A WALKING TARGET, TWICE. AS A JEW I'M A TARGET FOR TERRORISTS AND AS AN ARAB I'M A TARGET FOR THOSE WHO LOOK FOR SUSPECTS TO NEUTRALIZE. I BETTER STAY HOME.
EVEN WHEN GOD INTERVENES––LIKE HE DID IN THE BINDING OF ISAAC––IT ENDS IN BLOOD.

SMILE

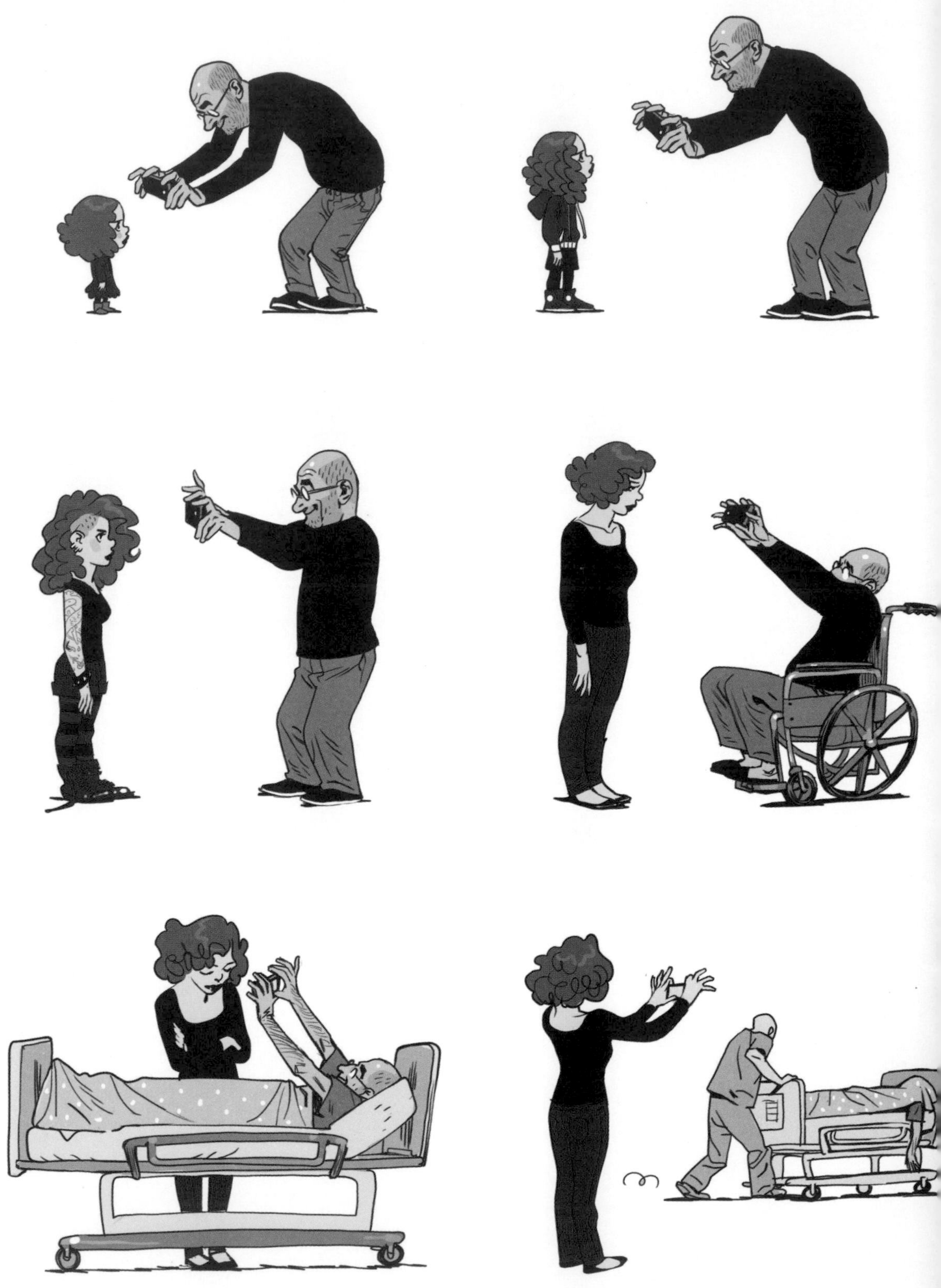

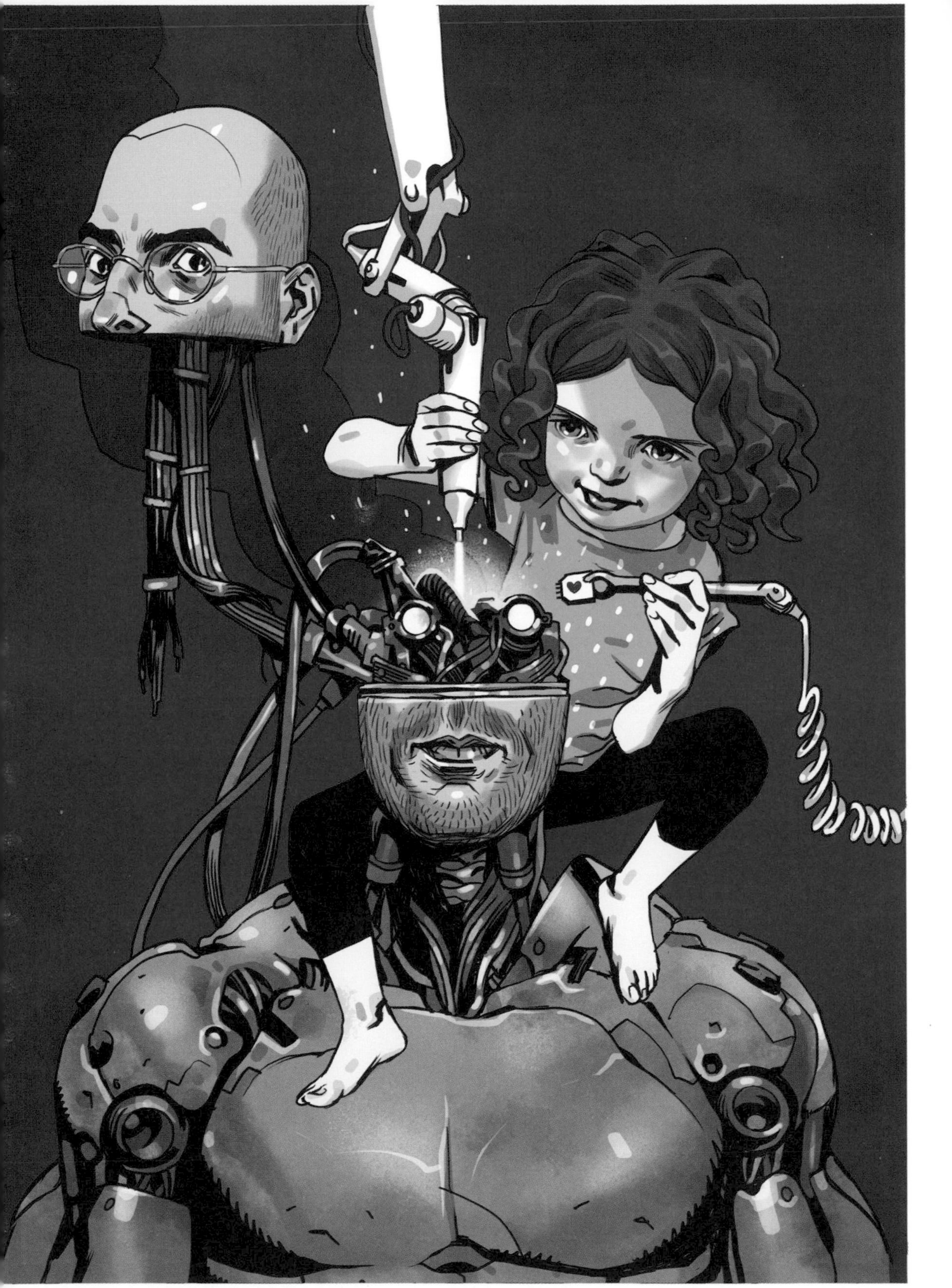

SOULS

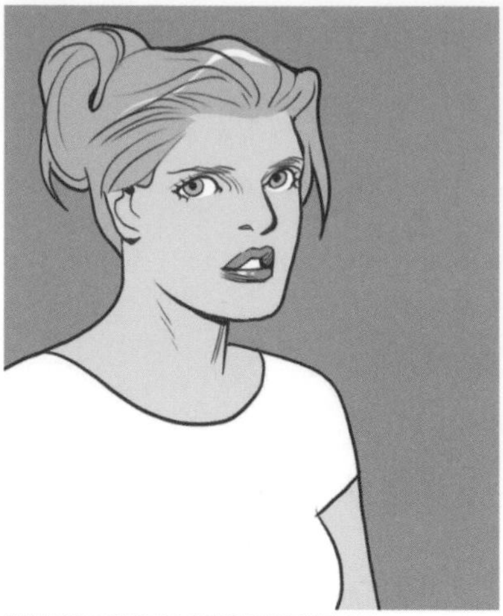

MY WIFE BELIEVES IN REINCARNATION.

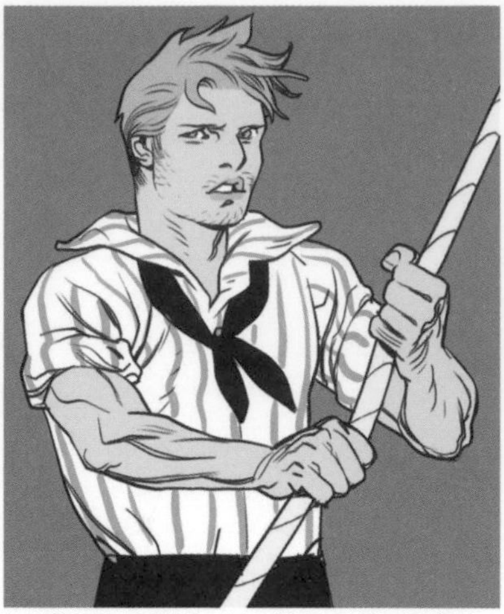

SHE BELIEVES THAT IN A PAST LIFE SHE WAS A SAILOR WHO DROWNED DURING THE BATTLE OF TRAFALGAR, IN WHICH THE BRITISH NAVY BEAT NAPOLEON AND HIS ALLIES.

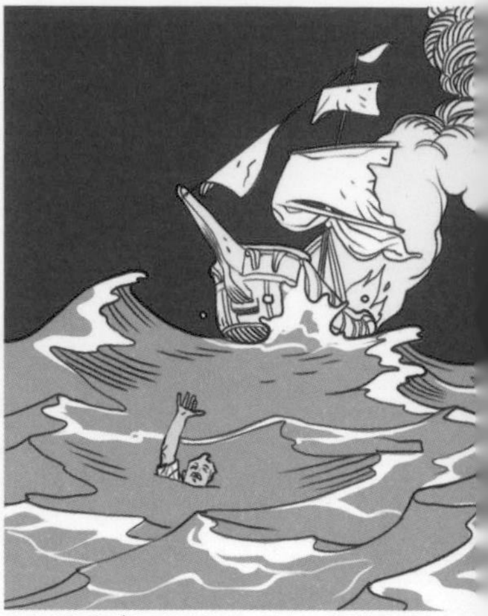

SHE DOESN'T LIKE FISH. IT ALL STARTED THERE. HIS POOR SOUL REINCARNATED ALL TH WAY TO HER.

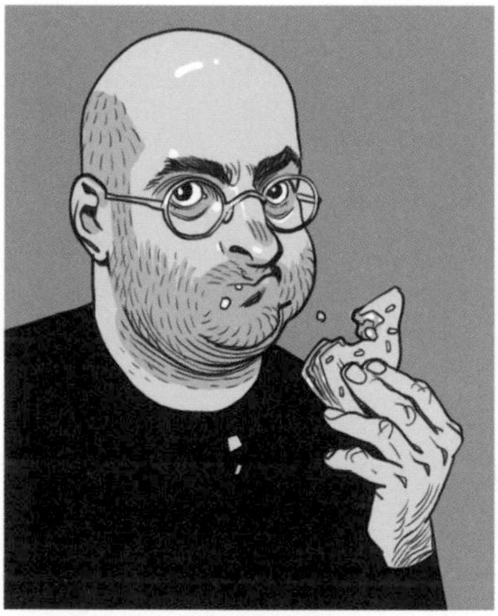

I DON'T BELIEVE IN REINCARNATION. I DON'T REALLY BELIEVE IN ANYTHING.

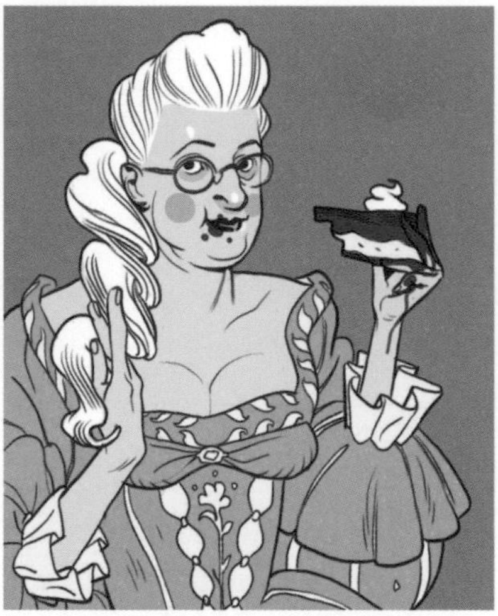

BUT JUST FOR THE SAKE OF ARGUMENT, IF I HAD TO, I'D SAY I WAS A REINCARNATION OF MARIE ANTOINETTE, QUEEN OF FRANCE, WHO WAS EXECUTED BY GUILLOTINE.

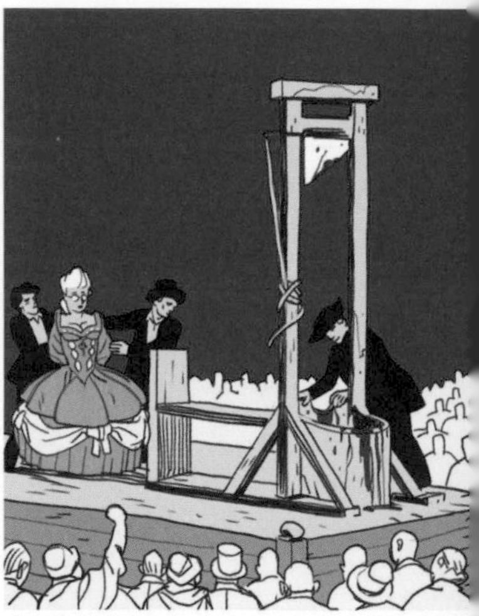

BUT I CAN'T BUY INTO THE IDEA. PEOPLE ARE JUST ANIMALS WHO LEARNED HOW TO TALK, SOULS ARE A RELIGIOUS IDEA MEANT TO HEL DEAL WITH THE CONCEPT OF DEATH.

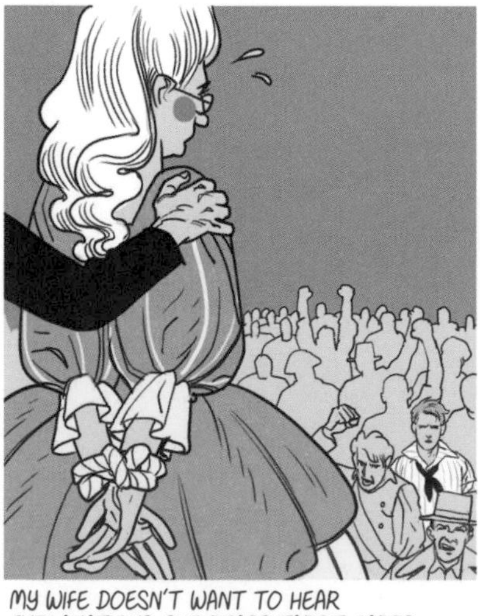

MY WIFE DOESN'T WANT TO HEAR EXPLANATIONS. SHE READS TAROT CARDS AND INTERPRETS COINCIDENCES. I'M A SERIAL DOUBTER, A COMPULSIVE HERETIC.

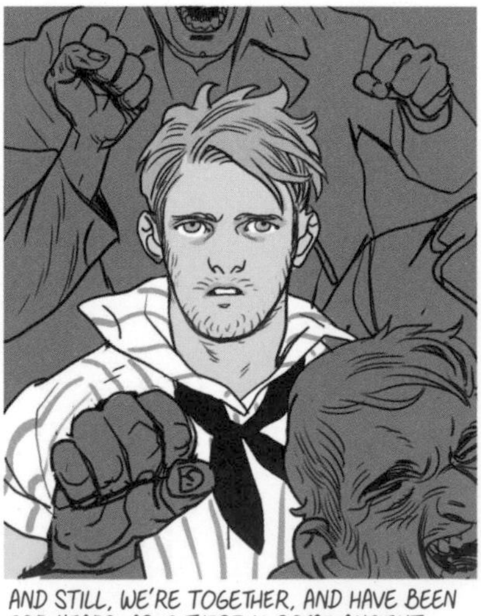

AND STILL, WE'RE TOGETHER, AND HAVE BEEN FOR YEARS, AS IF THERE IS SOME ANCIENT CONNECTION BETWEEN US. MAYBE WE'RE SOULMATES. MAYBE WE MET IN A PAST LIFE.

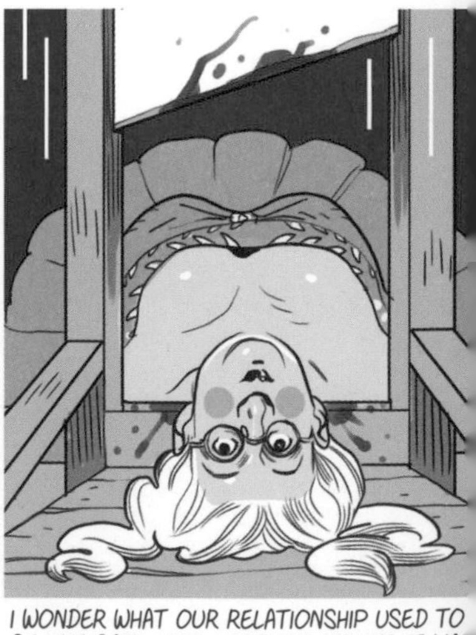

I WONDER WHAT OUR RELATIONSHIP USED TO BE LIKE BACK THEN. I GET THE FEELING IT WA PRETTY MUCH THE SAME.

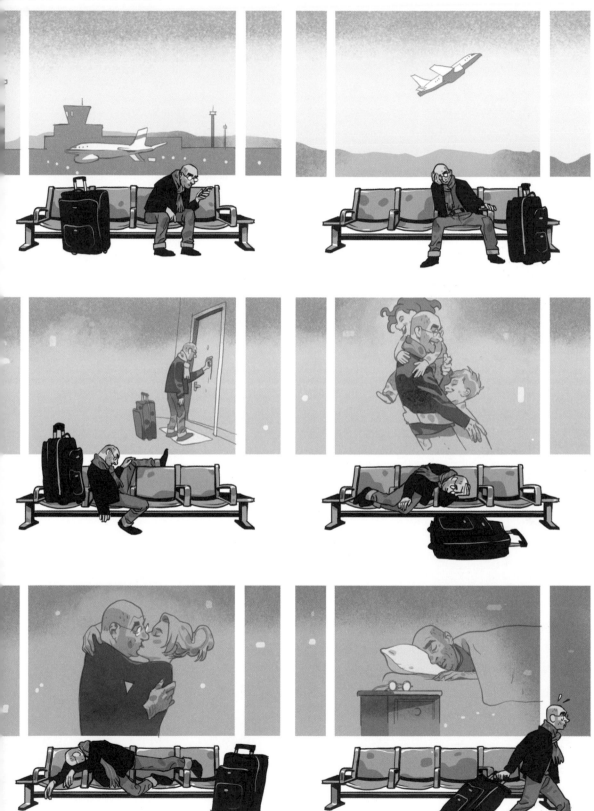

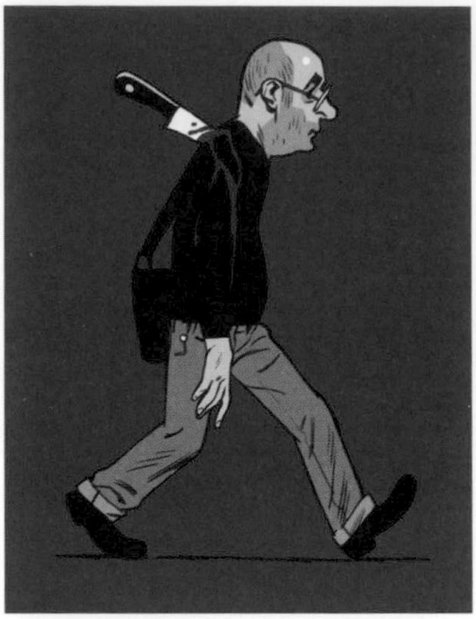

I'M THE WALKING DEAD.
THIS CONFLICT IS KILLING ME.

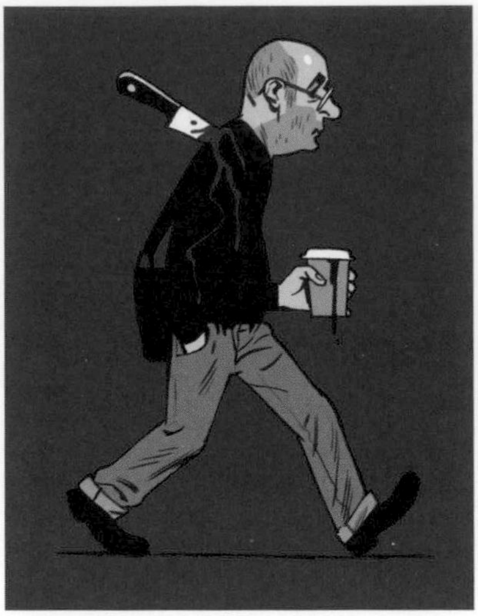

DON'T WORRY ABOUT ME. I CAN GO ON LIKE THIS FOR YEARS. PEOPLE HAVE GOTTEN USED TO MUCH WORSE.

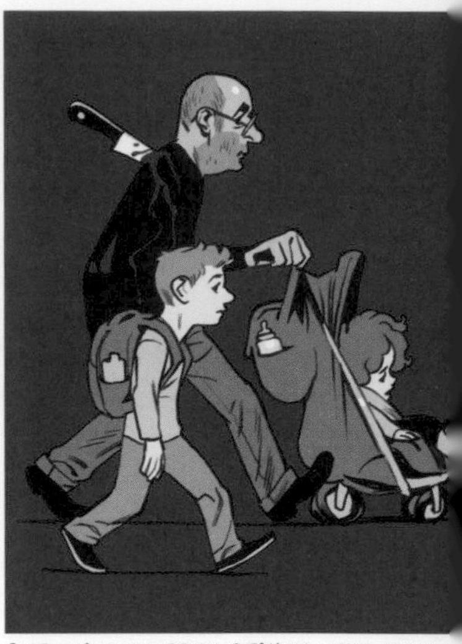

BUT I HAVE CHILDREN. STAYING HERE, NOW, FEELS LIKE PASSIVELY ACCEPTING A REALITY THAT MIGHT PUT THEM IN DANGER.

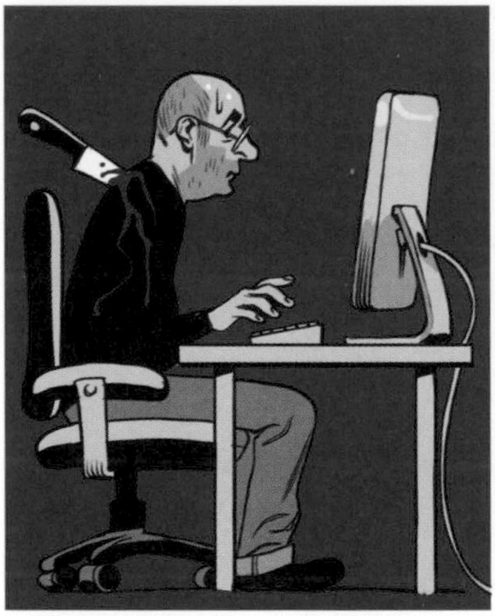

THE OBVIOUS SOLUTION IS TO MOVE TO A COUNTRY WITH NO TERROR, OR AT LEAST WITH NO TERRITORIAL CONFLICT ENHANCED BY RELIGIOUS BELIEFS.

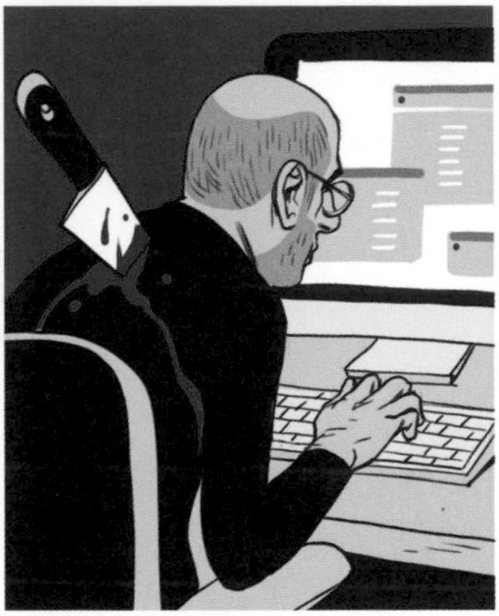

I TOOK THE FIRST STEP TO A NEW LIFE: I WROTE A RELATIVE IN LOS ANGELES, ASKING HIM ABOUT COST OF LIVING AND PUBLIC SCHOOLS.

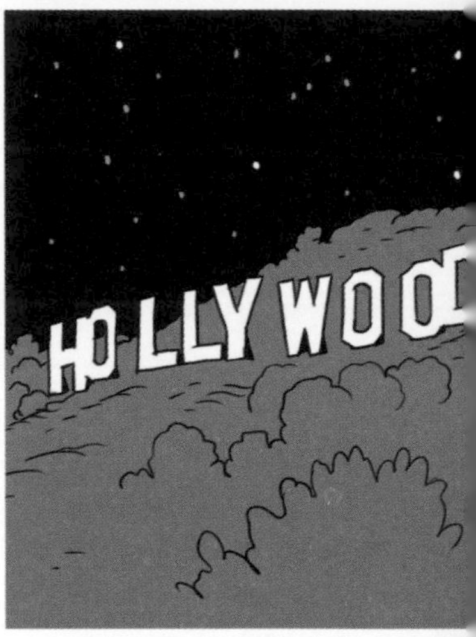
HOLLYWOO

HE GOT BACK TO ME WITH DATA. ISRAELIS C
IT "DESCENDING" FROM ISRAEL, BUT IN FACT
AN ASCENT IN ALL AREAS OF LIFE.

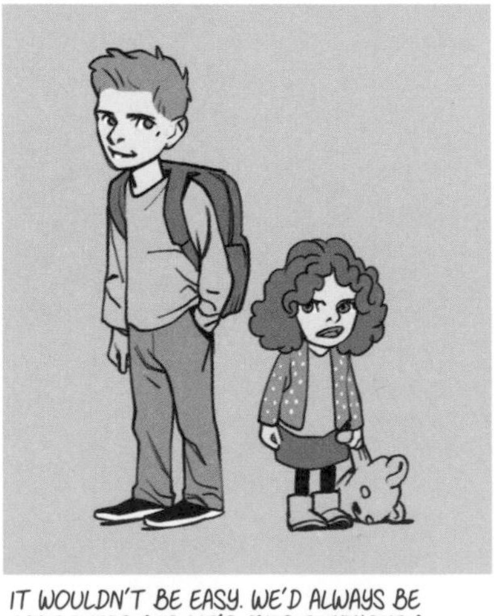

IT WOULDN'T BE EASY. WE'D ALWAYS BE FOREIGNERS AND WE'D MISS EVERYONE A LOT. WE WOULD TELL THEM THIS WAS JUST A TEMPORARY MOVE.

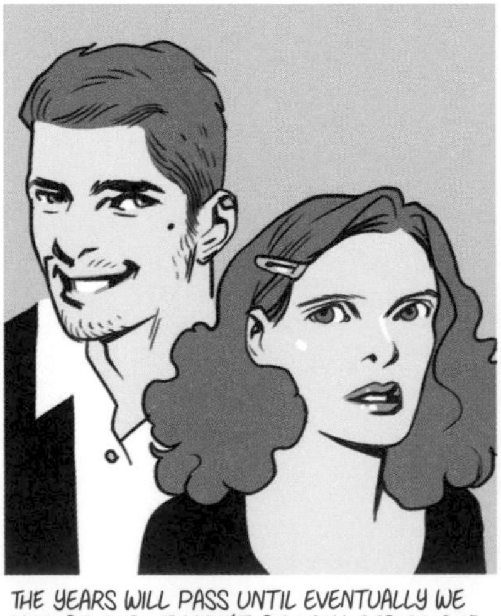

THE YEARS WILL PASS UNTIL EVENTUALLY WE WILL BE OLD. IT WON'T BE LONG BEFORE OUR CHILDREN HAVE THEIR OWN CHILDREN. THEY WON'T HAVE A FUNNY ACCENT.

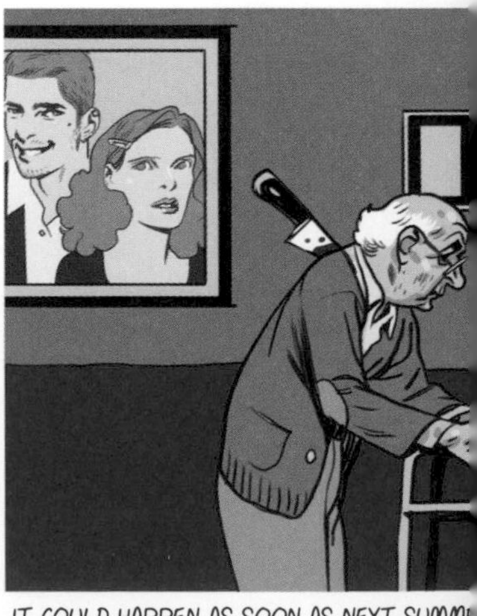

IT COULD HAPPEN AS SOON AS NEXT SUMM
WE JUST NEED TO PACK UP OUR HOME INTO
A CONTAINER AND BAM, WE'D BE IN AMERICA
IT'S THE RIGHT THING TO DO, FOR OUR
CHILDREN.

VEMBER 13TH

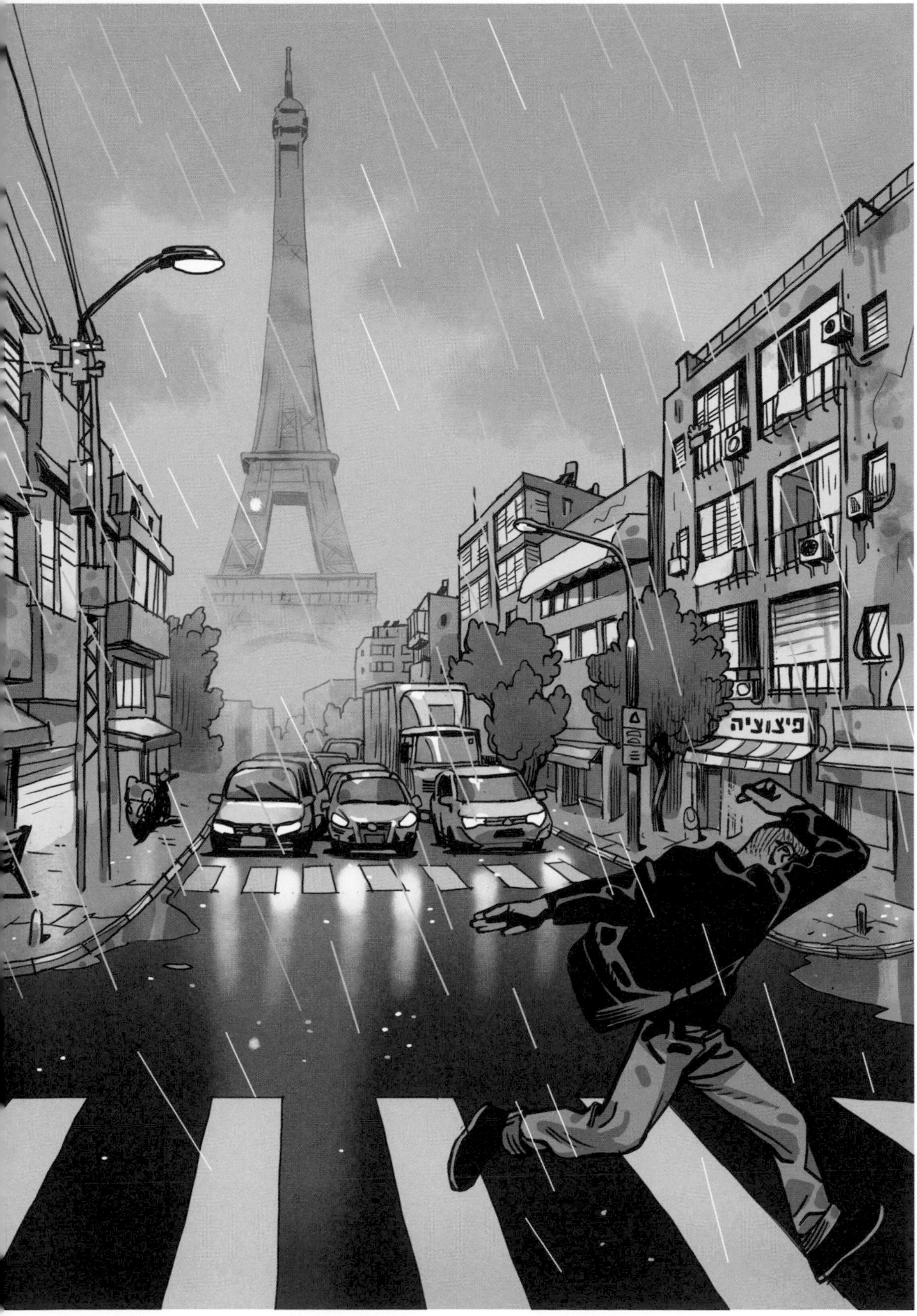
פיצוציה

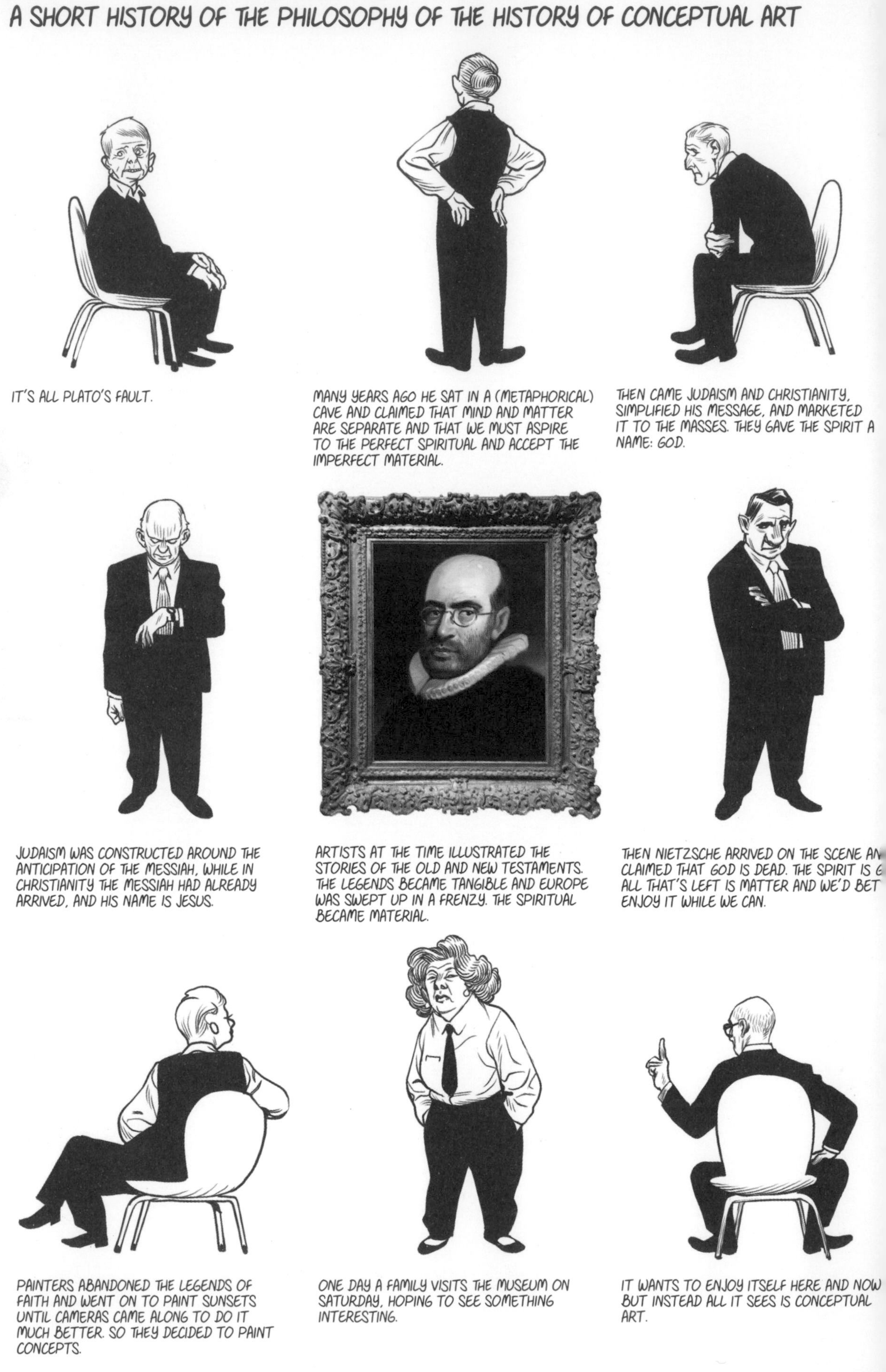
A SHORT HISTORY OF THE PHILOSOPHY OF THE HISTORY OF CONCEPTUAL ART
IT'S ALL PLATO'S FAULT.
MANY YEARS AGO HE SAT IN A (METAPHORICAL) CAVE AND CLAIMED THAT MIND AND MATTER ARE SEPARATE AND THAT WE MUST ASPIRE TO THE PERFECT SPIRITUAL AND ACCEPT THE IMPERFECT MATERIAL.
THEN CAME JUDAISM AND CHRISTIANITY, SIMPLIFIED HIS MESSAGE, AND MARKETED IT TO THE MASSES. THEY GAVE THE SPIRIT A NAME: GOD.
JUDAISM WAS CONSTRUCTED AROUND THE ANTICIPATION OF THE MESSIAH, WHILE IN CHRISTIANITY THE MESSIAH HAD ALREADY ARRIVED, AND HIS NAME IS JESUS.
ARTISTS AT THE TIME ILLUSTRATED THE STORIES OF THE OLD AND NEW TESTAMENTS. THE LEGENDS BECAME TANGIBLE AND EUROPE WAS SWEPT UP IN A FRENZY. THE SPIRITUAL BECAME MATERIAL.
THEN NIETZSCHE ARRIVED ON THE SCENE AN CLAIMED THAT GOD IS DEAD. THE SPIRIT IS G ALL THAT'S LEFT IS MATTER AND WE'D BET ENJOY IT WHILE WE CAN.
PAINTERS ABANDONED THE LEGENDS OF FAITH AND WENT ON TO PAINT SUNSETS UNTIL CAMERAS CAME ALONG TO DO IT MUCH BETTER. SO THEY DECIDED TO PAINT CONCEPTS.
ONE DAY A FAMILY VISITS THE MUSEUM ON SATURDAY, HOPING TO SEE SOMETHING INTERESTING.
IT WANTS TO ENJOY ITSELF HERE AND NOW BUT INSTEAD ALL IT SEES IS CONCEPTUAL ART.

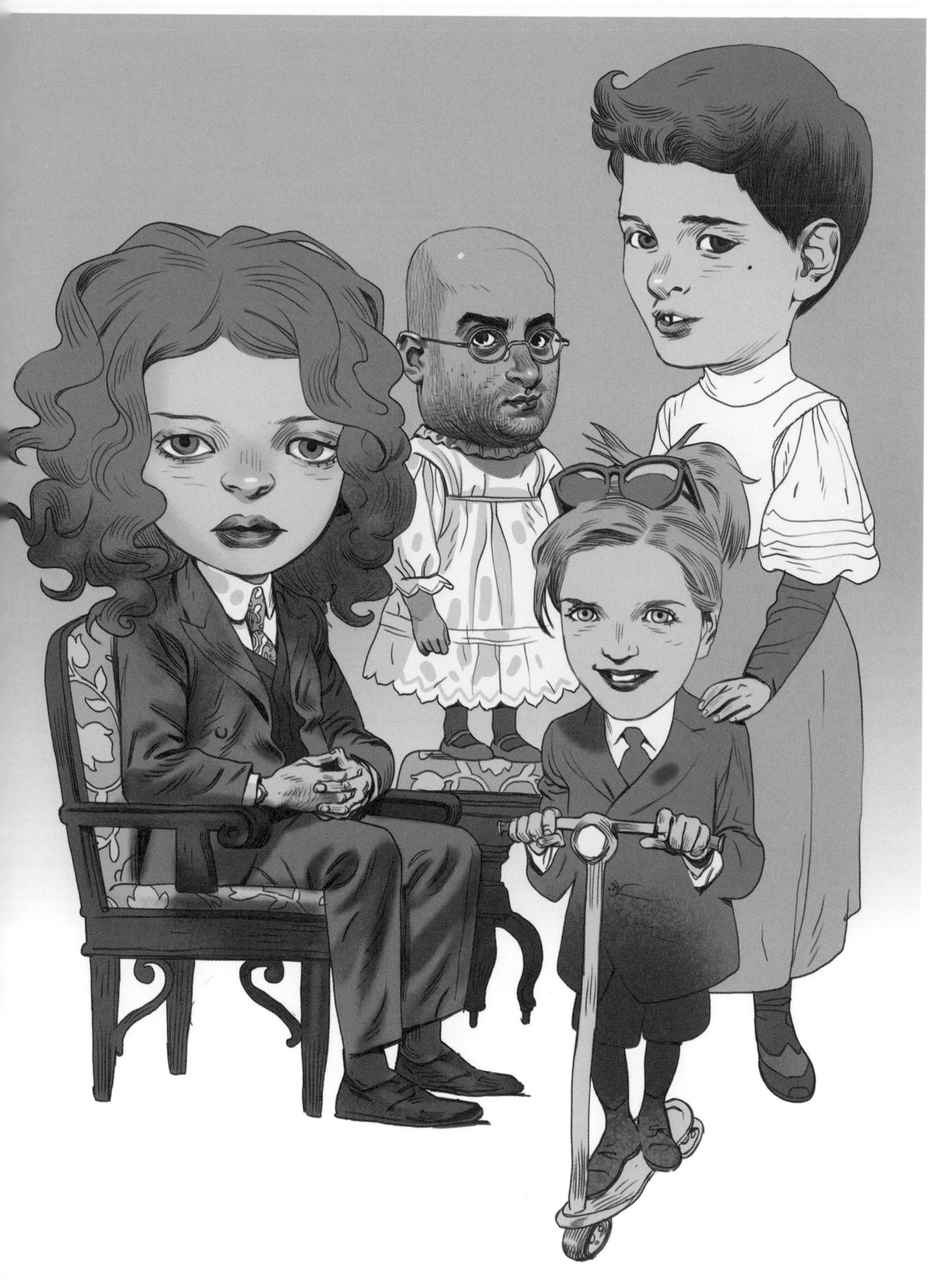

WHO?

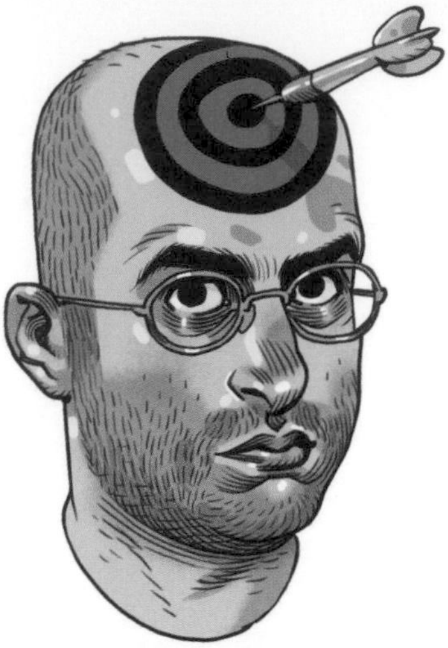

I'M THE RADICAL LEFT WING, I'M THE EXTREME RIGHT WING, I'M THE FINANCIAL CENTRALIST, I'M THE SOCIAL ECONOMIST.

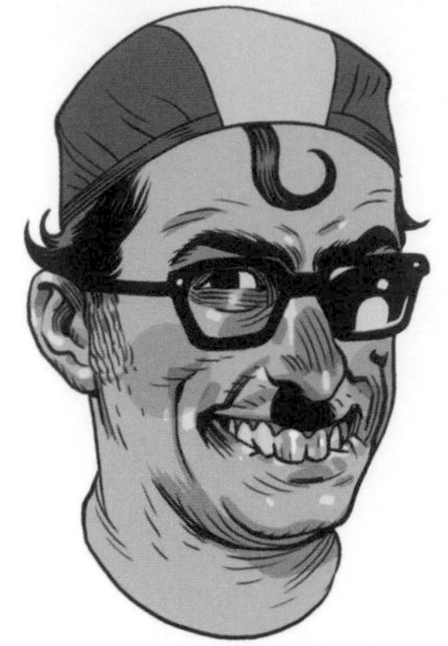

I'M THE USEFUL IDIOT, THE PRESENTABLE MIZRAHI, I'M THE ISRAELI 'OTHER', I'M AN EDUCATIONAL TRACKING SURVIVOR.

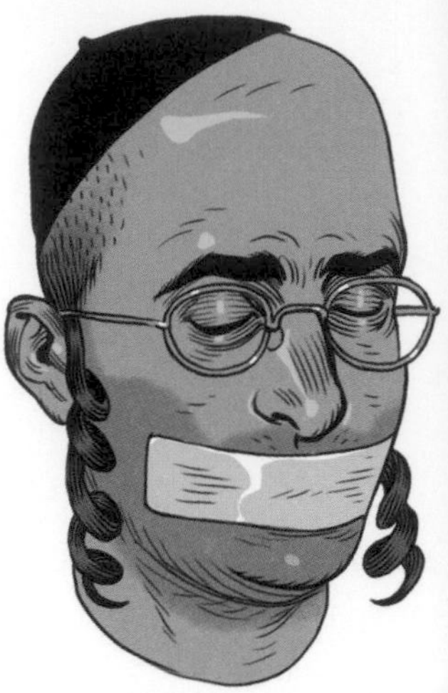

I'M THE SILENCED MINORITY, THE TRADITIONA INFERIORITY, THE RECYCLED WHINER, THE BITTER COMIC BOOK WRITER.

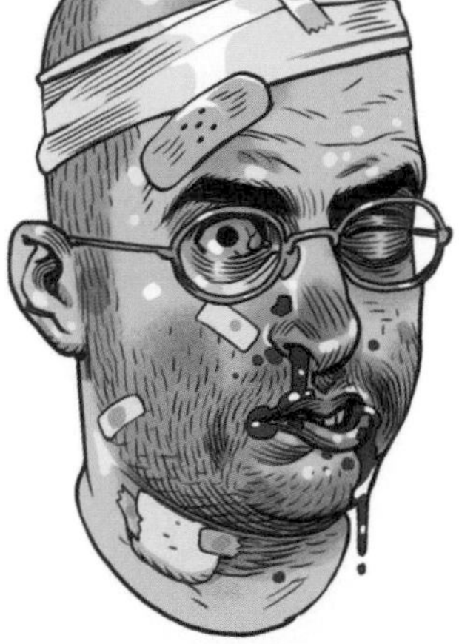

I'M A JEW UNDER PERSECUTION, AN ISRAELI SUFFERING EXHAUSTION. I'M THE NEW MAN, HOPELESS AND WITHOUT A PLAN.

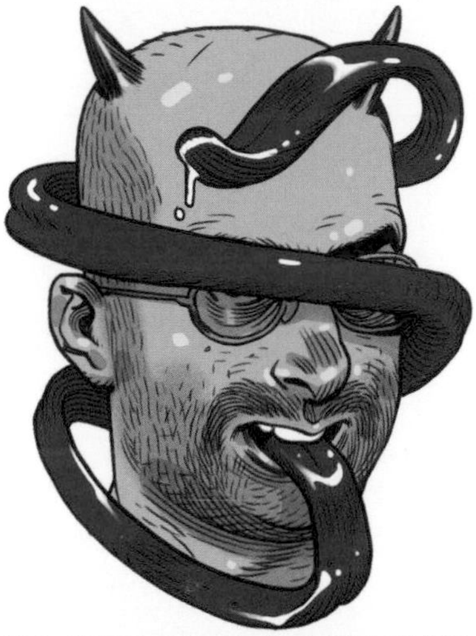

I'M A HARASSER FOR LIFE, BUT ONLY TOWARD MY WIFE. I'M AN ARDENT FATHER, I'M AN ABSENT FATHER.

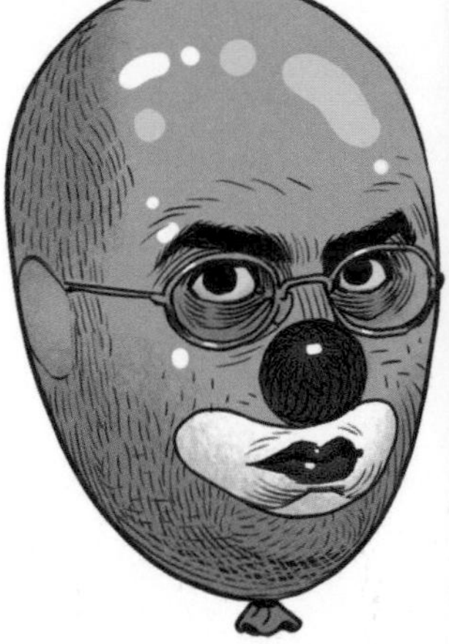

MY CHILDREN ARE CHARMING, YOURS ARE BC WE GO TO THE PARK, YOU GO TO A PROTES MAKE YOUR MARK.

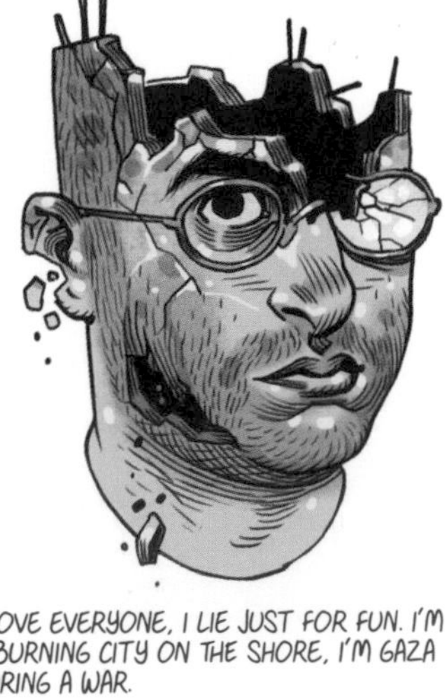

I LOVE EVERYONE, I LIE JUST FOR FUN. I'M A BURNING CITY ON THE SHORE, I'M GAZA DURING A WAR.

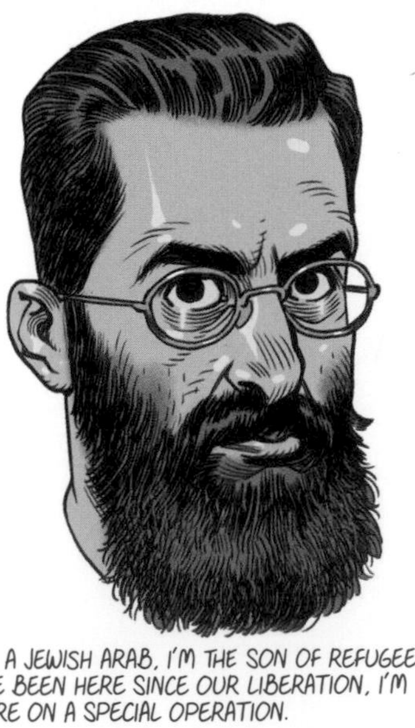

I'M A JEWISH ARAB, I'M THE SON OF REFUGEES. I'VE BEEN HERE SINCE OUR LIBERATION, I'M HERE ON A SPECIAL OPERATION.

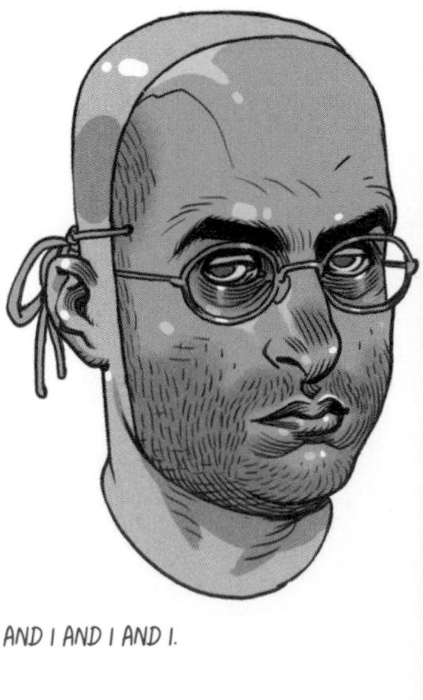

I AND I AND I AND I.

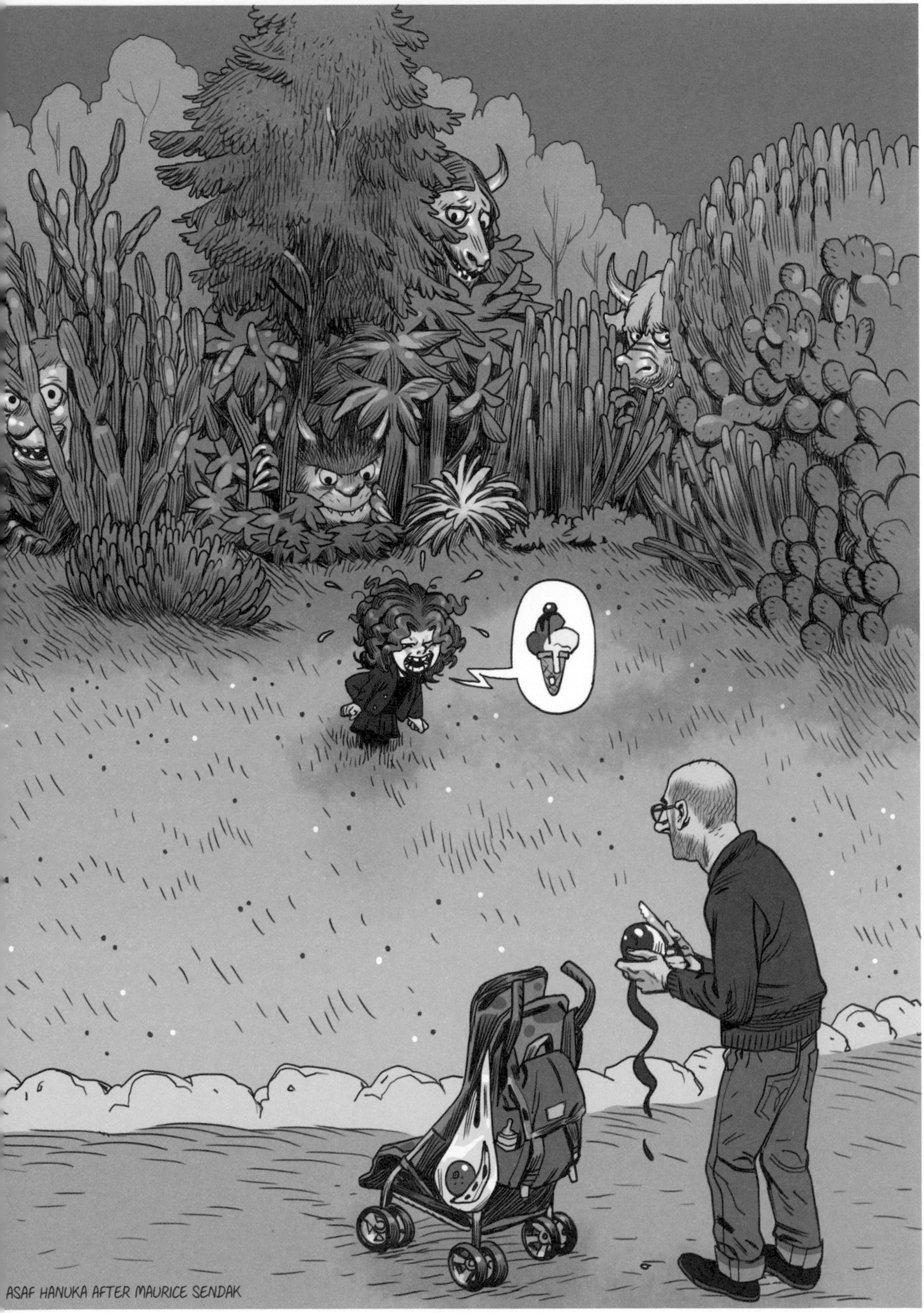
ASAF HANUKA AFTER MAURICE SENDAK

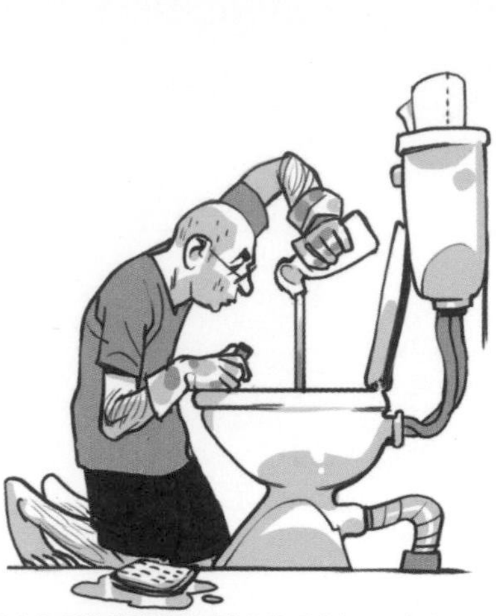

ON FRIDAY MORNING, RATHER THAN GO HAVE COFFEE AT OUR USUAL SPOT, MY WIFE AND I ROLLED UP OUR SLEEVES, DONNED RUBBER GLOVES, AND CLEANED THE HOUSE.

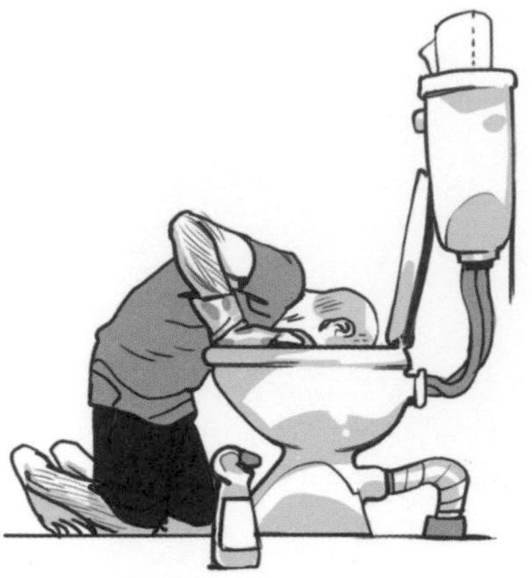

WE DID A DEEP CLEAN, USING SPECIAL SUBSTANCES. IT WAS HARD AND TIRING, BUT WE DIDN'T HAVE A CHOICE, BECAUSE WE'D HAD TO SAY GOODBYE TO OUR CLEANING WOMAN.

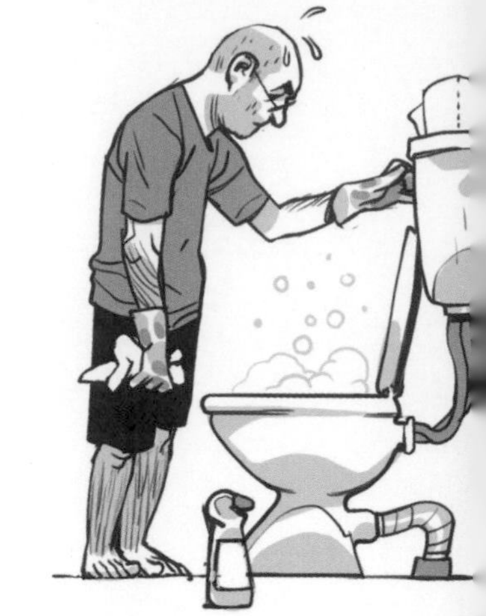

JUSTIFYING HIRING A CLEANING PERSON IS EAS IT'S CONVENIENT TO HAVE SOMEBODY ELSE TIDY AND CLEAN UP INSTEAD OF YOU.

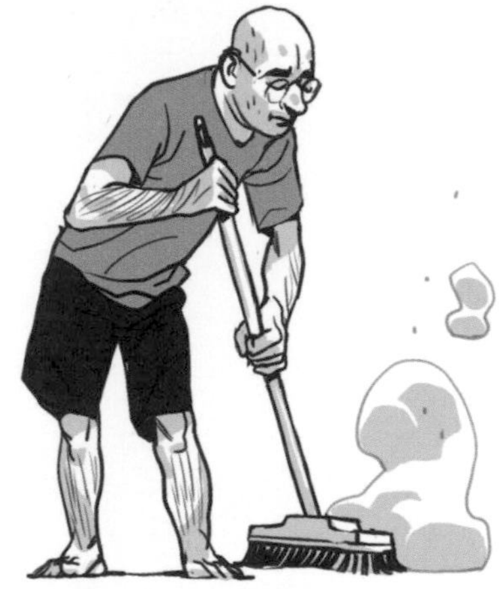

BUT I'VE ALWAYS FELT UNCOMFORTABLE WITH CLEANING WOMEN BECAUSE IT'S THE REMNANT OF ANOTHER, MORE OUTDATED PROFESSION: SERVANT.

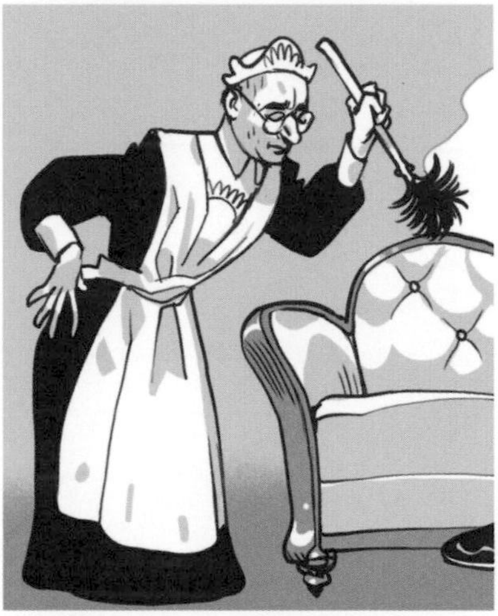

A CLEANING WOMAN SYMBOLIZES AN ENTIRE CLASS OF PEOPLE. THEY DON'T HAVE TO BE RICH, THEY JUST HAVE TO COME FROM A HIGHER CLASS THAN HER.

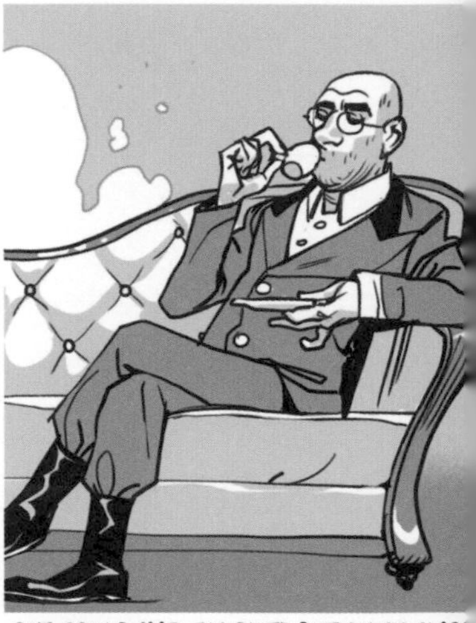

ONE COULD MAP THE DISTRIBUTION OF CLASS IN SOCIETY ACCORDING TO WHO CLEANS WHC HOUSE.

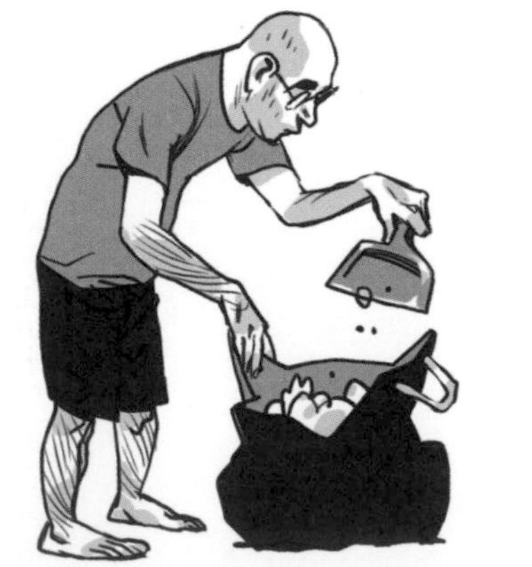

THE ONLY REASON WE FIRED OUR CLEANING WOMAN WAS TO TRY AND SAVE UP A FEW HUNDRED SHEKELS A MONTH AFTER A LONG SUMMER AND A CHALLENGING HOLIDAY SEASON.

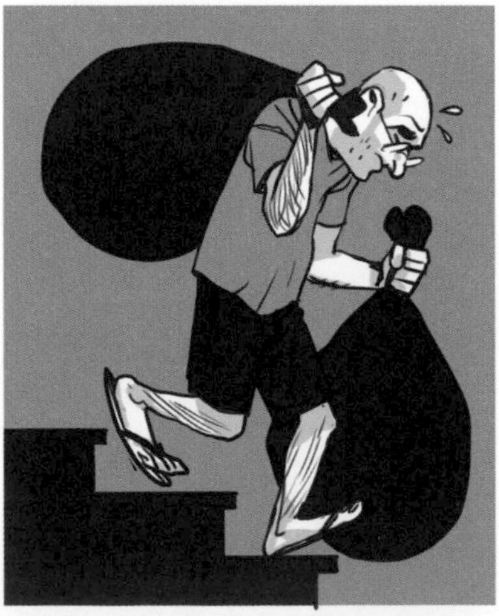

THIS MIGHT BE PART OF A PHASE IN WHICH WE GRADUALLY SAY GOODBYE TO OUR OLD CLASS AND ACCEPT OUR NEW ONE: THE CLASS OF PEOPLE WHO CHOOSE TO CLEAN THEIR OWN HOME.

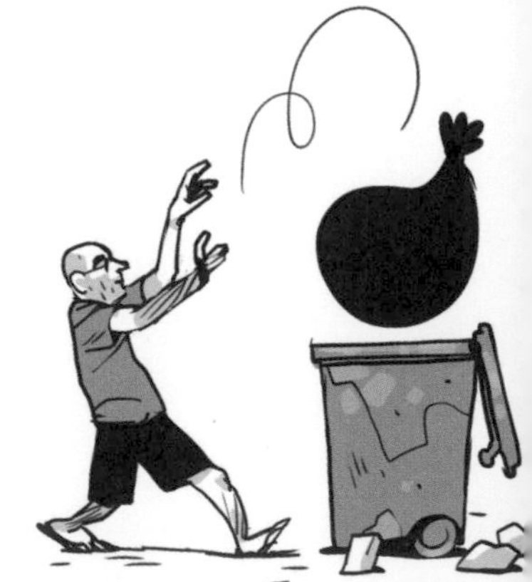

SCRUBBING IS A MEDITATIVE ACT THAT LEADS TO INTROSPECTION. PHYSICAL LABOR THAT SETS YOU FREE. THIS ARGUMENT SOUNDS MUCH MORE COMPELLING AFTER INHALING SOME BLEACH FUMES.

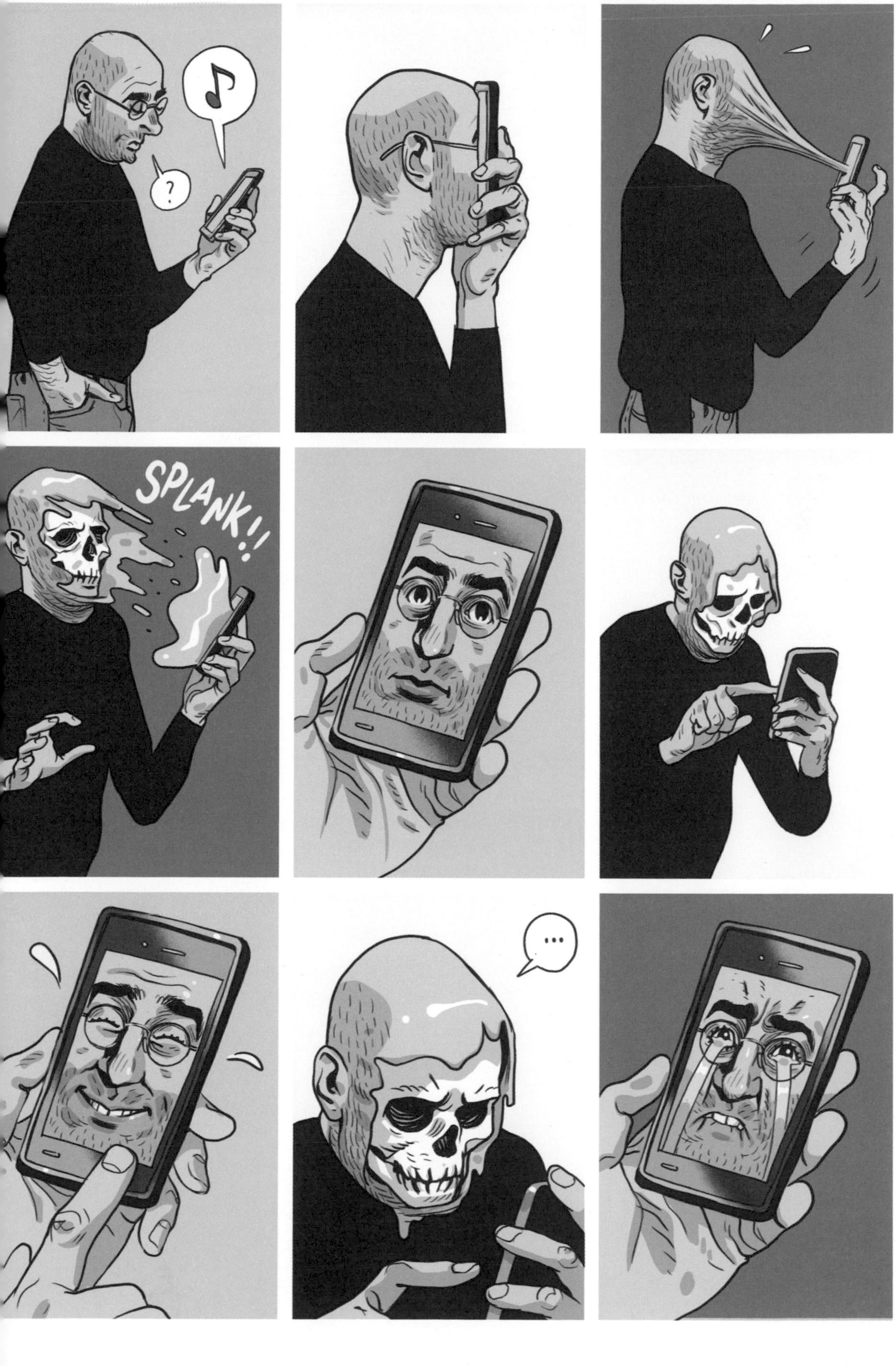
♪
?
SPLANK!!
...

A BEDTIME STORY

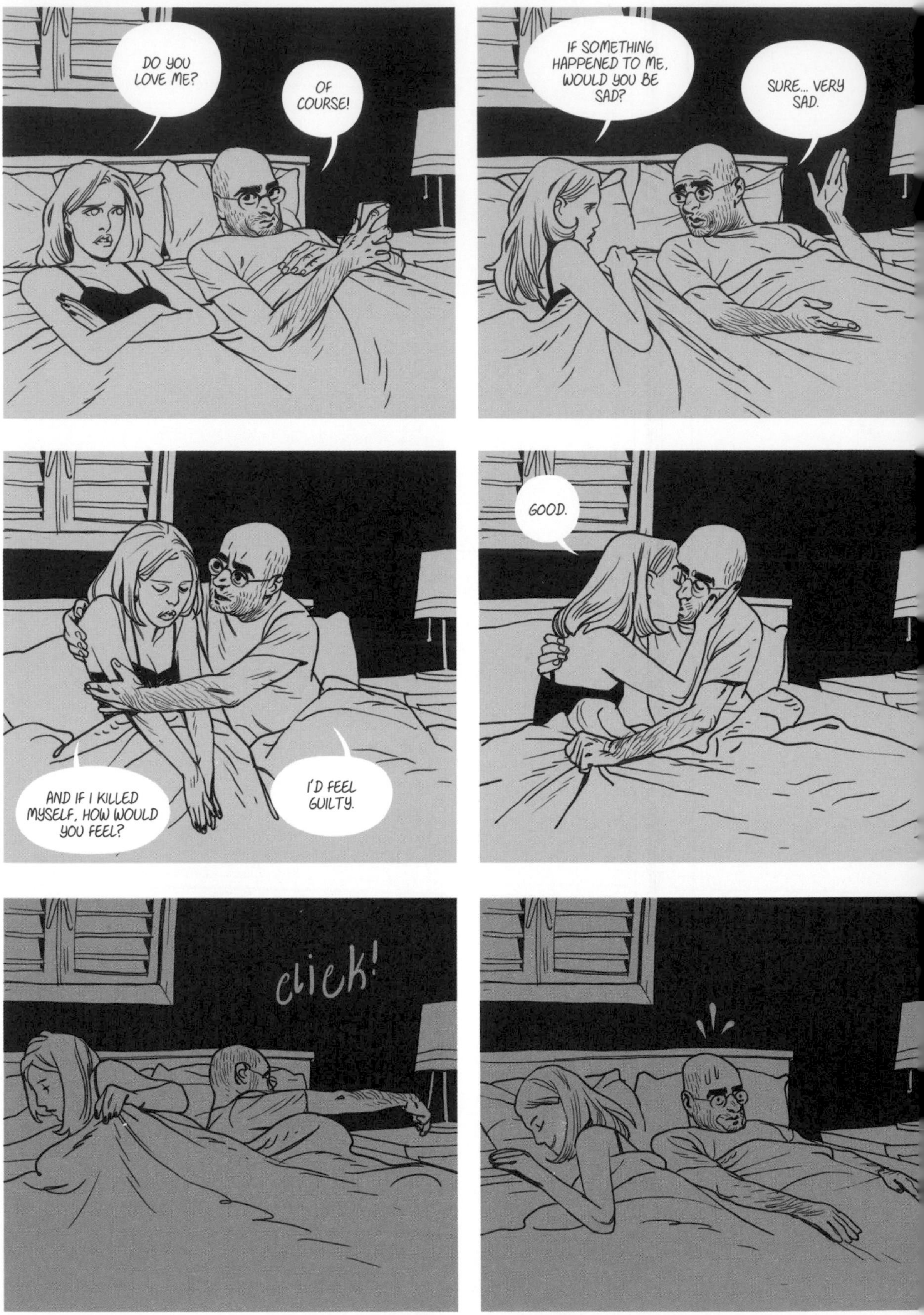
DO YOU LOVE ME?
OF COURSE!
IF SOMETHING HAPPENED TO ME, WOULD YOU BE SAD?
SURE... VERY SAD.
AND IF I KILLED MYSELF, HOW WOULD YOU FEEL?
I'D FEEL GUILTY.
GOOD.
click!

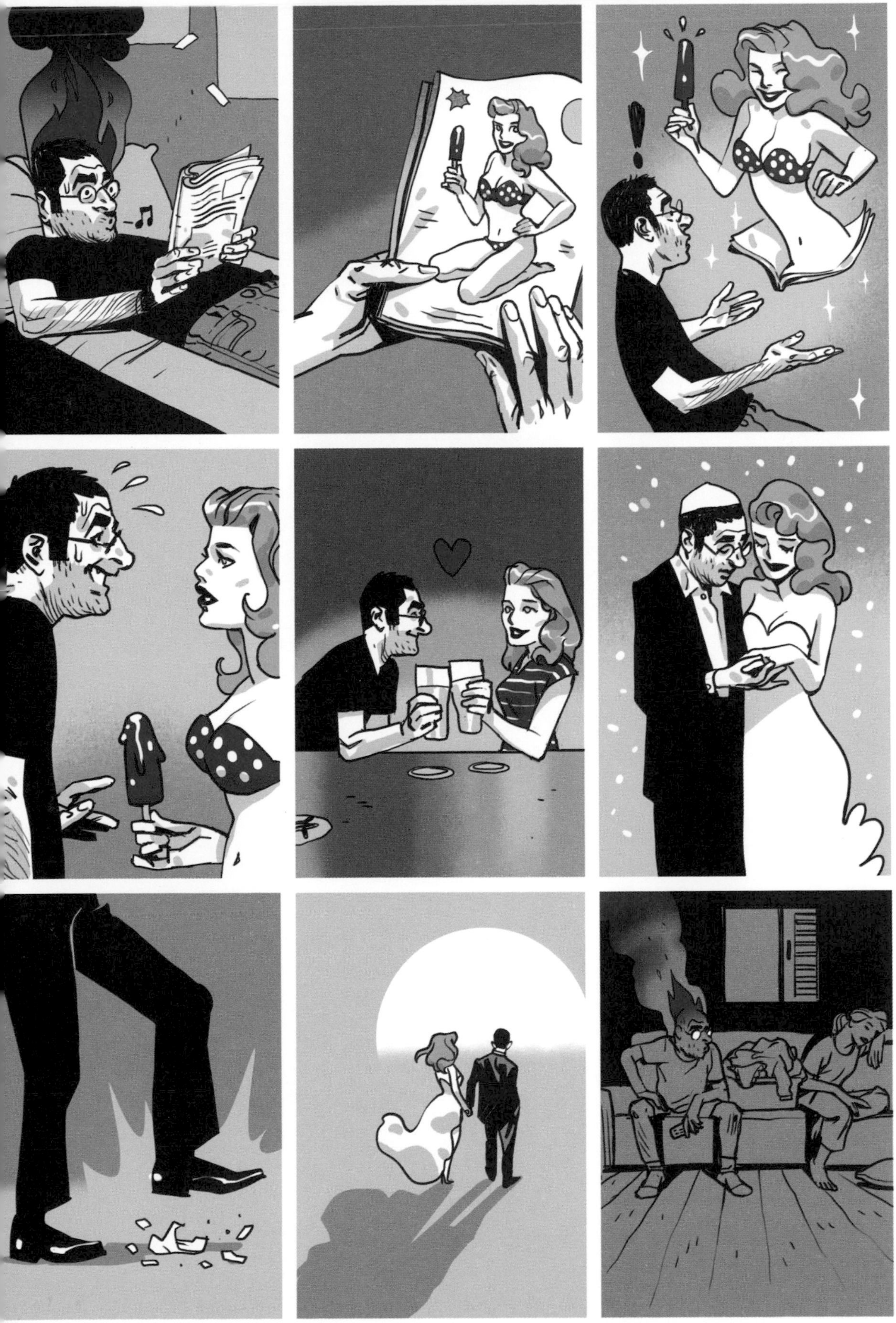

BOWING

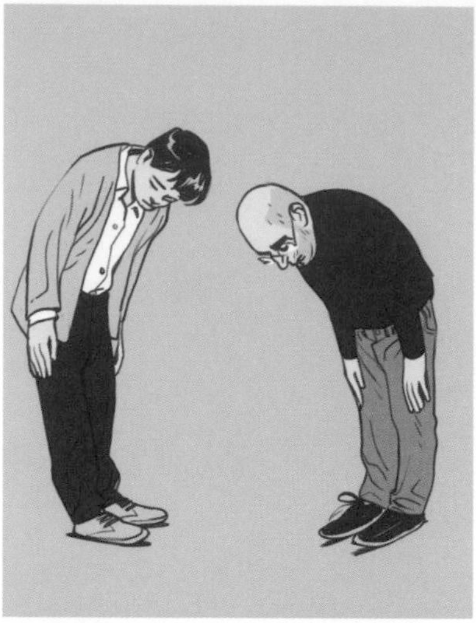

THE FIRST THING I LEARNED IN TOKYO IS THAT WHEN MEETING ANOTHER PERSON, A BOW IS CUSTOMARY IN PLACE OF A HANDSHAKE.

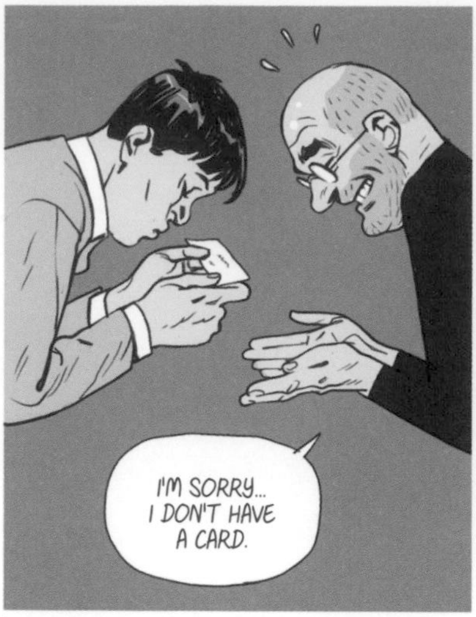
I'M SORRY...
I DON'T HAVE
A CARD.

AFTER BOWING, THERE IS THE CEREMONY OF EXCHANGING BUSINESS CARDS.

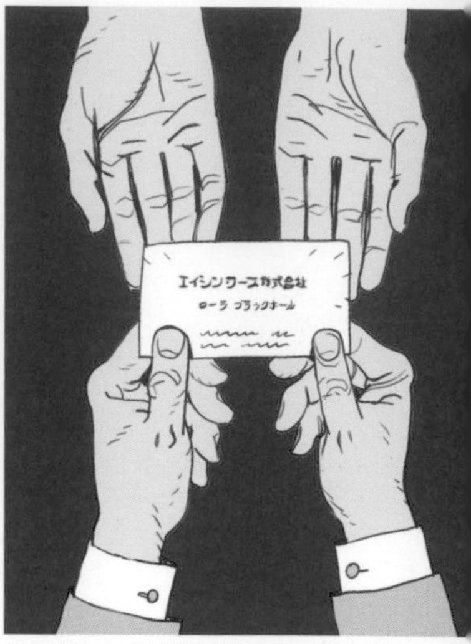

THE CARD IS ALWAYS OFFERED WITH TWO HANDS AND ACCEPTED WITH TWO HANDS.

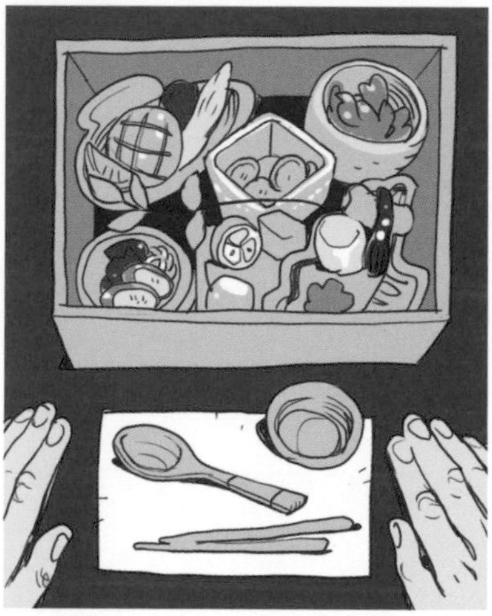

THE BUSINESS CARD IS JUST ONE SMALL EVIDENCE OF THE JAPANESE AFFINITY FOR LABELING. ORDER AND FUNCTIONALITY ARE CENTRAL VALUES IN JAPANESE CULTURE.

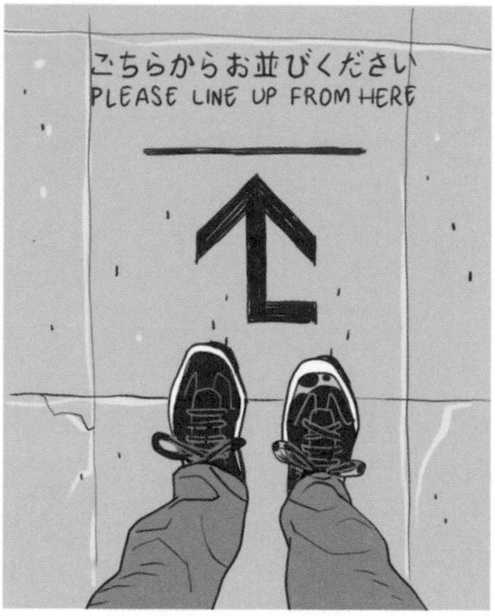
こちらからお並びください
PLEASE LINE UP FROM HERE

EACH THING HAS ITS PLACE AND ITS ROLE, AND EVERYBODY HAPPILY OBEYS.

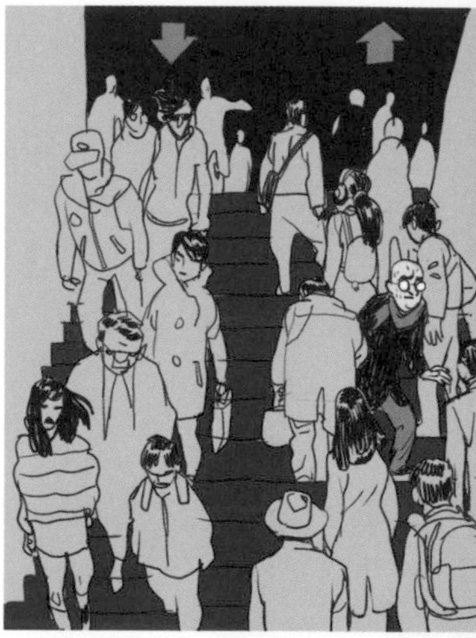

THIS BEHAVIOR ELIMINATES ANY CHANCE OF VIOLENCE OR CHAOS, EVEN IN THE BUSIEST, MOST CROWDED PLACES.

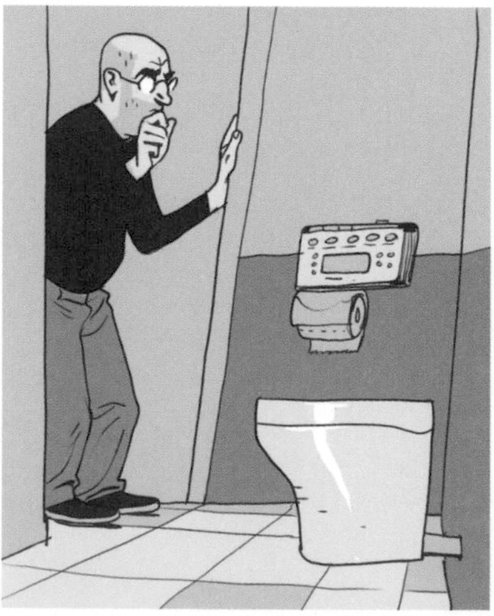

IT'S NICE TO LIVE IN A WORLD WHERE EVERYTHING WORKS AND THE BATHROOM IS ALWAYS CLEAN.

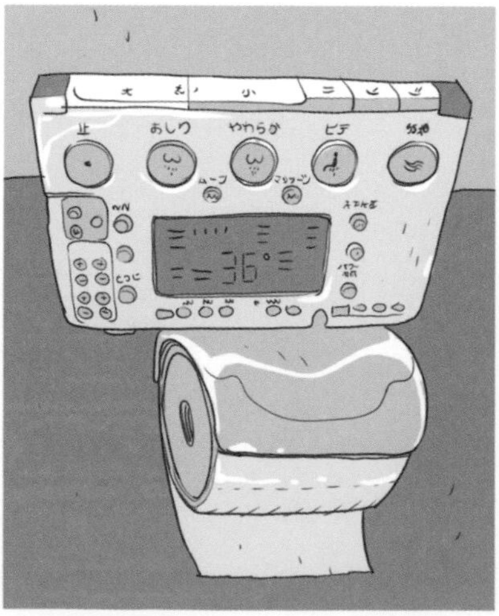
止
おしり
やわらか
ビデ
36°

IT TURNS OUT THERE ARE MANY WAYS OF FLUSHING, BUT I WASN'T ABLE TO DISCERN THE DIFFERENCES BETWEEN THEM.

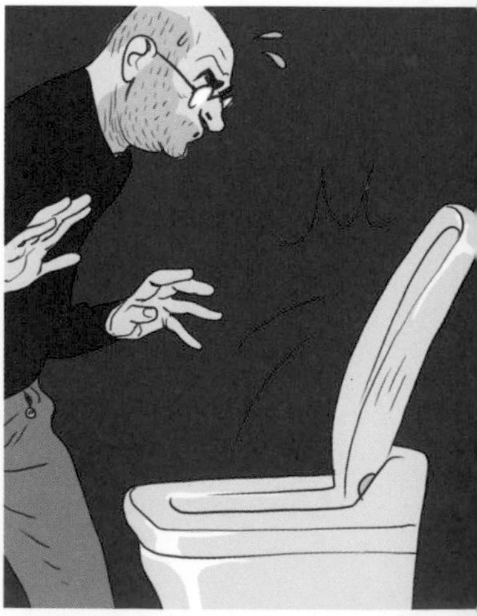

WHEN I WAS ABOUT TO SIT DOWN THE TOILET LID LIFTED AUTOMATICALLY, ELIMINATING ANY CHANCE FOR VIOLENCE.

VISIT TO TOKYO WAS THE ONLY TIME I EVER T THAT MY APPEARANCE WAS UNUSUAL, IN A CH MORE PROFOUND WAY THAN THE NUANCES ETHNICITY AND TRIBAL ORIGINS.

BUT IN SPITE OF RACE DIFFERENCES I COULD HAVE BEEN BORN JAPANESE. I LIKE ORDER, I LIKE THINGS TO COME IN BOXES, AND I NEVER LAUGH OUT LOUD IN PUBLIC.

A FACE IS JUST A MASK. DEEP INSIDE, WE'RE ALL PEOPLE. LIKE THE JEWS, THE JAPANESE HAVE A HISTORY OF MAINTAINING THEIR IDENTITY IN SPITE OF OUTSIDE FORCES.

THE 17TH CENTURY JAPAN CLOSED ITSELF F TO THE WORLD FOR 250 YEARS TO DEFEND SELF AGAINST CATHOLIC MISSIONARIES AND HER OUTSIDE INFLUENCES AND THREATS.

ITS ISOLATION ALLOWED JAPANESE CULTURE TO EVOLVE SEPARATELY FROM THE WEST, CREATING A UNIQUE VISUAL LANGUAGE.

I WAS WONDERING IF ALL THE CUTE CHARACTERS WERE A REACTION TO THE DEVASTATION OF HIROSHIMA AND NAGASAKI. I WISH COLLECTIVE TRAUMAS WERE TRANSLATED INTO SOMETHING HUGGABLE IN ISRAEL.

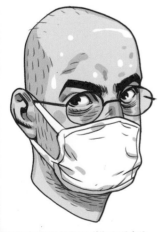 

CAUGHT A COLD DURING MY VISIT AND UICKLY BEGAN WEARING A WHITE CLOTH ASK, AS IS THE JAPANESE CUSTOM. IT'S THE DIVIDUAL'S WAY OF BEING CONSIDERATE OF E GROUP.

AT NIGHT I DREAMT THAT MY COUGH GREW WORSE AND WORSE UNTIL MY ENTIRE FACE TURNED INTO SOMETHING THAT WOULD BE MUCH MORE DIFFICULT TO HIDE.

THE NEXT MORNING MY COUGH WAS GONE. I TOOK OFF THE MASK. MY FOREIGNNESS BECAME COMFORTABLE. LIKE ANYTHING ELSE IN JAPAN, IT TOO FOUND ITS RIGHTFUL PLACE.

FISTS

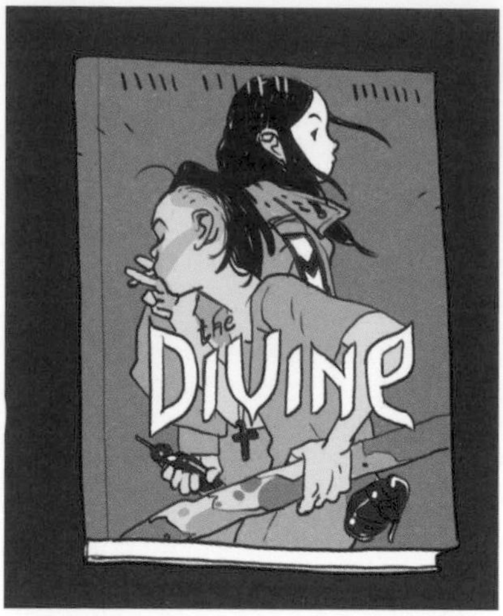
the DIVINE

THE DIVINE, A COMIC BOOK I CO-CREATED WITH TOMER HANUKA (ILLUSTRATION), BOAZ LAVIE (WRITING), AND RON PROPPER (PRODUCTION), WON THE INTERNATIONAL MANGA AWARD.

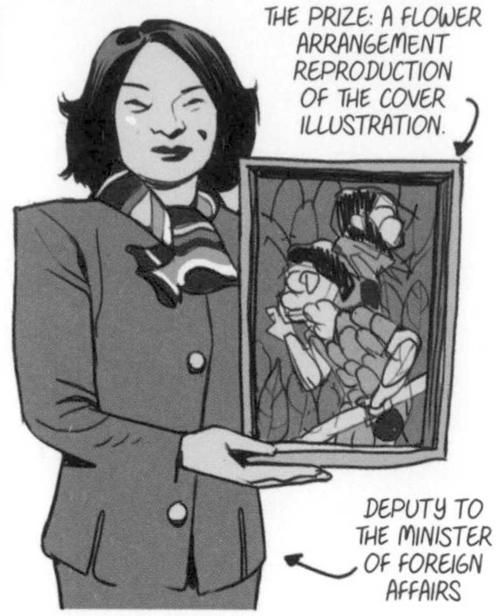
THE PRIZE: A FLOWER ARRANGEMENT REPRODUCTION OF THE COVER ILLUSTRATION.
DEPUTY TO THE MINISTER OF FOREIGN AFFAIRS

WE WERE INVITED TO A FORMAL AWARD CEREMONY IN TOKYO. COMIC BOOKS ARE A SERIOUS BUSINESS IN JAPAN, AND COMIC BOOK ARTISTS ARE SUPERSTARS.

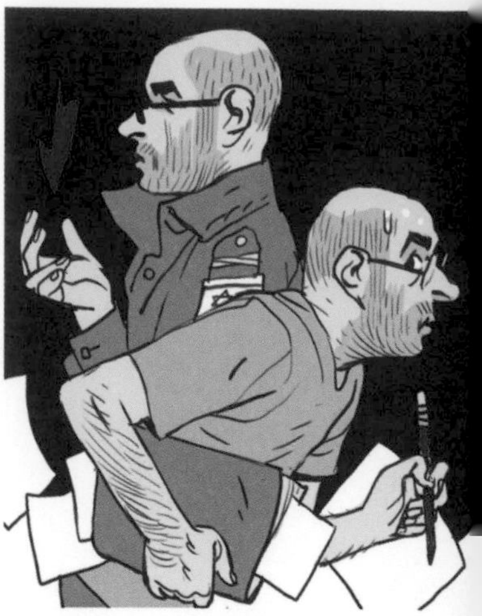

IN ISRAEL, I GET EMBARRASSED WHENEVER I HAVE TO EXPLAIN WHAT I DO FOR A LIVING. I'VE ACCEPTED MY POSITION IN THE MARGINS OF LEISURE CULTURE A LONG TIME AGO.

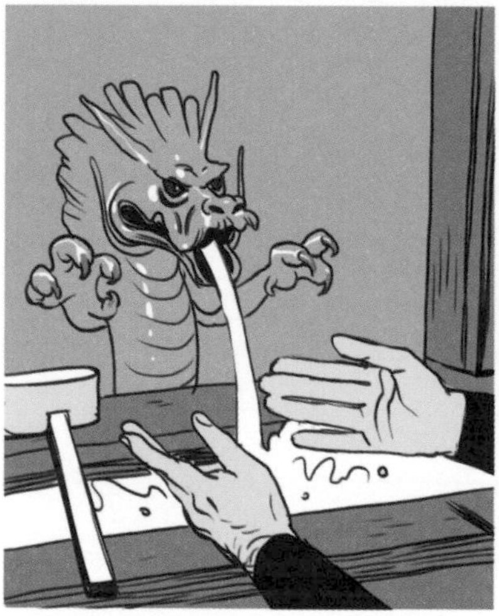

IN A TEMPLE IN TOKYO, I NOTICED A BASIN OUTSIDE FOR HAND WASHING, SIMILAR TO THE ONES THAT CAN BE FOUND IN JEWISH CEMETERIES.

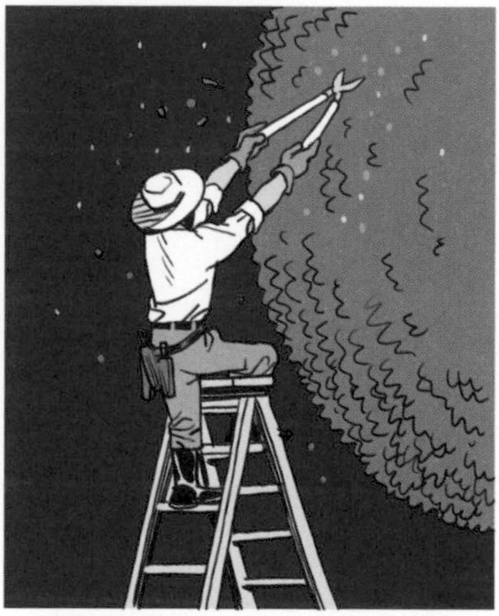

A GARDENER WAS TRIMMING THE TOP OF ONE OF THE TREES WITH GEOMETRIC PRECISION, SLOWLY TURNING IT INTO A BALL. THAT DIDN'T REMIND ME OF ANYTHING IN ISRAEL.

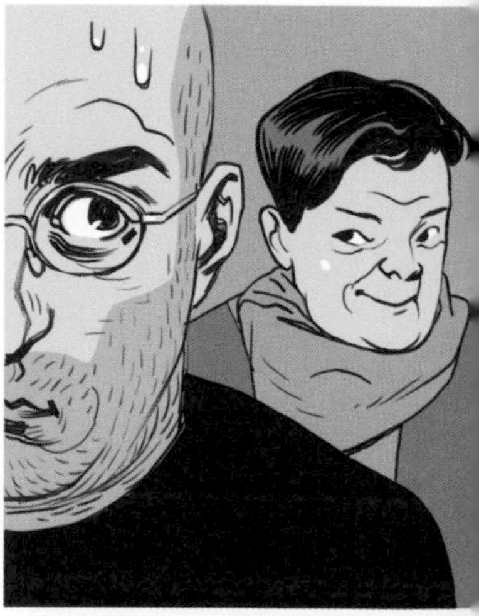

OUR INTERPRETER EXPLAINED THAT IN JAPAN PUBLIC EMBARRASSMENT IS THE LOWEST POI A MAN CAN REACH, WHICH IS WHY EVERYONE DOES THEIR JOBS PERFECTLY.

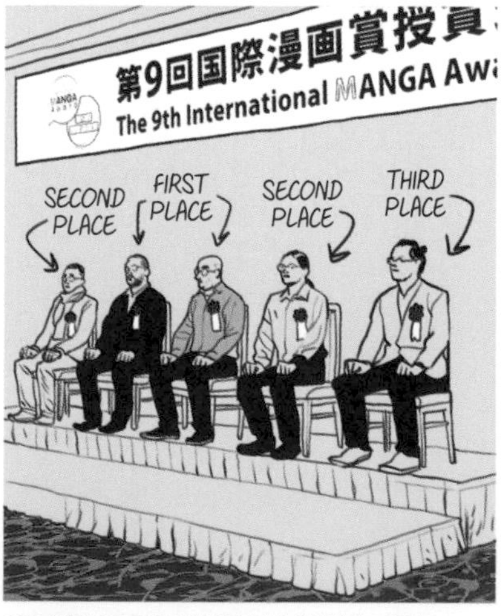
第9回国際漫画賞授賞
The 9th International MANGA Awa
SECOND PLACE
FIRST PLACE
SECOND PLACE
THIRD PLACE

THE DAY OF THE CEREMONY BEGAN WITH A REHEARSAL. A KIND PERSON EXPLAINED THAT WE SHOULD SIT WITH OUR HANDS BUNCHED INTO FISTS.

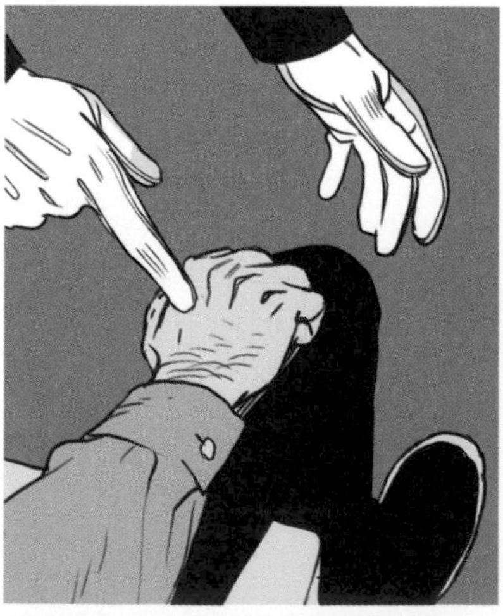

FINGERS SHOULD NOT BE SEEN IN ANY OF THE PHOTOGRAPHS. THEY ARE PERSONAL, AND THEY ARE MESSY. FINGERS SULLY PERFECTION AND AMASS UNNECESSARY DETAILS.

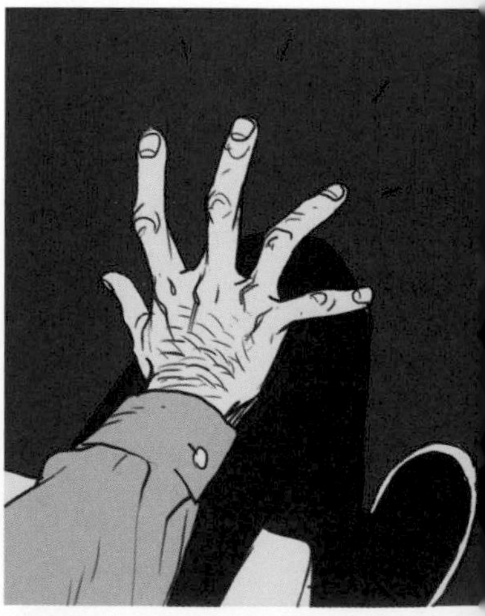

WHEN THEY STARTED TAKING PICTURES I OPENED MY FISTS. EVERYONE LOOKED AT ME. I WAS AT MY LOWEST SOCIAL POINT. IN ONE SINGLE MOMENT I FOUND MYSELF BACK IN THE MARGINS. BACK HOME.

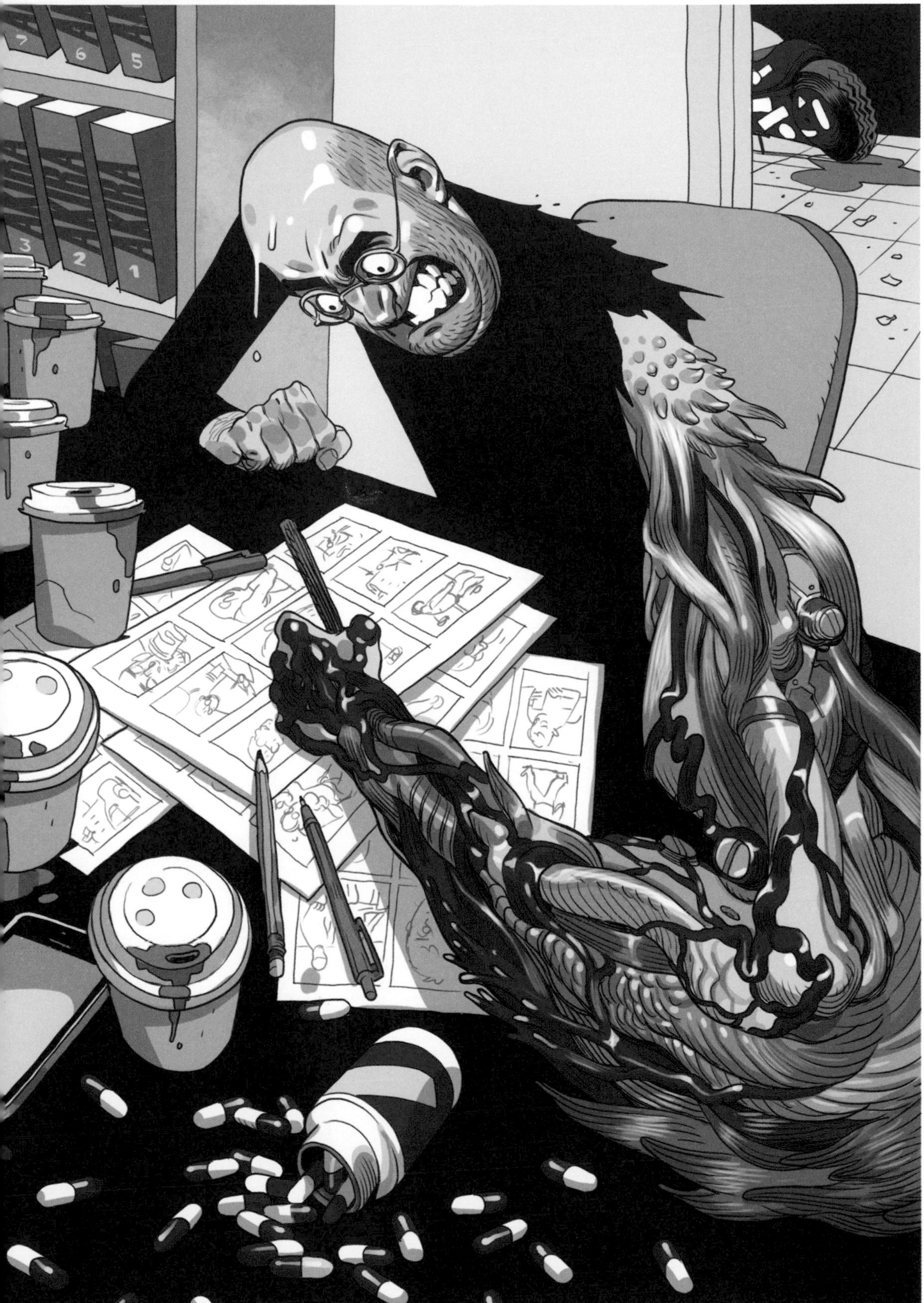

I NEED A HERO

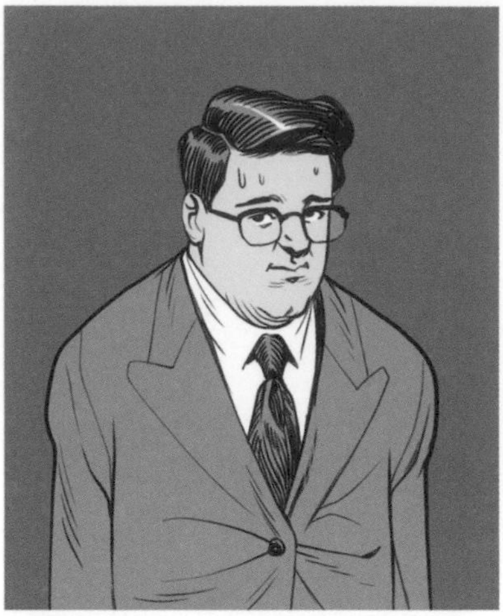

JERRY SIEGEL, A SHY AMERICAN JEW OF RUSSIAN DESCENT, INVENTED SUPERMAN, THE FIRST SUPERHERO, IN 1938, ALONG WITH ILLUSTRATOR JOE SHUSTER.

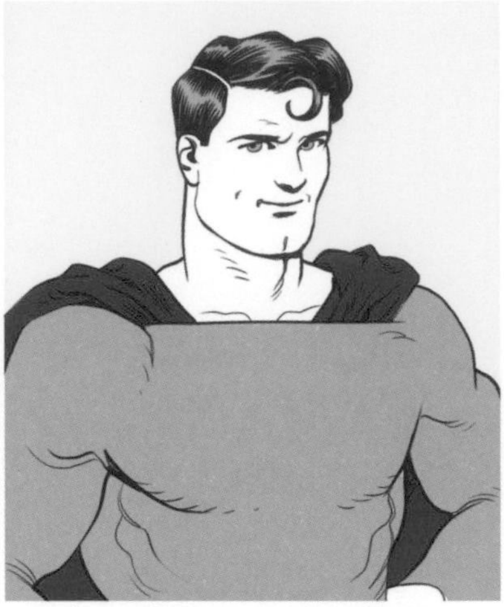

SIEGEL'S FATHER DIED OF A HEART ATTACK WHEN ROBBERS BROKE INTO HIS STORE. SUPERMAN WAS EVERYTHING SIEGEL DREAMED OF BEING: A HERO WHO SHOWS UP WHENEVER SOMEONE NEEDS SAVING.

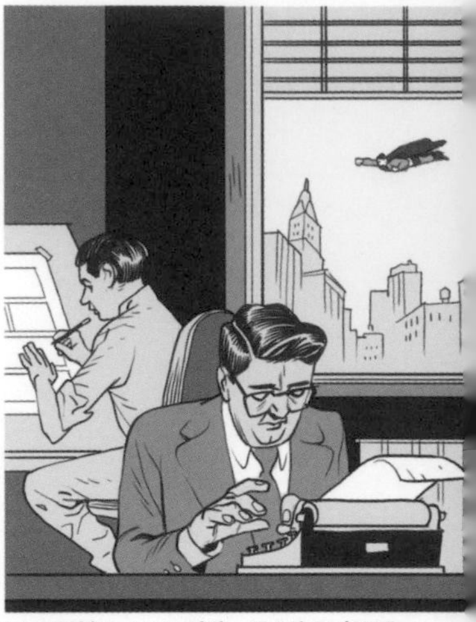

SUPERMAN, WHO CAME FROM PLANET KRYPTON, BECAME A SYMBOL OF AMERICA'S ECONOMIC POWER AND MORAL SUPERIORITY. HE EMBODIED THE PROMISE OF CAPITALISTIC EQUAL RIGHTS.

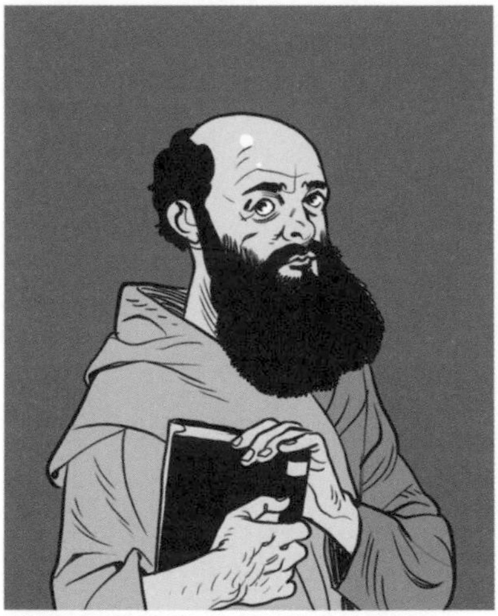

PAUL THE APOSTLE, A JEWISH GUY WHO SUFFERED FROM A MYSTERIOUS ILLNESS, CONVERTED TO CHRISTIANITY AFTER EXPERIENCING AN EPILEPTIC SEIZURE ON HIS WAY TO DAMASCUS IN 34 AD.

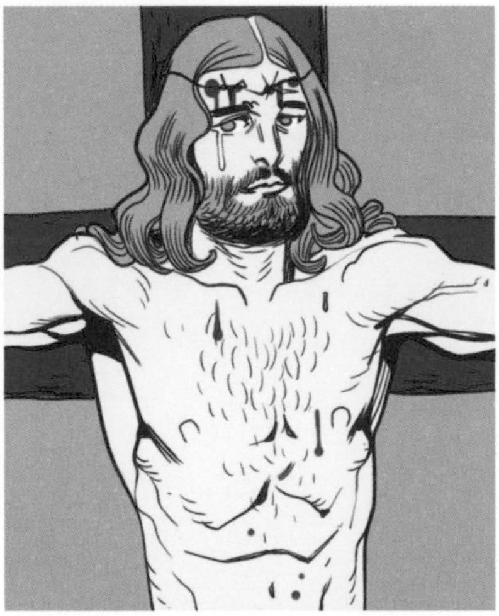

HE BECAME A MISSIONARY, SPREADING STORIES ABOUT JESUS, A CONCEPTUAL CHARACTER THAT EMBODIED EVERYTHING PAUL DREAMED OF BEING: HANDSOME, BELOVED, AND POSSESSING OF MAGICAL HEALING POWERS.

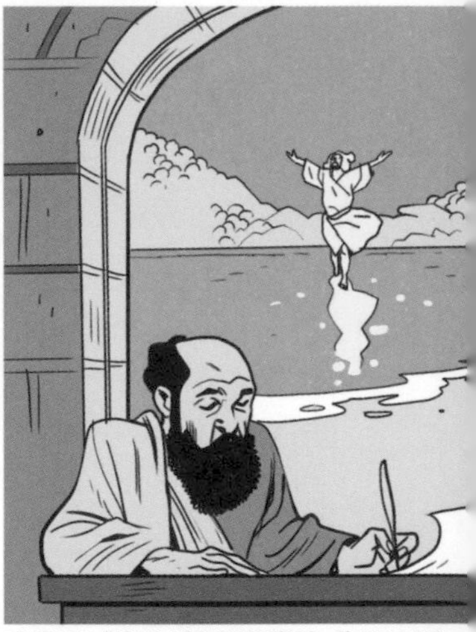

THOUGH JESUS HAD SUFFERED, MUCH LIKE PAUL, HE WAS ABLE TO FIND REDEMPTION IN SUFFERING. CHRISTIANITY WAS TRANSFORMED FROM A PERSECUTED CULT TO THE OFFICIAL FAITH OF THE ROMAN EMPIRE.

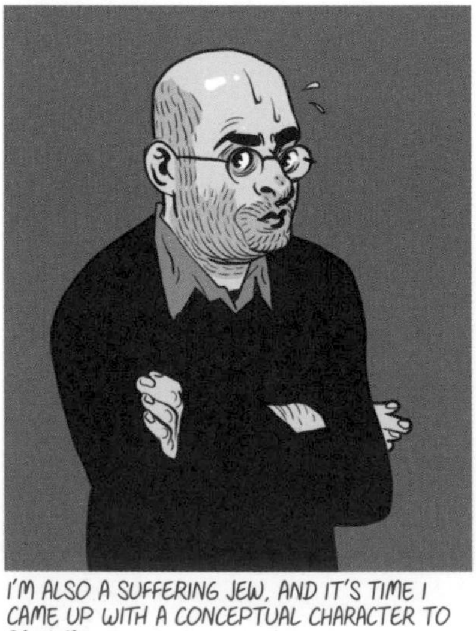

I'M ALSO A SUFFERING JEW, AND IT'S TIME I CAME UP WITH A CONCEPTUAL CHARACTER TO SAVE ME.

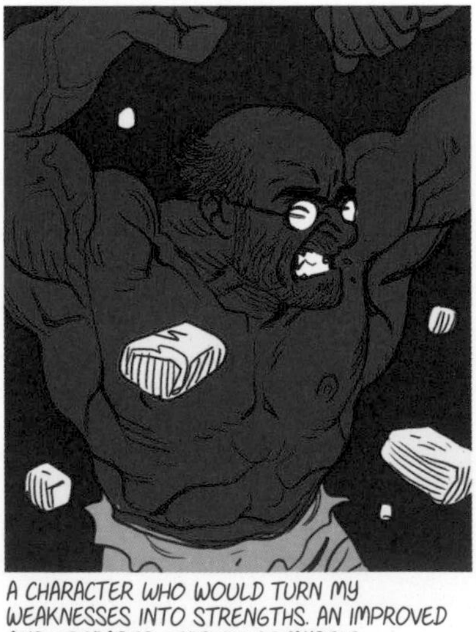

A CHARACTER WHO WOULD TURN MY WEAKNESSES INTO STRENGTHS. AN IMPROVED AND UPGRADED VERSION OF MYSELF, EMBODYING EVERYTHING I'VE EVER WANTED TO BE BUT COULDN'T.

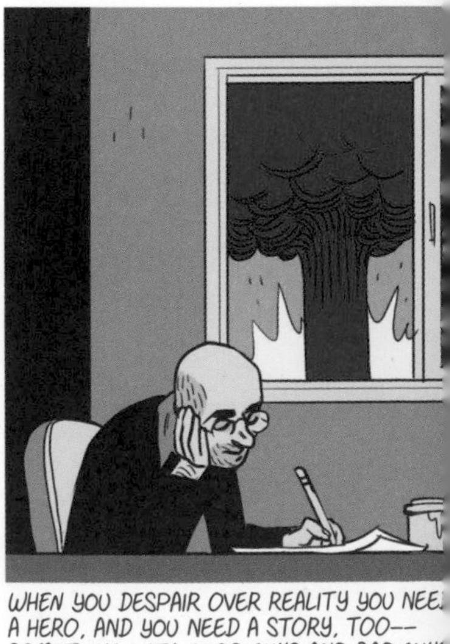

WHEN YOU DESPAIR OVER REALITY YOU NEED A HERO, AND YOU NEED A STORY, TOO—SOMETHING WITH GOOD GUYS AND BAD GUYS, A DIVINE PROMISE AND REDEMPTION.

FORE AND AFTER

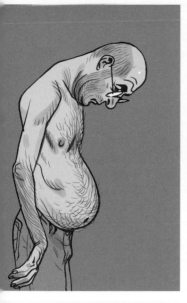

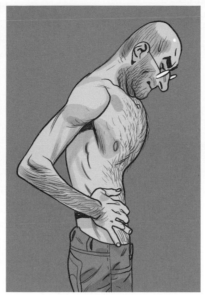

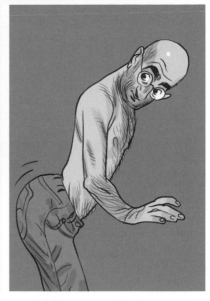

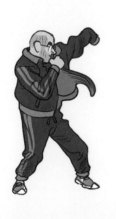

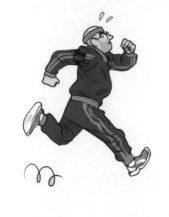

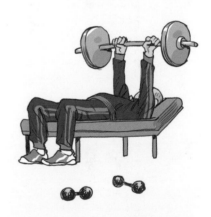

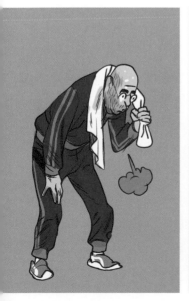

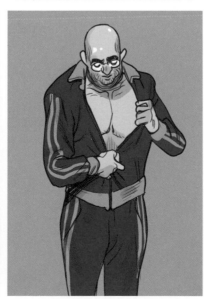

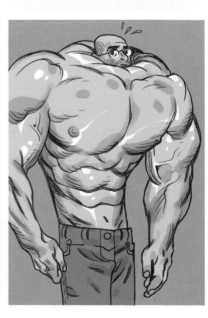

COSTUMES

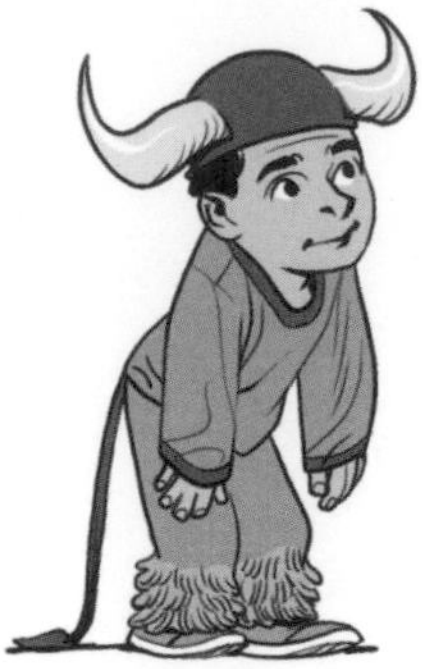

UNTIL I WENT TO MIDDLE SCHOOL I DIDN'T EVEN KNOW WHAT "MIZRAHI" MEANT. I DON'T KNOW IF MY PARENTS WERE TRYING TO PROTECT ME, OR IF THEY TRULY BELIEVED IT DIDN'T MATTER ANYMORE.

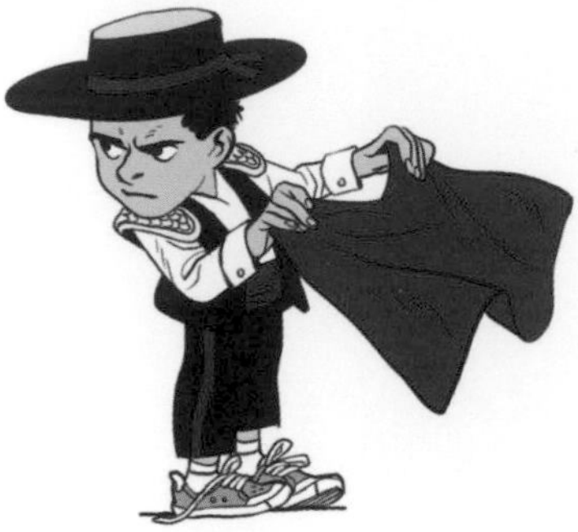

I DIDN'T KNOW WHERE MY FAMILY HAD COME FROM AND WHEN I ASKED, I WAS TOLD WE WERE "SEPHARDIC." I NATURALLY ASSUMED THAT MEANT WE WERE FROM SPAIN, CALLED "SEPHARAD" IN HEBREW.

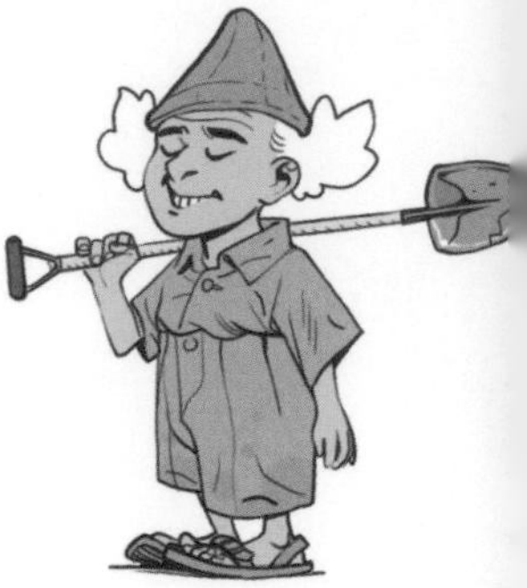

THE JEWS OF KURDISTAN WERE NOT MENTIONED IN HISTORY CLASS, AND THE JEW OF IRAQ WERE DESCRIBED ONLY BRIEFLY. TH MAIN STORY WAS THE ZIONIST MOVEMENT, LED BY RUSSIANS AND POLES.

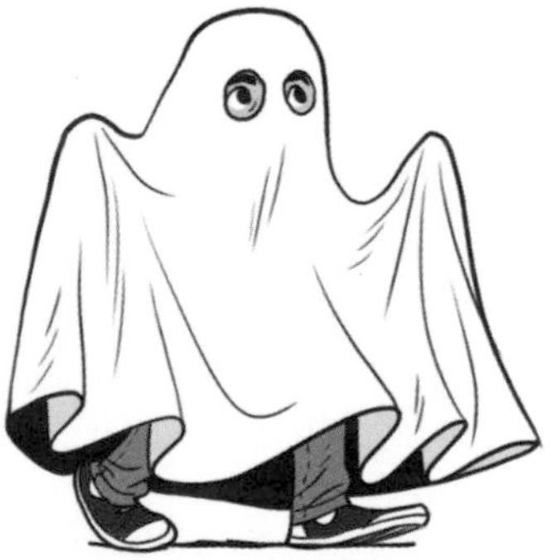

DUE TO THE CUMULATIVE EFFECT OF LONG TERM REPRESSION, BY THE TIME I SORT OF FIGURED OUT WHERE I'D COME FROM, IT WAS ALREADY TOO LATE. I'D LOST THE ABILITY TO BE AN AUTHENTIC MIZRAHI.

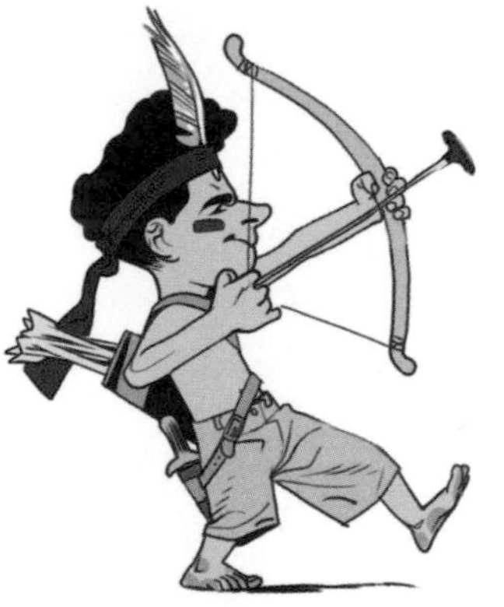

THE ISRAELI CLICHÉ OF THE AUTHENTIC MIZRAHI IS SOMEONE WHO'S CONNECTED TO FOLKSY CULTURE, TO A PARTICULAR TYPE OF FOOD, NEIGHBORHOOD FRIENDS, MIZRAHI MUSIC, AND JEWISH TRADITION.

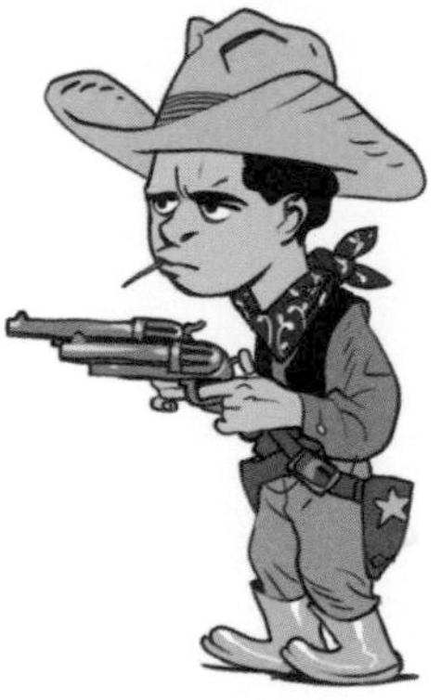

AN AUTHENTIC MIZRAHI LOVES THIS COUNTR EVEN THOUGH ITS ESTABLISHMENTS HAVE H HIM. HE'S A ZIONIST, EVEN THOUGH ZIONISM TAKEN ADVANTAGE OF HIM.

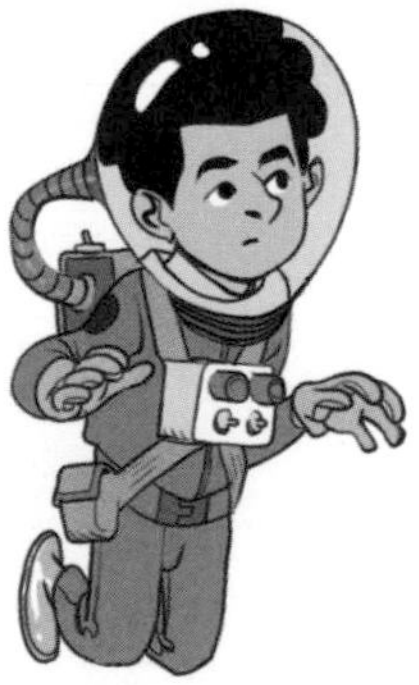

ASHKENAZIS DON'T CARE IF I'M AUTHENTIC. TO THEM I'M MIZRAHI. OTHER MIZRAHIS CAN INSTANTLY TELL I'M FAKE, NOT A REAL PART OF THE STRUGGLE. I'M STUCK IN THE VACUUM BETWEEN CAMPS.

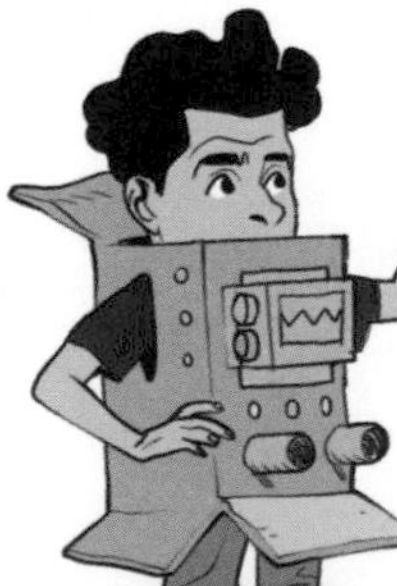

SO I START MY OWN STRUGGLE: I FIGHT FOR THE RIGHT TO BE A GENETIC MIZRAHI WHO SUFFERS FROM A LACK OF AWARENESS RATHER THAN AN INFERIORITY COMPLEX.

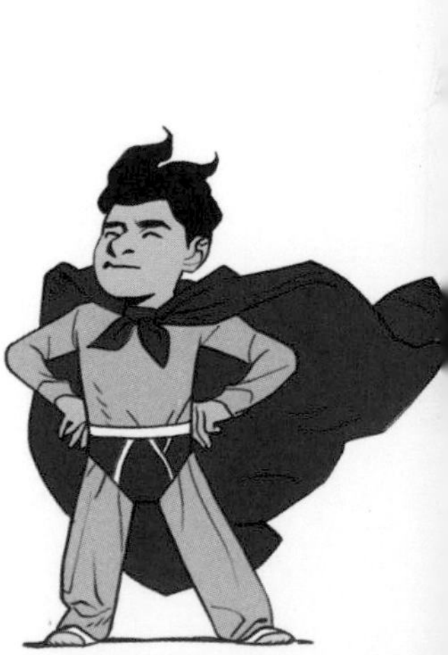

THERE ARE MANY OTHERS LIKE ME, I'M SURE DON'T BE ASHAMED OF WHO YOU ARE. ALW BE PROUD, EVEN IF YOU DON'T KNOW OF WHAT.

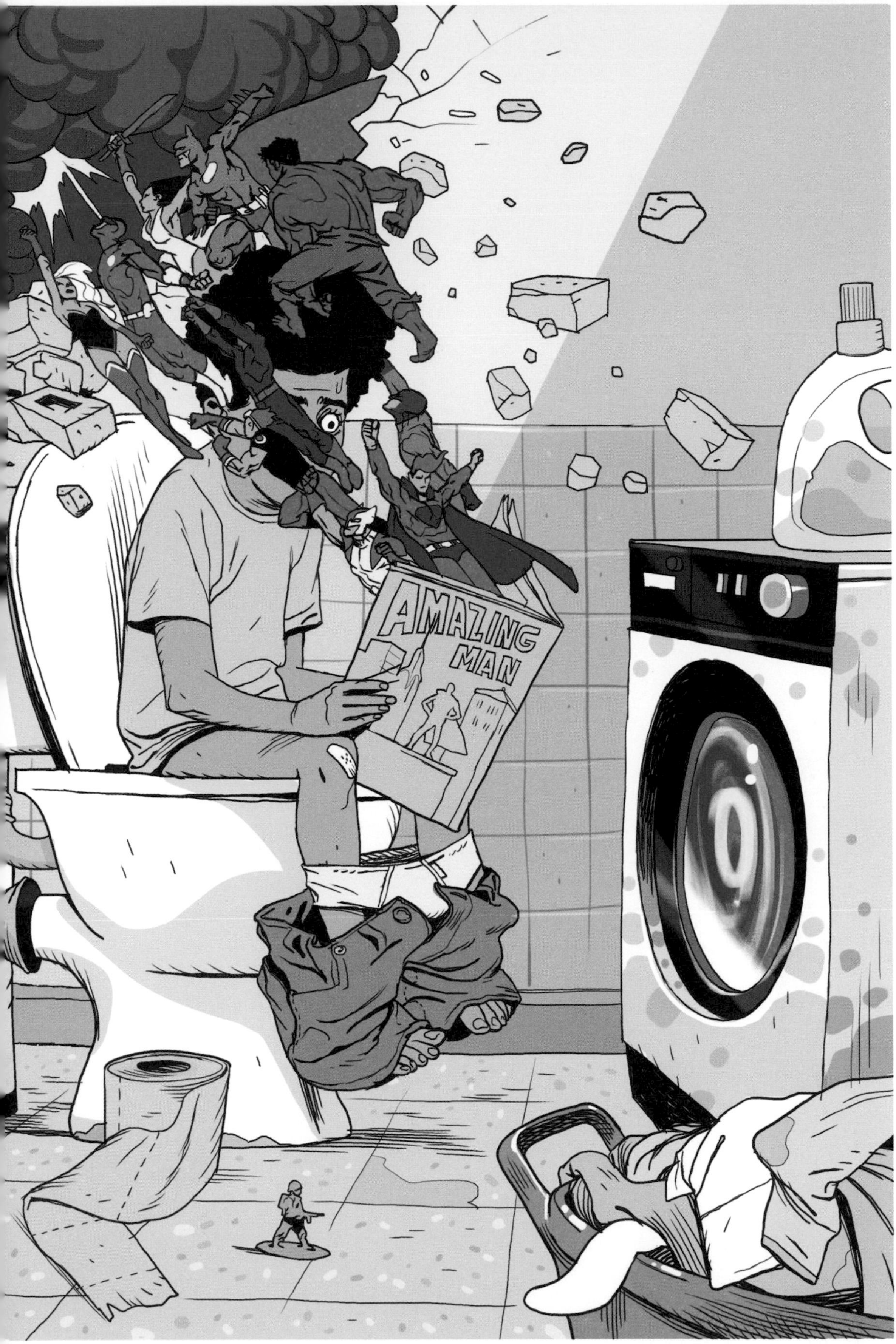
AMAZING
MAN

THE MOMENT I REALIZED ANXIETY CAN BECOME INSPIRATION

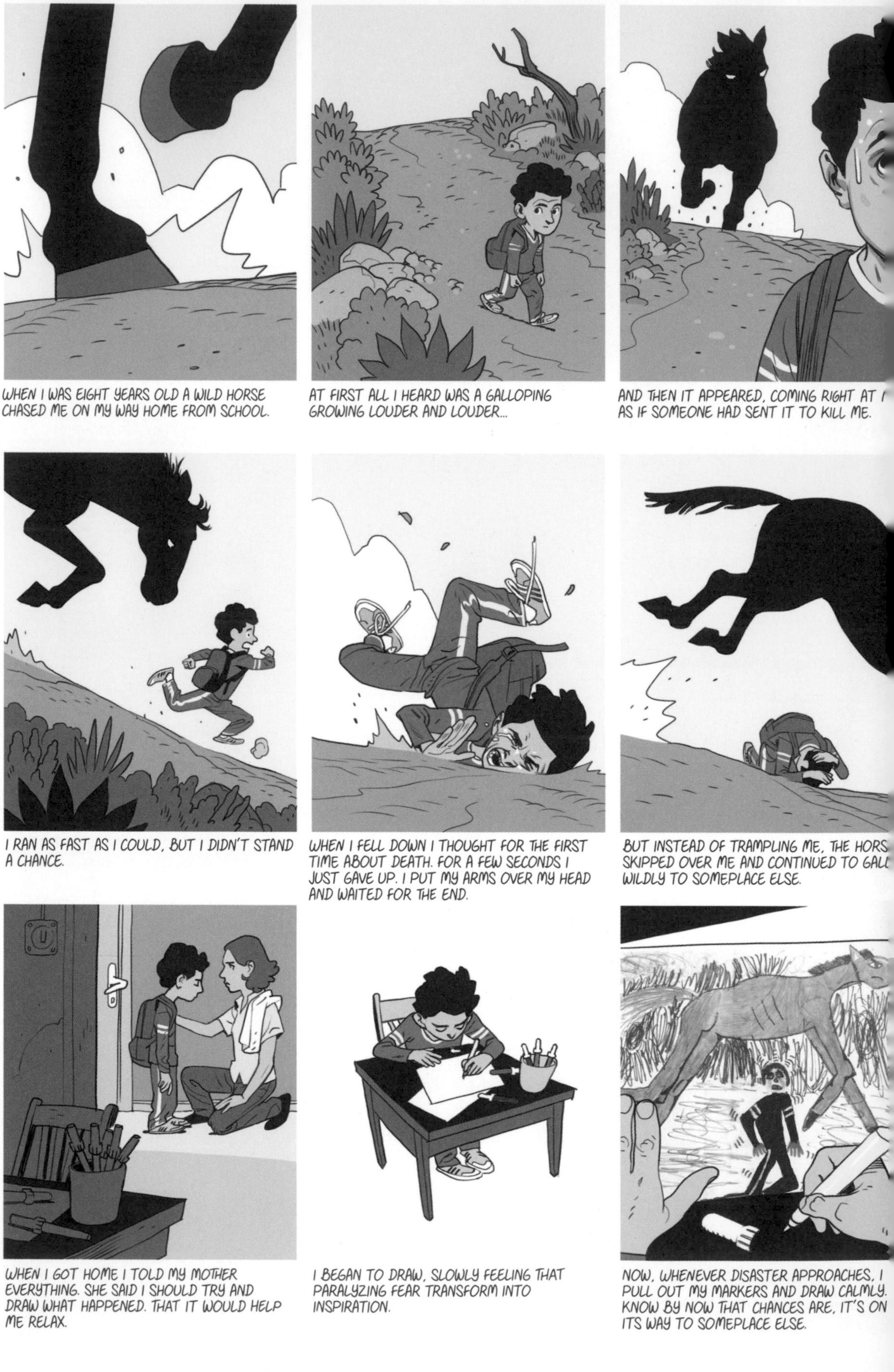
WHEN I WAS EIGHT YEARS OLD A WILD HORSE CHASED ME ON MY WAY HOME FROM SCHOOL.
AT FIRST ALL I HEARD WAS A GALLOPING GROWING LOUDER AND LOUDER...
AND THEN IT APPEARED, COMING RIGHT AT AS IF SOMEONE HAD SENT IT TO KILL ME.
I RAN AS FAST AS I COULD, BUT I DIDN'T STAND A CHANCE.
WHEN I FELL DOWN I THOUGHT FOR THE FIRST TIME ABOUT DEATH. FOR A FEW SECONDS I JUST GAVE UP. I PUT MY ARMS OVER MY HEAD AND WAITED FOR THE END.
BUT INSTEAD OF TRAMPLING ME, THE HORS SKIPPED OVER ME AND CONTINUED TO GAL WILDLY TO SOMEPLACE ELSE.
WHEN I GOT HOME I TOLD MY MOTHER EVERYTHING. SHE SAID I SHOULD TRY AND DRAW WHAT HAPPENED. THAT IT WOULD HELP ME RELAX.
I BEGAN TO DRAW, SLOWLY FEELING THAT PARALYZING FEAR TRANSFORM INTO INSPIRATION.
NOW, WHENEVER DISASTER APPROACHES, I PULL OUT MY MARKERS AND DRAW CALMLY. KNOW BY NOW THAT CHANCES ARE, IT'S ON ITS WAY TO SOMEPLACE ELSE.

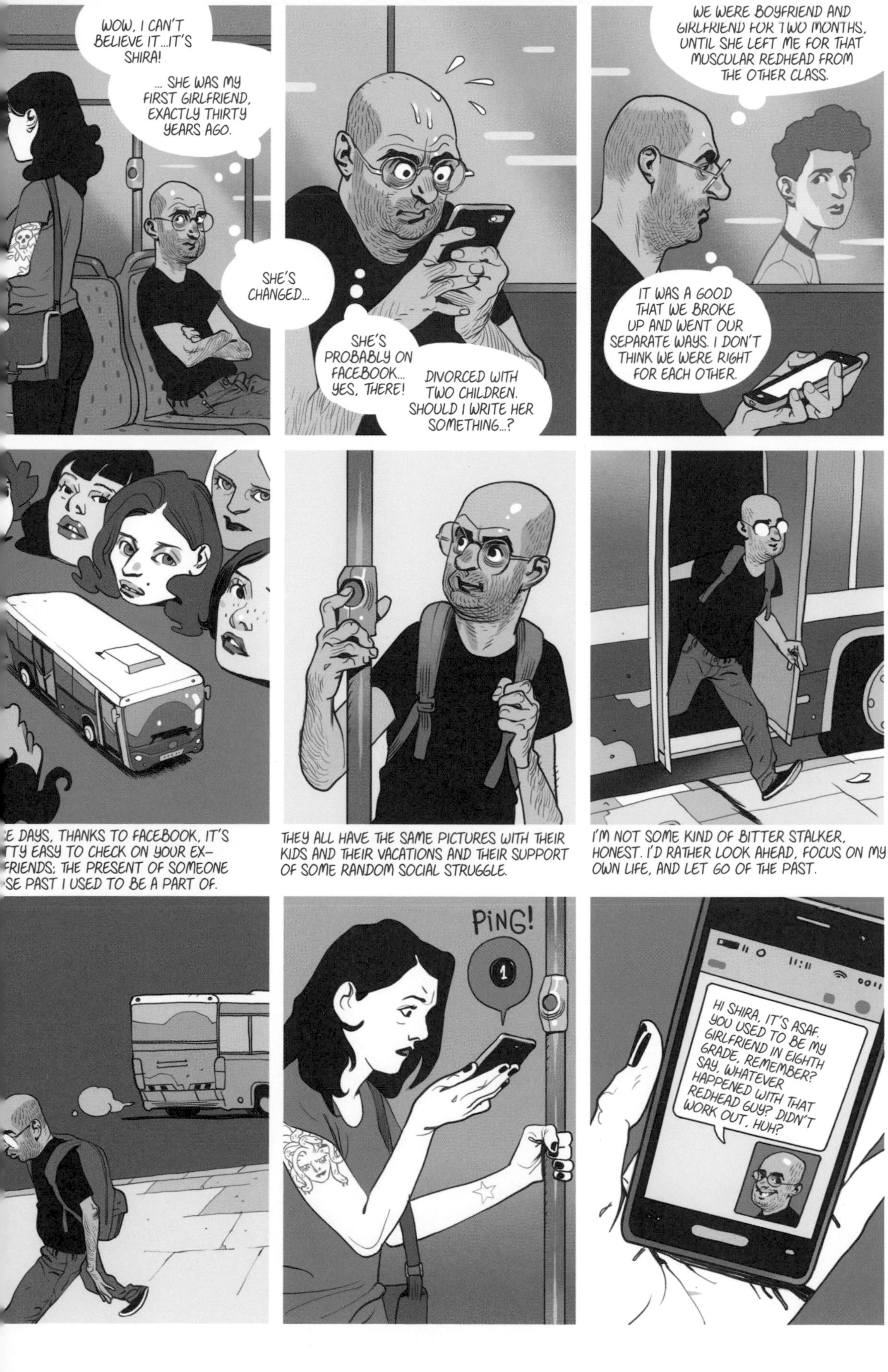
WOW, I CAN'T BELIEVE IT...IT'S SHIRA!
... SHE WAS MY FIRST GIRLFRIEND, EXACTLY THIRTY YEARS AGO.
SHE'S CHANGED...
SHE'S PROBABLY ON FACEBOOK... YES, THERE!
DIVORCED WITH TWO CHILDREN. SHOULD I WRITE HER SOMETHING...?
WE WERE BOYFRIEND AND GIRLFRIEND FOR TWO MONTHS, UNTIL SHE LEFT ME FOR THAT MUSCULAR REDHEAD FROM THE OTHER CLASS.
IT WAS A GOOD THAT WE BROKE UP AND WENT OUR SEPARATE WAYS. I DON'T THINK WE WERE RIGHT FOR EACH OTHER.
E DAYS, THANKS TO FACEBOOK, IT'S TTY EASY TO CHECK ON YOUR EX-FRIENDS; THE PRESENT OF SOMEONE SE PAST I USED TO BE A PART OF.
THEY ALL HAVE THE SAME PICTURES WITH THEIR KIDS AND THEIR VACATIONS AND THEIR SUPPORT OF SOME RANDOM SOCIAL STRUGGLE.
I'M NOT SOME KIND OF BITTER STALKER, HONEST. I'D RATHER LOOK AHEAD, FOCUS ON MY OWN LIFE, AND LET GO OF THE PAST.
PING!
1
HI SHIRA, IT'S ASAF. YOU USED TO BE MY GIRLFRIEND IN EIGHTH GRADE, REMEMBER? SAY, WHATEVER HAPPENED WITH THAT REDHEAD GUY? DIDN'T WORK OUT, HUH?

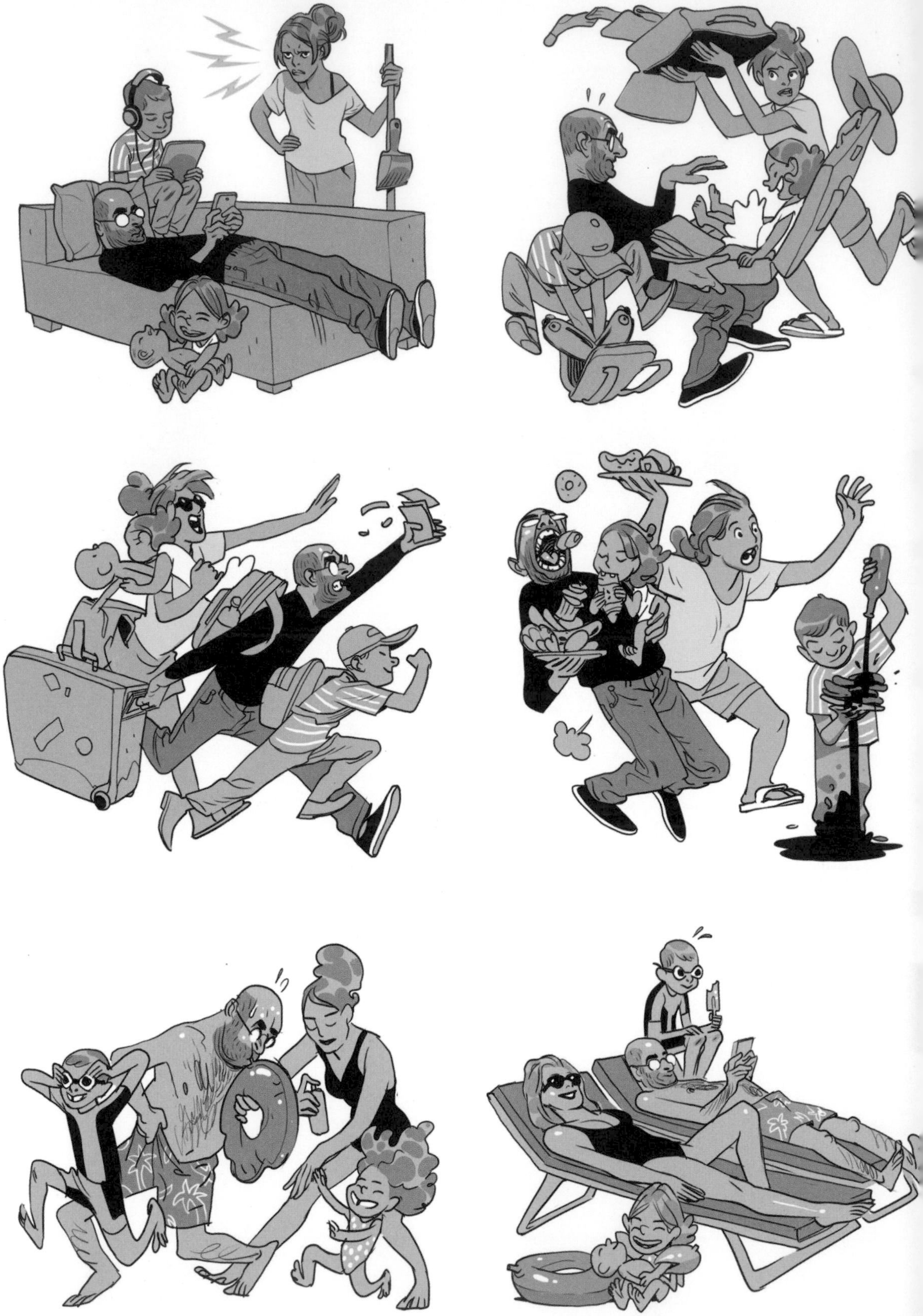

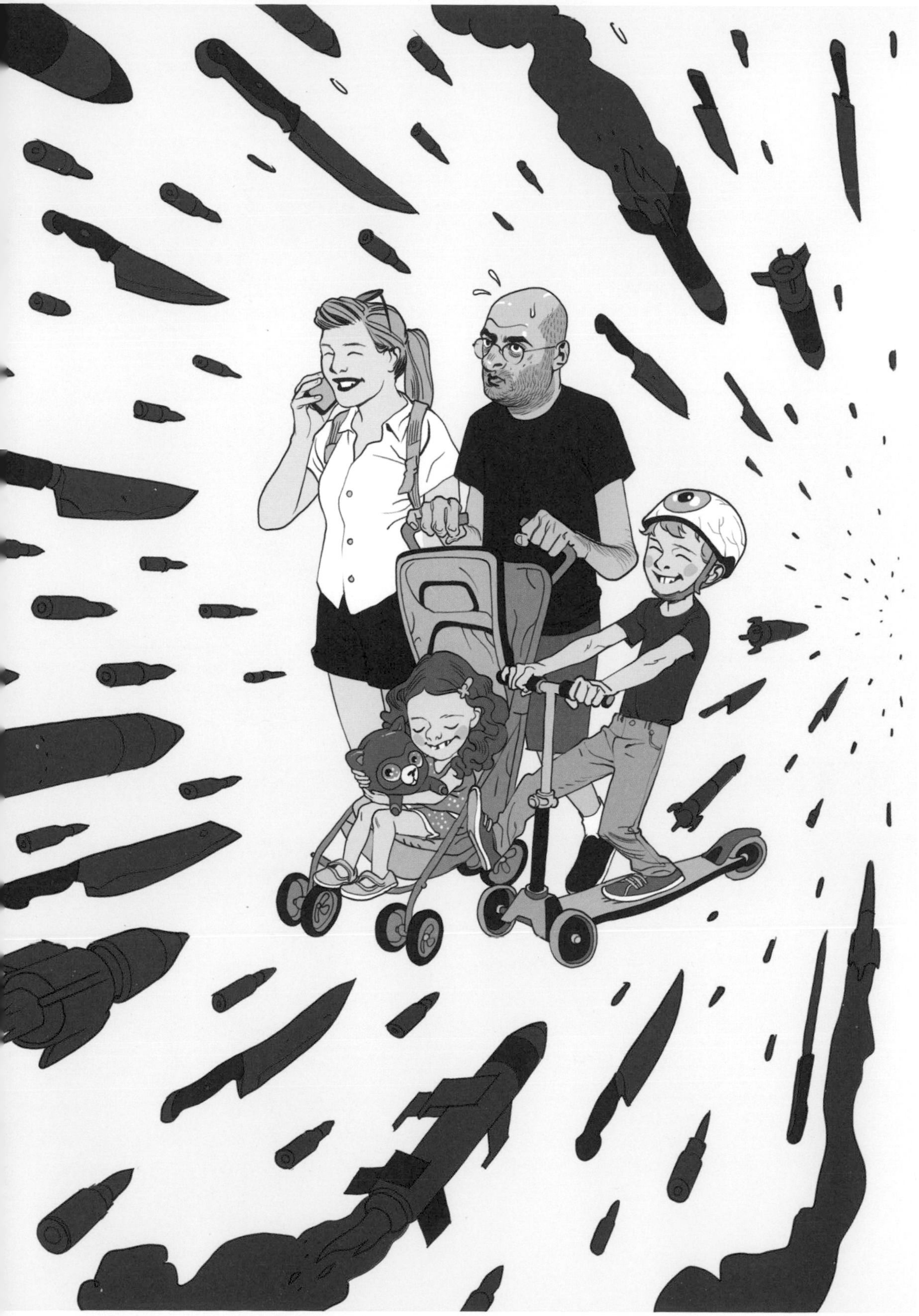

A PREVIEW OF HELL

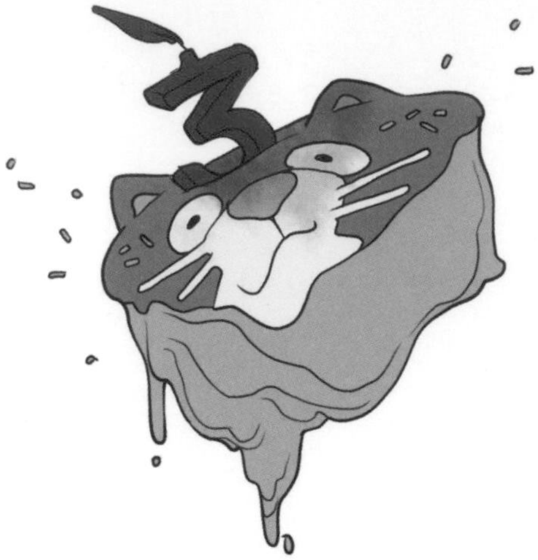

IT ALL BEGAN AT OUR DAUGHTER'S BIRTHDAY PARTY AT THE PARK, WHICH BECAME A MULTI-CASUALTY SWEAT BATH. EVERYONE'S GOOD INTENTIONS DRIPPED AWAY, LEAVING ONLY HUMAN REMAINS, WHISPERING "HAPPY BIRTHDAY TO YOU."

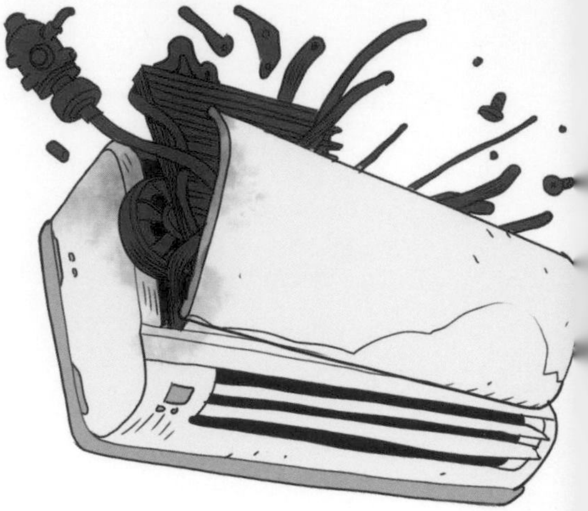

THEN THINGS STARTED TO FALL APART. "IT ISN'T COOLING!" MY WIFE SAID OVER DINNER, POINTING HER FORK AT THE AIR CONDITIONER. "ARE YOU SURE? MAYBE IT'S JUST TIRED," I SAID, TRYING TO INSPIRE HER EMPATHY, THOUGH I KNEW SHE WAS RIGHT.

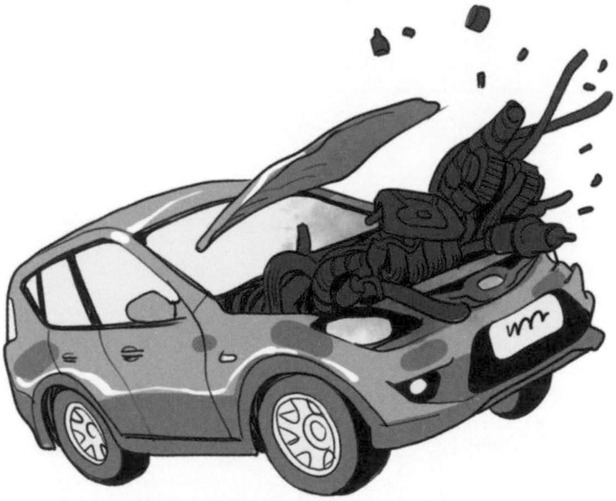

THE CAR BATTERY WAS NEXT. "IT'S GOT NOTHING TO DO WITH SUMMER," THE MECHANIC ASSURED ME. "IT'S JUST EXPIRED." STRANGE HOW EVERYTHING JUST EXPIRES ALL AT ONCE DURING THE FIRST WEEK OF JULY. EVERYTHING THAT USED TO WORK NO LONGER DOES.

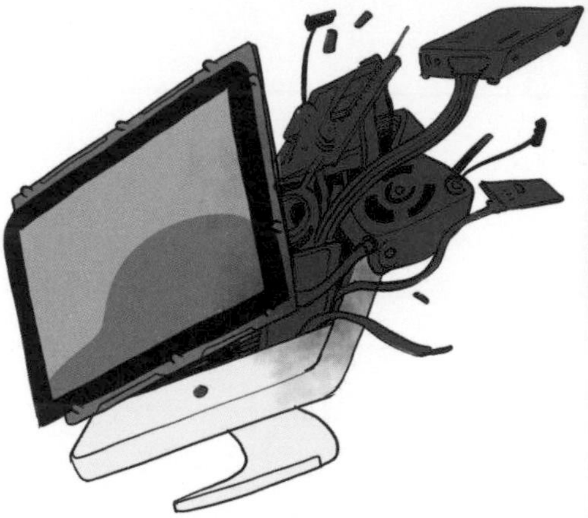

THEN THE COMPUTER MALFUNCTIONED AT THE SAME TIME AS THE BACKUP DRIVE. WHAT ARE THE ODDS? ACCORDING TO THE RESTORATION COMPANY, THERE WAS A 50% CHANCE OF SAVING THE FILES. THE PROCESS COST AS MUCH AS A WEEKEND GETAWAY IN AUGUST.

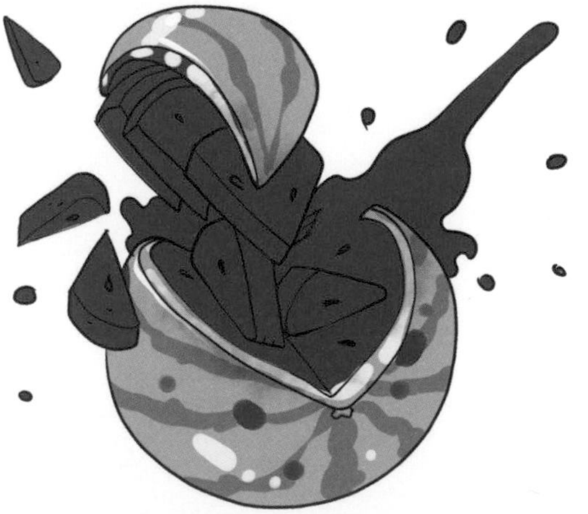

A VACATION WOULD MAKE ALL THIS AGONY WORTH SOMETHING. SUMMER WILL END ON THE SIDE OF A POOL SOMEPLACE FARAWAY. IT DOESN'T EVEN MATTER HOW MUCH IT COSTS OR IF THERE'S EVEN A POOL. AS LONG AS IT ISN'T HERE.

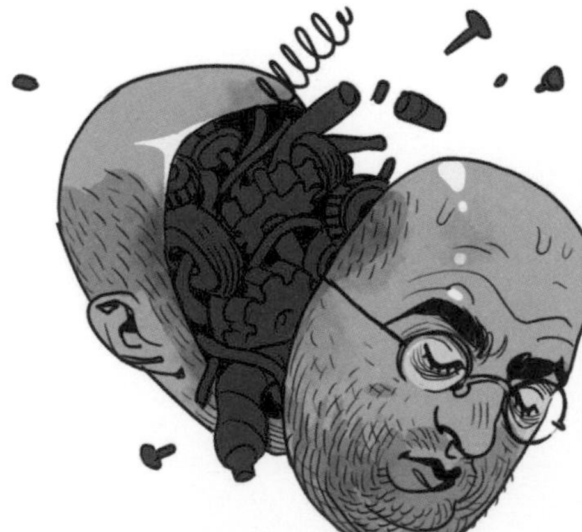

THIS MORNING I WOKE UP WITH A BACKACHE. THAT'S IT, I'M MALFUNCTIONING TOO. SOMEONE TAKE ME TO BE FIXED, HAVE MY PARTS CHANGED. I PROMISE TO RETURN, NEW AND IMPROVED, IN THE FALL.

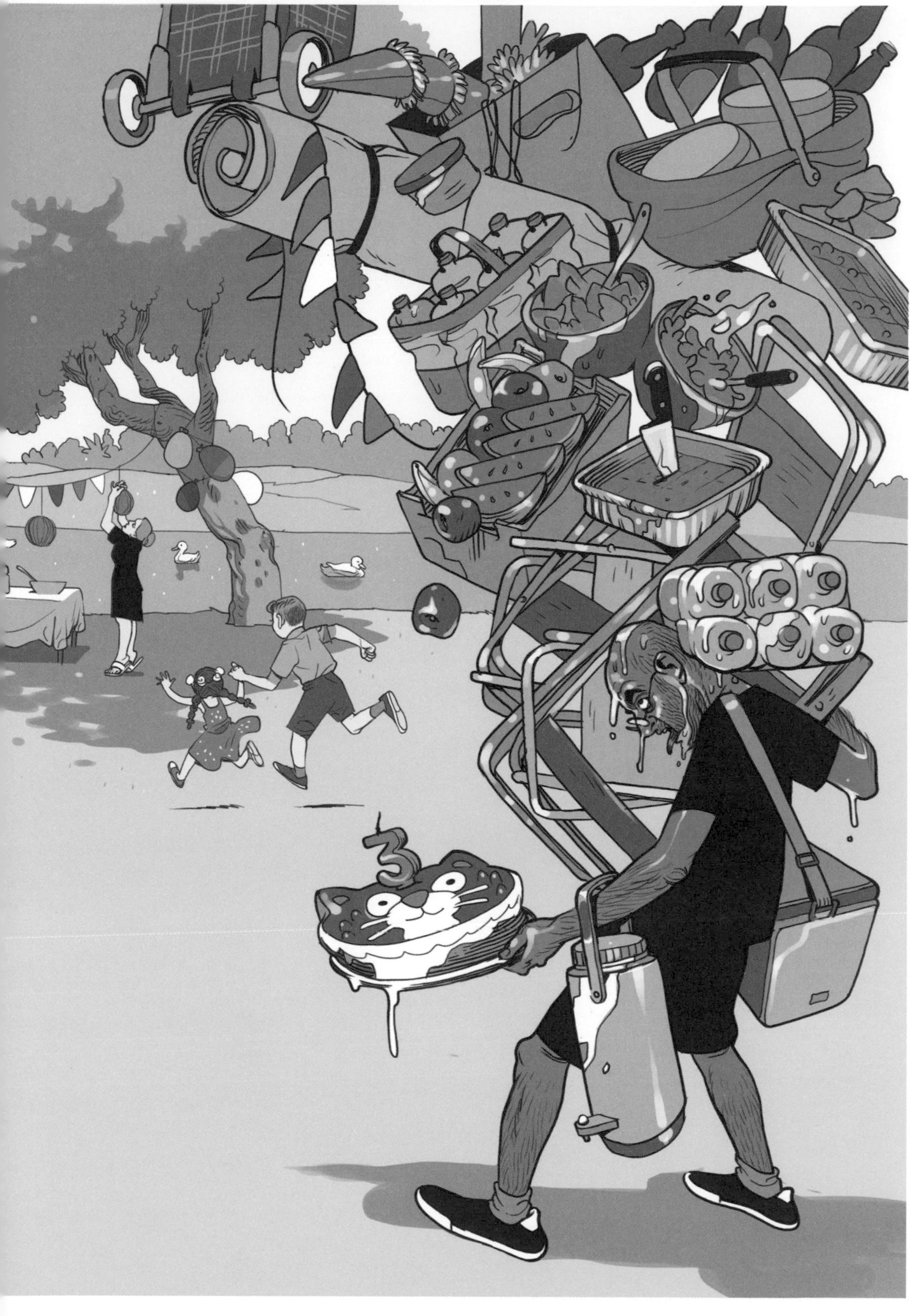
3

POINT OF VIEW

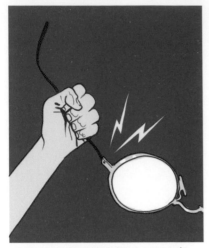

MY DAUGHTER BENT MY GLASSES. SHE DIDN'T DO IT ON PURPOSE, SHE'S ONLY THREE YEARS OLD. THOUGH I'VE GOT TO SAY SHE LOOKED QUITE PLEASED AS SHE WAS DOING IT.

SINCE THEN, EVERY TIME I LEANED FORWARD JUST A LITTLE BIT, THEY FELL OFF.

I TRIED NOT LOOKING DOWN, UNTIL ONE TIM WHEN I WAS PEEING, I GLANCED DOWN AT MY ZIPPER AND MY GLASSES FELL INTO THE TOILET. I DECIDED TO GIVE THEM UP.

REALITY IS MUCH SIMPLER WHEN ALL YOU SEE IS BLURRY SPOTS. THERE'S MORE SPACE FOR INTERPRETATION. MY WIFE MIGHT BE ANGRY, BUT PERHAPS SHE'S JUST VERY BUSY...?

MY KIDS MIGHT HAVE BEEN CRYING IN THE BATHTUB, BUT I CHOOSE TO BELIEVE THEY WERE LAUGHING. IT'S JUST A LITTLE SOAPY WATER!

I DON'T UNDERSTAND THE NEWS AT ALL ANYMORE. I WAS HAVING TROUBLE FOLLOWIN EVEN BEFORE MY GLASSES GOT BENT, AND I'M MOSTLY GUESSING AND QUESTIONING.

I DON'T KNOW IF THERE IS OR ISN'T AN OCCUPATION, IF THE I.D.F. IS A MORAL MILITARY FORCE OR NOT. SO I DECIDE FOR MYSELF. YOU MIGHT CALL IT, "MY POINT OF VIEW."

THE ADVANTAGE OF HAVING A PERSONAL POINT OF VIEW IS THAT I CHOOSE WHICH WAY TO LOOK, AND MORE IMPORTANTLY, I DECIDE WHAT TO SEE.

I RECOMMEND IT. IT'S A WONDERFUL FEELIN

WIFE HATES HUMMUS. THAT'S WHY I WAS SO [TOU]CHED WHEN SHE TEXTED ME, "SHOULD I [BRING] YOU SOME HUMMUS? I'M NEAR THE PLACE."

I LOVE HUMMUS BUT I DON'T MAKE A BIG DEAL OUT OF IT, UNLIKE SOME PEOPLE I KNOW, WHO ARE SELF-PROCLAIMED HUMMUS CONNOISSEURS.

I'VE GIVEN UP ON THE FANTASY OF TAKING HER TO THE BEST HUMMUS PLACE IN ISRAEL THAT ONLY I KNOW ABOUT. I COULD NEVER DO THAT TO HER.

[THE] ROOTS OF THE CONFLICT: WHEN MY WIFE [WA]S IN KINDERGARTEN, THE TEACHER GAVE [HE]R A HUMMUS SANDWICH PREPARED THAT [MO]RNING.

NO ONE SHOULD BE MADE TO EAT GROCERY STORE HUMMUS THAT HAS BEEN COAGULATING IN BREAD FOR HOURS. HUMMUS SHOULD BE EATEN FRESH FROM THE POT, IN A HOME COOKING STYLE RESTAURANT.

BUT ISRAEL WAS STILL A YOUNG STATE AND THERE WAS NO AWARENESS OF THAT SORT OF THING. THE TRAUMA FIXED AN EQUATION: HUMMUS=GROSS.

[I] TRIED TO EXPLAIN TO HER THAT IT'S [PA]RT OF ISRAELI AND MIDDLE EASTERN [CUL]TURE. IF WE DON'T LOVE HUMMUS, WHAT [MIGH]T HAVE WE GOT TO BE HERE, IN THE [LAN]D OF ISRAEL?

BUT NO ONE CAN CONTROL LOVE AND HATE, AND ANY ATTEMPT TO INFLUENCE THEM WITH RATIONALIZATIONS IS PRETENTIOUS AND DOOMED TO FAIL.

WHEN SHE BROUGHT ME THAT CONTAINER OF HUMMUS I WAS MOVED, BECAUSE I KNEW SHE WENT AGAINST HER OWN EMOTIONS JUST TO MAKE ME HAPPY. I WAS FILLED WITH HOPE AND LOVE, AND EVENTUALLY WITH HUMMUS, TOO.

THANK YOU THANK YOU

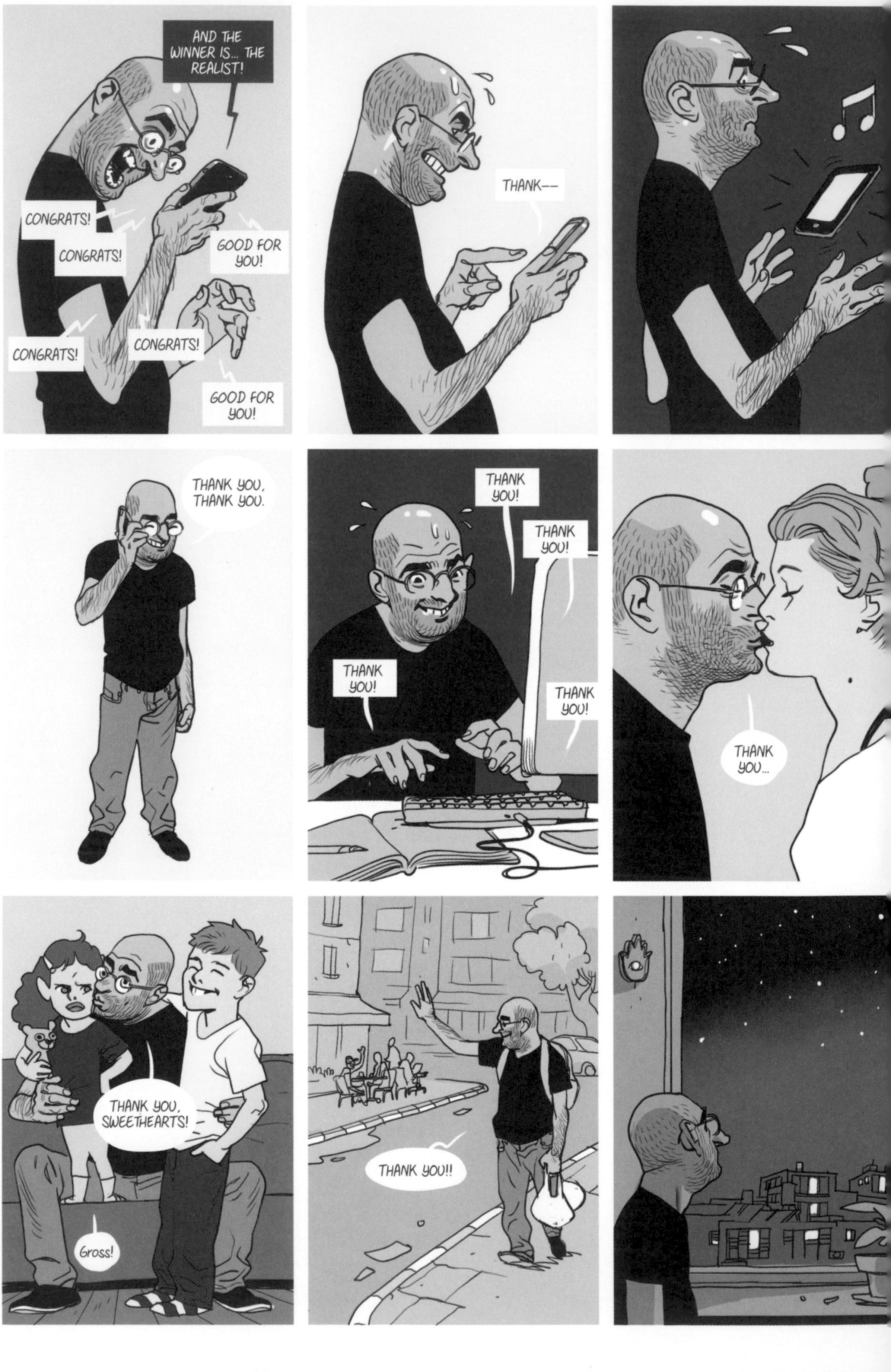
AND THE WINNER IS... THE REALIST!
CONGRATS!
CONGRATS!
GOOD FOR YOU!
CONGRATS!
CONGRATS!
GOOD FOR YOU!
THANK--
THANK YOU, THANK YOU.
THANK YOU!
THANK YOU!
THANK YOU!
THANK YOU!
THANK YOU...
THANK YOU, SWEETHEARTS!
Gross!
THANK YOU!!

OBAL MELTDOWN

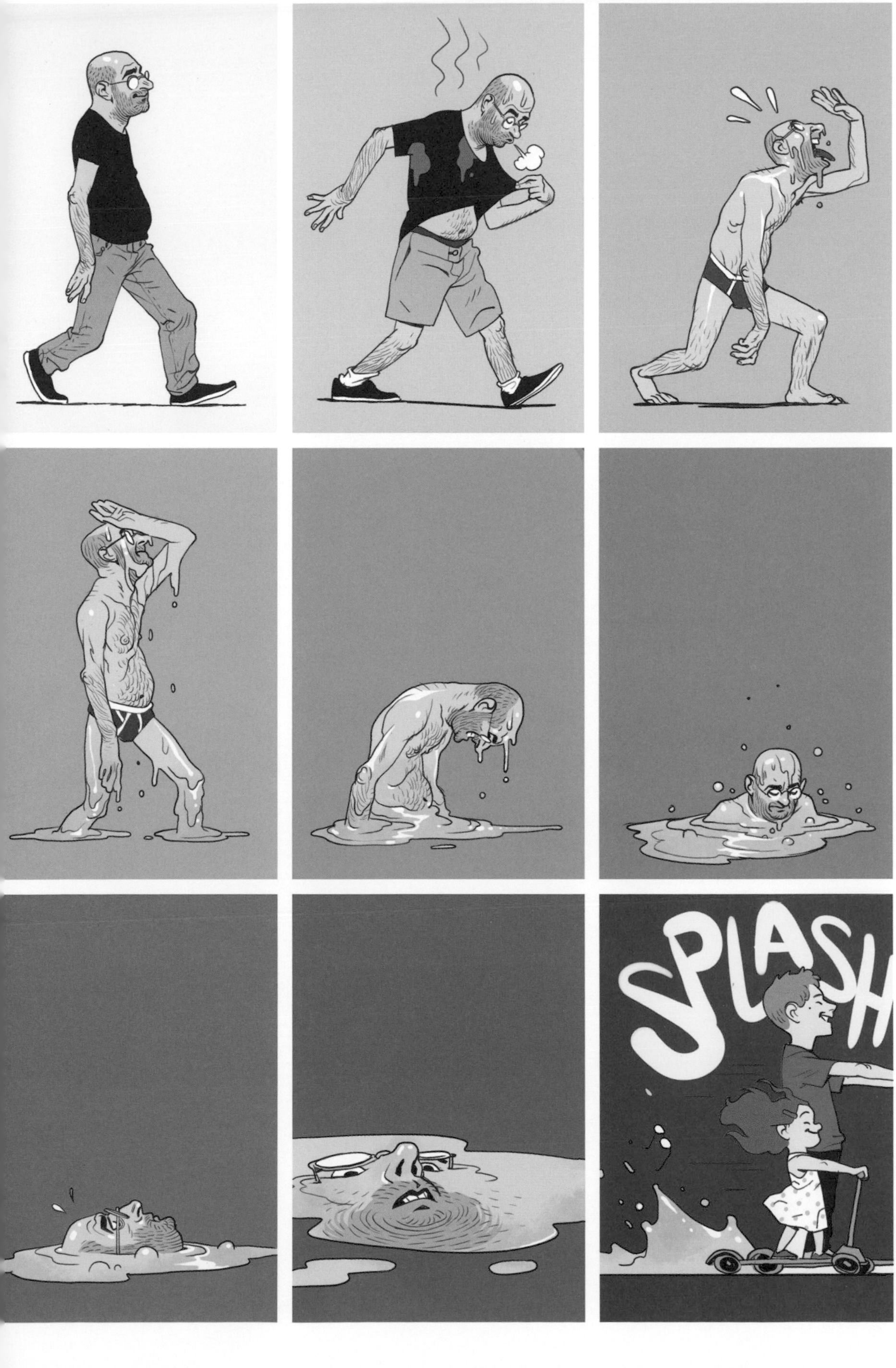
SPLASH

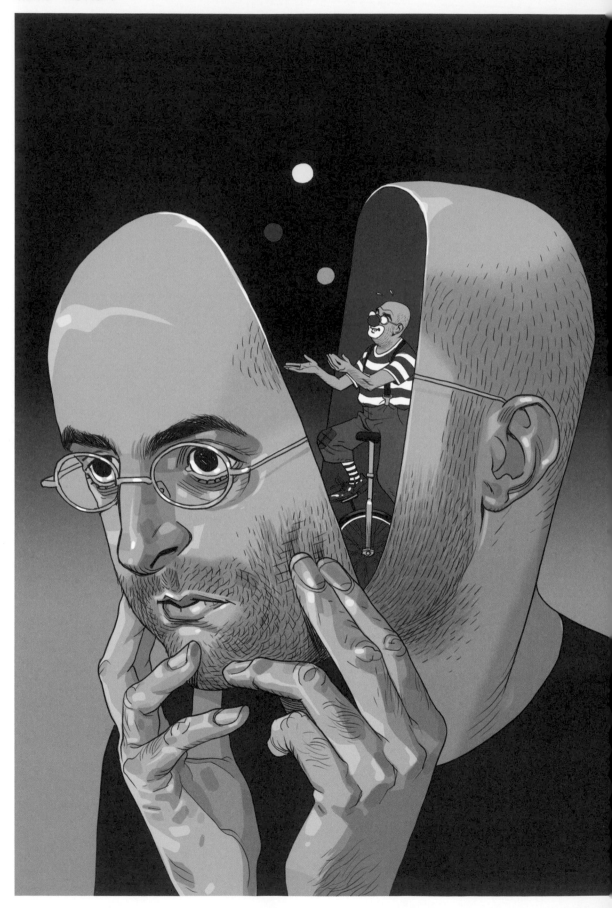

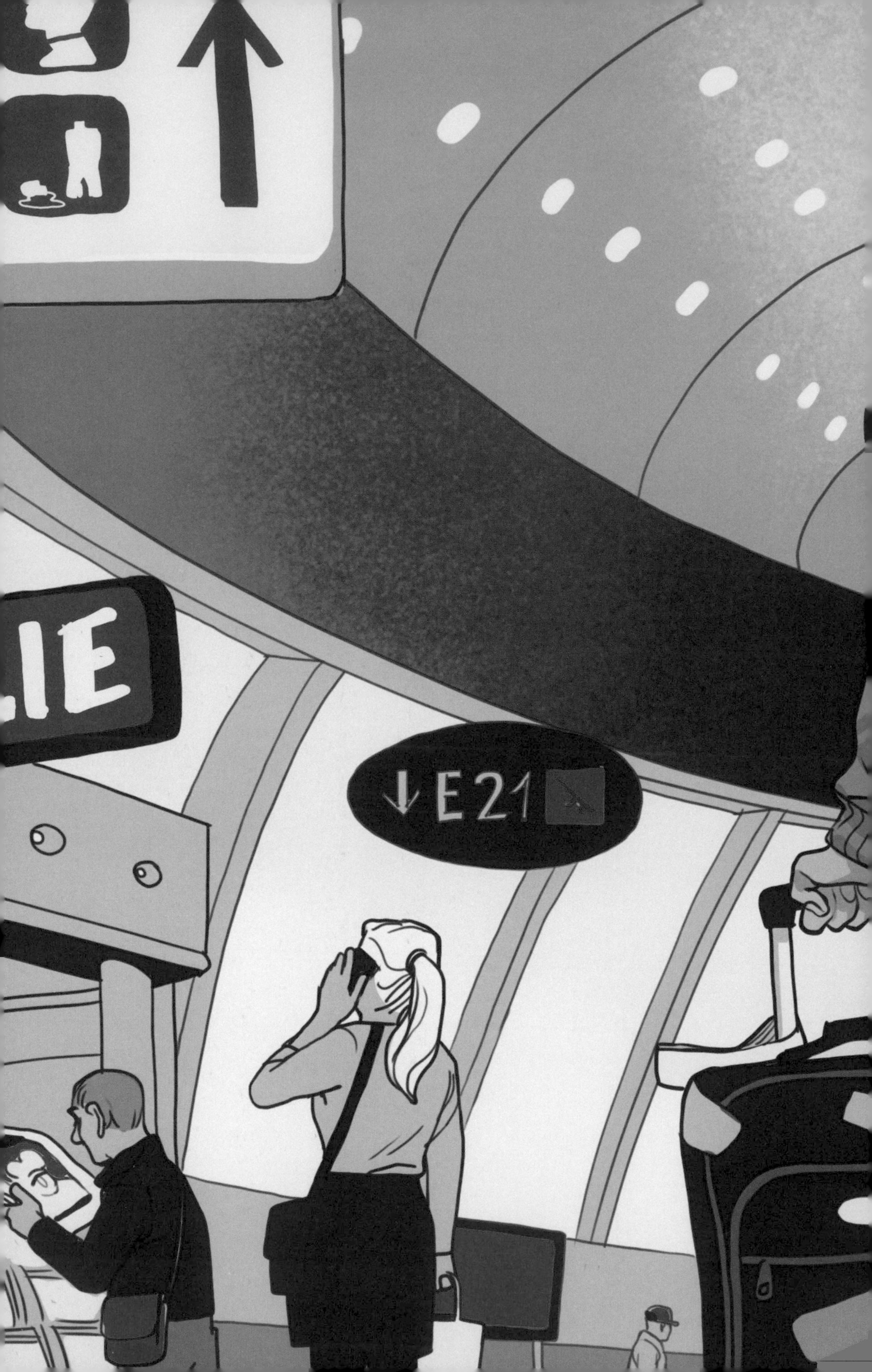
LIE
E21

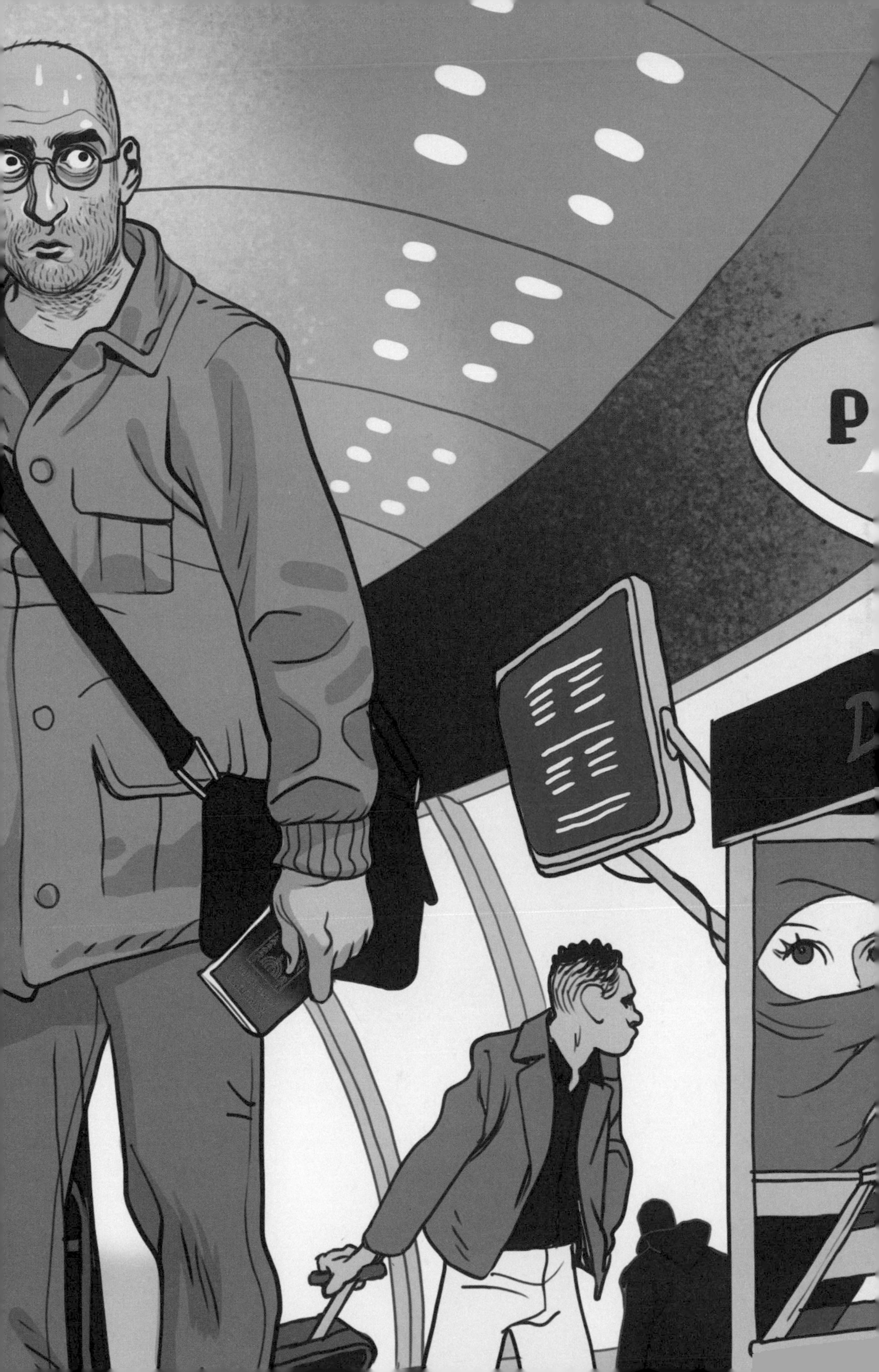

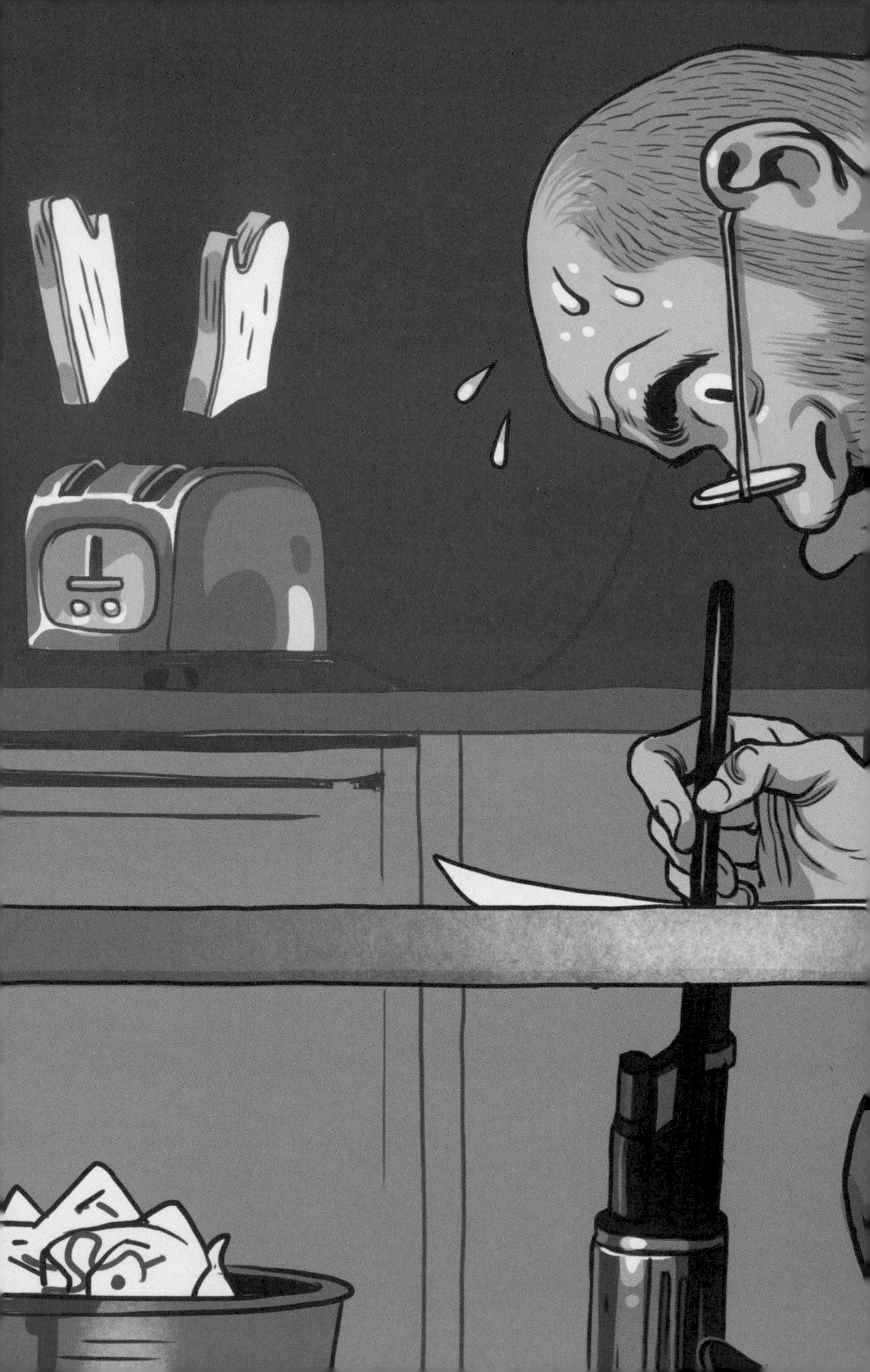

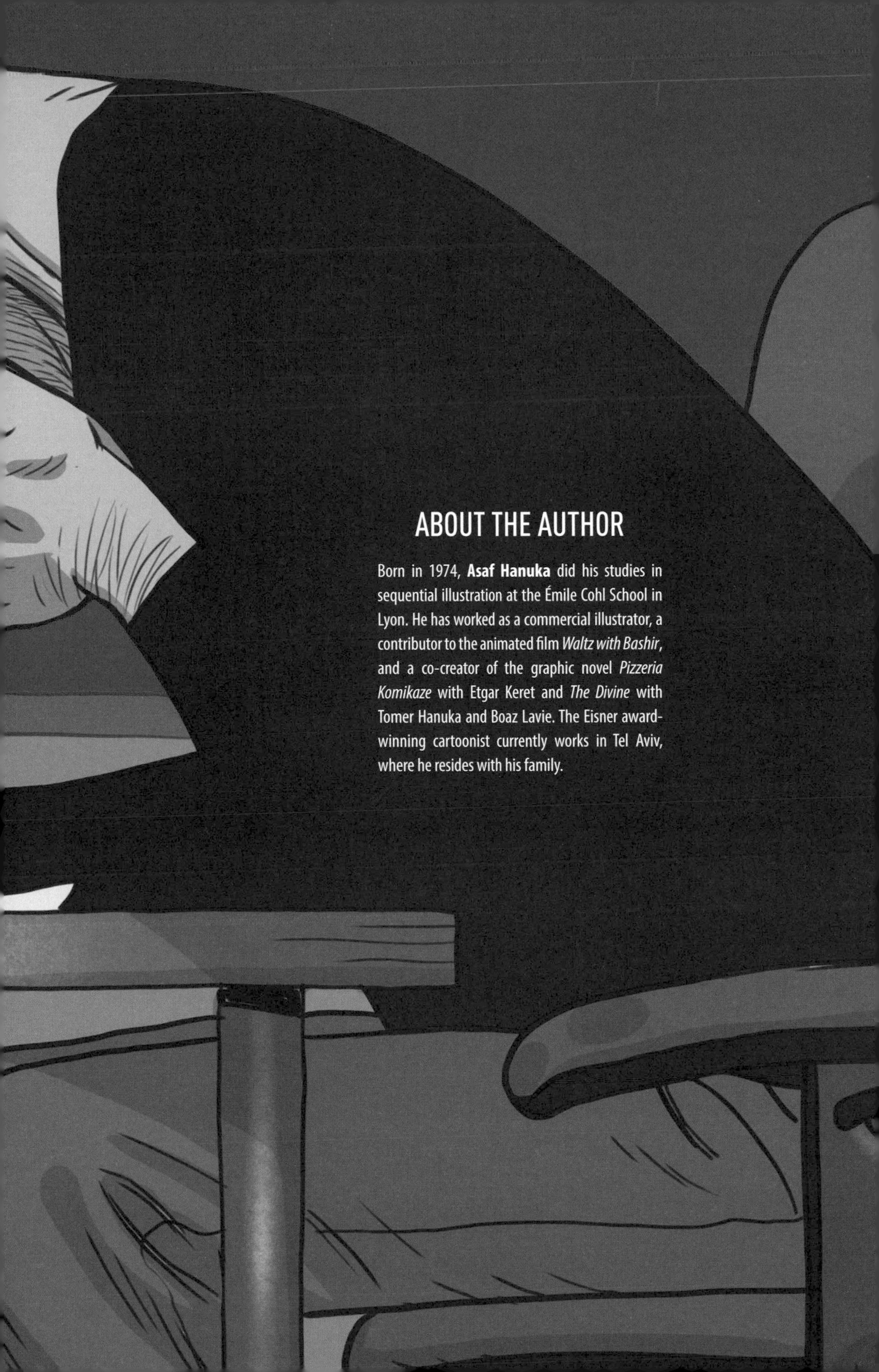

ABOUT THE AUTHOR

Born in 1974, **Asaf Hanuka** did his studies in sequential illustration at the Émile Cohl School in Lyon. He has worked as a commercial illustrator, a contributor to the animated film *Waltz with Bashir*, and a co-creator of the graphic novel *Pizzeria Komikaze* with Etgar Keret and *The Divine* with Tomer Hanuka and Boaz Lavie. The Eisner award-winning cartoonist currently works in Tel Aviv, where he resides with his family.

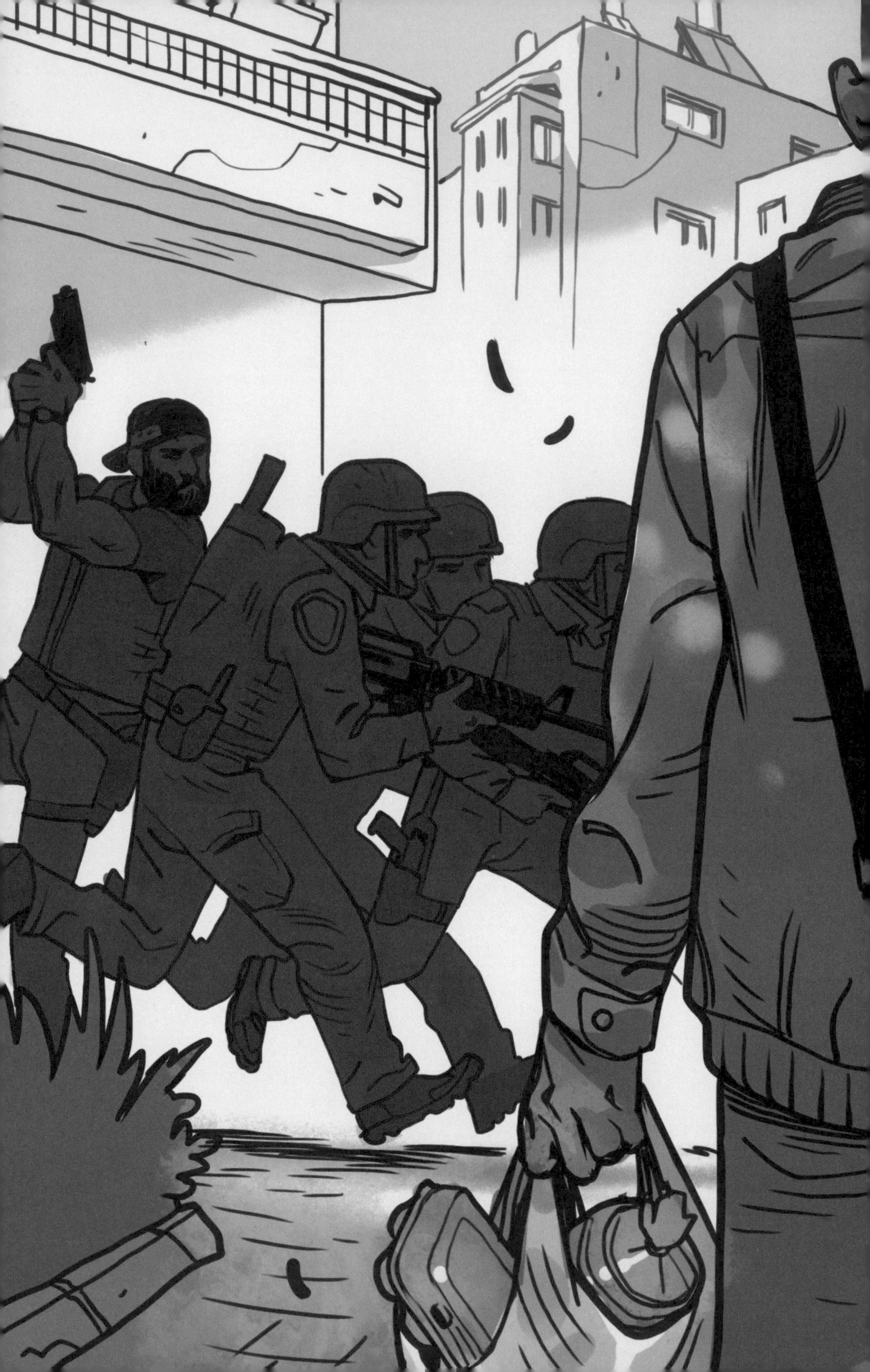

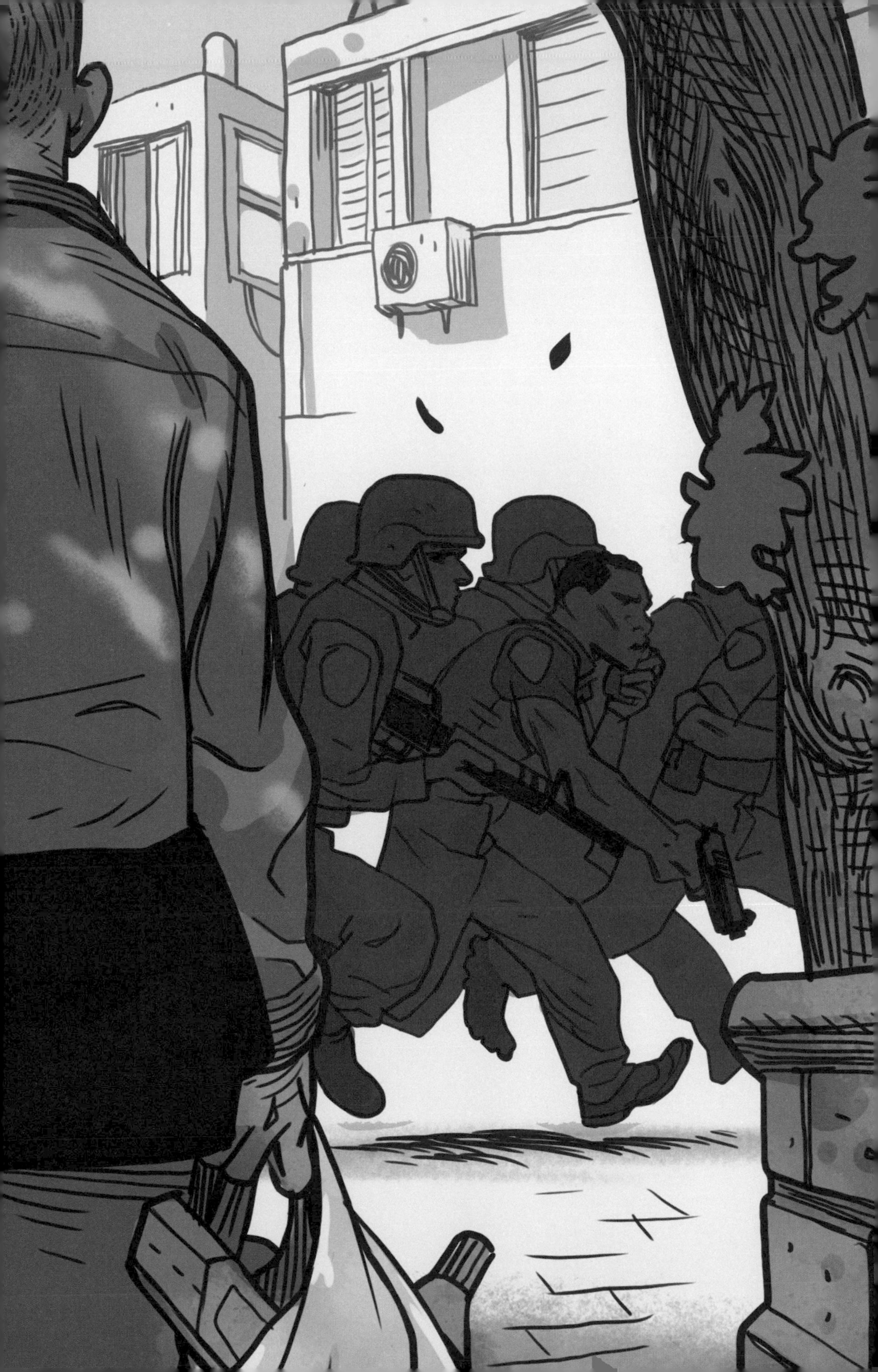